THE SPIRIT OF BUDDHISM

The Spirit of Buddhism

DAVID BURNETT

MONARCH
BOOKS
Mill Hill, London & Grand Rapids, Michigan

First published by Monarch Books 1996
Second edition published by Monarch Books 2003,
Concorde House, Grenville Place,
Mill Hill, London, NW7 3SA.

Distributed by:
STL, PO Box 300, Kingstown Broadway,
Carlisle, Cumbria CA3 0QS.

ISBN 1 85424 622 4

British Library Cataloguing Data
A catalogue record for this book is available
from the British Library.

Book design and production for the publishers by
Bookprint Creative Services
P.O. Box 827, BN21 3YJ, England.
Printed in Great Britain.

CONTENTS

LIST OF FIGURES

FOREWORD TO SECOND EDITION

Teachers always learn much from their students. The changes to this second edition of *The Spirit of Buddhism* have in a large part resulted from the questions and comments of the students I have taught over the last few years. I want to thank them for all their valuable comments.

This second edition is different in several ways. First, new and updated material has been included. Buddhism is a living religion that continues to grow and develop. This is especially seen in the new expressions of Buddhism that have emerged in the West. There have been many new books written by both academics and practitioners, and I have sought to include some of the latest ideas, especially with regards to Buddhism in the state of Gandhara, the debate over the *Dharma* protectors, and the so-called *Jesus Sutras* of early Christianity in China.

Second, I have framed the material more into the style of a text-book, starting each chapter with clear learning objectives to try and draw out the main issues of the particular chapter. There is also an extended and updated bibliography, glossary and index.

Third, at the end of each chapter there is a topic that may be used in interfaith discussions. They are not meant for Christians merely to score points over Buddhists, but to provide thoughtful discussions that will allow both Buddhists and Christians to come to a greater understanding of truth.

Finally, each chapter now has a section of web-based resources, called "Webwise". These provide the reader with details of some of the immense amount of resources currently available on the Internet. By following the links you will be able to read some of the Buddhist scriptures and look at the official sites of various

Buddhist schools to see how they present their history and teaching. To help with the various links you may go directly to the website for *The Spirit of Buddhism* where you are able to surf the net whilst having your book open at a particular chapter. Websites do occasionally change, but it is hoped to keep this site up-to-date, and to include additional material for your interest.

Log onto the site at http://www.burnett.uk.com/spiritofbuddhism

CHAPTER ONE

THE BUDDHA

What you can learn from this chapter

- the historical context at the time of the Buddha
- a description of the life of the Buddha
- the ways in which the story of the Buddha has been variously expressed in different Buddhist traditions

With two Buddhist monks I drove off the main road onto a narrow track into the forest region of central Sri Lanka. I was being taken to visit a former Sinhalese university professor who had renounced his former way of life and become a forest monk. At the end of the track, we left the vehicle and started to climb the steps that led to the cave. Walls and a door had been built to provide some privacy, and a flat stone provided a place to sleep. The venerable monk welcomed us warmly and invited us to sit on the rush mats that covered the floor. He provided us with fruit juice and we chatted warmly about his beliefs and his practice of meditation. He kindly gave me copies of the booklets that he had written on Buddhism. As we were about to take our leave he said, "Before you go, I must give you the address of my website." Seeing me look around for any signs of electricity, he explained that some supporters in Singapore had set up the website for him. Smiling at me, he said, "My laptop is my pen and paper, and I have to rely on snail mail." The ancient teaching has adapted to the modern world.

*   *   *

The word *buddha* has been used in various religious traditions in India to describe those who have had a transforming insight into the nature of reality. It is not a proper name but a title for a person who has achieved the highest level of consciousness. The original Pali word *budh* means to "wake up", "understand" or "perceive". No study of the Buddhist tradition can avoid commencing with the life of the person who came to be known as 'the Buddha'.

No one has questioned the actual existence of such a historical figure because there could not have been such an explosion of religious creativity without a most dynamic founder. The Buddhist scholar Lamotte writes: "Buddhism could not be explained if it were not based on a personality powerful enough to give it the necessary impetus and to have marked it with its essential features which will persist throughout all history."[1]

The Indian context

The Buddha lived and taught in the region of the Ganges basin in north-east India that was inhabited by people speaking an early form of Sanskrit. This language was brought into the Indian sub-continent around 1500 BC when nomadic people from the area of northern Iran migrated through what is now Pakistan. Local dialects were probably mutually comprehensible, so allowing communication throughout the region. The influx of these migrants brought to an end the sophisticated city-based civilisation of the Indus valley, but initiated a new Aryan civilisation.[2] The Aryans gradually settled in the wooded valley of the Ganges and formed small city-states claimed by tribal groups who were governed by monarchs or by an assembly of the leading families. These cities became complex societies of rulers, business people, traders, priests, musicians and prostitutes. Some people became wealthy and adopted a flamboyant lifestyle. Merchants travelled from city to city with trade items and local news. The society was based on agriculture with the growth of rice, millet, wheat, bananas, mangoes and dates. Despite these settlements, there were still vast areas of forest with tigers, elephants and monkeys.

The religion of the Aryans was based upon a body of oral hymns and teaching known as the *Vedas*. The people worshipped a multitude of gods known as *devas* who were essentially nature deities expressing active principles of nature and human life. The central rite of the Aryan religion was one in which the priest sang the praises of the particular *deva* and offered sacrifices by placing them in the sacred fire. Early sacrifices were of grain and milk but later, animal sacrifices were added. The role of the priests in enunciating the sacred sacrificial verses, known as *mantras,* placed them at the head of what was regarded as a divinely ordered social hierarchy. Beneath the Brahmin priests were the warrior-leaders of the society (*ksatriya*), then the traditional cattle-rearers and cultivators (*vaisya*), and then the servants (*sudra*). The individual's place in this social system was seen as determined by birth. Later, the social hierarchy incorporated thousands of lesser social groups to form what is known as the caste system.

At the time of the Buddha, the Brahmin priests dominated religious life with their knowledge of the ancient *Vedic* hymns and the complex rituals. However, for the majority of Aryans, Brahmanism incorporated beliefs in spirits (*devas*) and ghosts, and the practice of divination and protective magic. Although the Buddha was critical of these folk beliefs, he did not denounce them. For this reason, right from the beginning up to the present time, Buddhism has happily co-existed with folk beliefs, as can be seen in Buddhist countries today.

India in the sixth century BC was, however, a country of changing social conditions, where the small kinship-based communities were being drawn into expanding city-states. Several of these cities developed into major centres of trade and administration based upon a money economy. New wealth for some resulted in new social problems for all. The concentration of population encouraged disease, and some individuals decided to leave these settlements to find a new basis to life in an insecure world. These wandering ascetics, known as *sramana*, were somewhat akin to the early Greek philosophers and mystics. The *sramanas* rejected the *Vedic* tradition and wandered free from family ties in order to think, debate, and investigate. Out of the teaching of the more orthodox of these *sramanas* was compiled the *Upanishads*.

As a result of the complex philosophical speculations of the *Upanishads*, three major and related assumptions appeared. These are important for an understanding of the emergence of the teaching of the Buddha. The first was a monistic assumption in which an element, known as *Brahman,* was conceived as underlying the whole cosmos. This contrasted markedly with the monotheism of the Middle East in which an eternal, self-sufficient God was believed to have created the universe out of nothing. The second assumption argued that because the human soul (*atman*) was part of *Brahman,* the soul must also be eternal. In contrast, the Judaeo-Christian tradition regards the life of a single being as a unique phenomenon, which begins at birth and ends in death. The third assumption was that of reincarnation, which provided an explanation of the eternal nature of the *atman.* In the Indian tradition, a given being passes eternally from one existence to another, assuming different forms each time. Allied to this idea was the notion that the quality of a person's *karma,* or "action", determines the nature of his or her future reincarnation. The consequence was that the main aim in life was to find a way of release from this eternal circle of birth and death.

During this period of Indian history, many people seem to have set out to discover the way of liberation, and the Buddha must be seen initially as one among many such searchers. Around notable teachers gathered groups of disciples. One of the major *sramana* groups at the same time as the Buddha was that of the Jains called, in Buddhist texts, *nigantha.* The movement was founded by Vardhamana the *Mahavira,* or "Great Hero". He taught that all things, even rocks, are alive and possess a life principle (*jiva*). The aim of Jainism was to liberate the *jiva* from the round of rebirths by freeing it from its bondage of *karma.* This was achieved by wearing out the results of previous *karma* by severe austerities such as self-denial, fasting, and going unwashed. To avoid the generation of new *karma,* total non-violence (*ahimsa*) to any form of life was advocated, to the extent of avoiding the killing of an insect. While the teaching of the Buddha had much in common with that of the Jains, he opposed their asceticism as too extreme and proposed a "Middle Path".

The Buddha lived in a time of social change, and as Karen Armstrong comments, this makes his life and message significant for many today.

The story of Gotama [Buddha] has particular relevance for our own period. We too live in a period of transition and change, as was North India during the sixth and fifth century B.C.E. Like the people of North India, we are finding that the traditional ways of experiencing the sacred and discovering an ultimate meaning in our lives are either difficult or impossible. As a result, a void has been an essential part of the modern experience.[3]

The life of Sakyamuni Buddha

The full story of the life of the Buddha took some centuries to develop, and scholars have much debated the issue of when a continuous narrative was first composed. Most scholars now follow Lamotte in suggesting three phases.[4] First, there were biographical fragments found in canonical texts presenting episodes in the life of the Buddha. Second, there were fuller accounts written in Sanskrit or Pali such as the "Acts of the Buddha" (*Buddhacarita*). Finally, there are many late biographies composed in various parts of Asia in the local language. Some of these are simple narratives but most are ornate renderings that show particular local expressions. From these accounts, one can draw out a basic rendering of the life of the man who has come to be known as the Buddha.

Indian society was not concerned with the record of exact dates as were the Graeco-Roman and Chinese societies. The dates for the events in the life of the Buddha are therefore subject to some speculation. The Theravada school of Buddhism accepts the date of birth of the Buddha as 624 BC. Western scholars have tended to work back from King Asoka who, according to Hellenistic sources, ascended the throne of Magadha in about 268 BC. Buddhist writings state that the Buddha died either 218 or 100 years before the consecration of Asoka. As all sources agree that he died when he was 80 years old, he would have lived either 566–486 BC or 448–368 BC. In the past, Western scholars have accepted the earlier dates, but today some consider that the evidence for the early date is insufficient and so they prefer the later date. Thus, some uncertainty remains about the exact date of the birth of the Buddha. Today, most scholars are still uncertain but would place the date of the death of the Buddha much nearer 400 BC than 500 BC.[5]

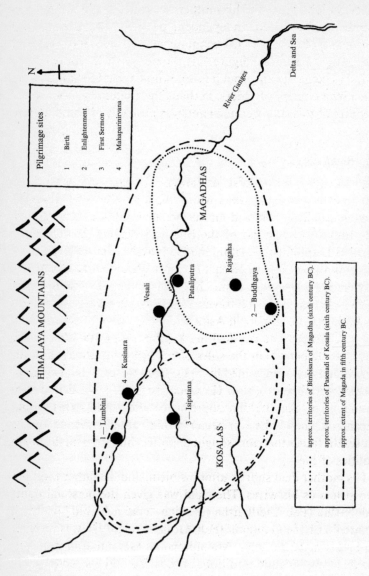

Figure 1.1 Map of Ganges basin at the time of the Buddha

Pilgrimage sites

1 — Birth
2 — Enlightenment
3 — First Sermon
4 — Mahaparinirvana

N

HIMALAYA MOUNTAINS

River Ganges

Delta and Sea

MAGADHAS

KOSALAS

1 — Lumbini
4 — Kusinara
Vesali
3 — Isipatana
Pataliputra
Rajagaha
2 — Buddhgaya

.... approx. territories of Bimbisara of Magadha (sixth century BC).

– – – approx. territories of Pasenadi of Kosala (sixth century BC).

– — – approx. extent of Magada in fifth century BC.

He is said to have had a father who was a warrior nobleman called Suddhadana, and his mother was called Maya.[6] They were members of a proud, independent people called Sakyas who were probably already tied economically to the larger states of the Ganges basin (see figure 1.1). Some accounts speak of his father as being the king, but it is now known that the Sakyas were ruled by a council of elders. Perhaps the Buddha's father was a member of this ruling council and was probably of the *kshatriya* class.

The Buddha's early life

The story told by Buddhists usually commences with his mother's dream of a great six-tusked white elephant entering her womb. This is usually considered an auspicious symbol of sovereignty. The traditional location of the Buddha's birth is the village (or park) of Lumbini, now within the southern borders of Nepal. The Pali commentaries explain that his mother wanted the child to be delivered at her family home, but he was born at Lumbini just halfway between the two towns. Five days after his birth, an old Brahmin astrologer named Asita came to the home. Asita noticed the 32 characteristic physical marks of a future Buddha on the body of the baby.[7] On the soles of his feet were wheels, and his fingers and toes were joined by webs. Asita forecast that two great careers were open to him. He would become either a universal monarch, or the Buddha supreme of the world. This would depend on whether he ever began to think about suffering and its cause. His father therefore sought to protect him from all the harsh realities of life.

His mother died shortly after his birth, and his father took her two sisters as his wives. The child was given the personal name Siddhartha (Pali: Siddhattha meaning "goal achieved" or "wish granted") of the Gautama (Pali: Gotama) clan. He was brought up by his maternal aunt, Mahaprajapati Gotami, and was educated in the ethics and traditions of the tribe, and instructed in the Brahminical lore. There is no evidence that he could read or write but, as was common then, he probably memorised much of the teaching.

When Gautama was 16, he married a beautiful princess called

Yasodhara from a neighbouring clan. Legend says that Yasodhara was the most beautiful of women, who dressed in the finest fabrics. His father built for them three palaces – one for the rainy season, one for winter, and one for the heat of summer. Each palace was filled with every kind of enjoyment for the five senses, according to the season of the year. Yasodhara eventually bore her husband a son, whom he named Radula (meaning "impediment"), a name that suggests Guatama's growing dissatisfaction.

Then, one day when he was 29 years of age, he went out with his charioteer, driving in the park. On his way, Gautama suddenly observed an old man whose back was bent double and whose hair was grey. Gautama had seen only healthy young people and was shocked at the sight. He enquired of his charioteer what was the matter with the man and was told that this was old age. The sight left the young prince brooding and sorrowful. On another day, Gautama went out again with his charioteer, and he saw the so-called "second sight", which was of a man desperately ill. For the first time, Gautama realised that physical misery attends the whole of human life. Later, the prince came across the "third sight", when according to legend, he saw a group of people constructing a funeral pyre. This time, he learned that all human beings are subject to death. These three sights left Gautama saddened and depressed. His father tried to interest him with greater pleasures but Gautama had been radically changed. The "fourth sight" showed Gautama a way out of his predicament. As he and his charioteer were driving in the park, a shaven-headed mendicant, wearing a yellow robe, appeared before him.

Buddhist stories often describe in loving detail the lonely struggle of the prince in deciding to renounce all the luxuries of palace life. His father commanded ever more sensuous entertainment to satisfy Gautama's every desire but his needs could not be met. Finally, one night, Gautama quietly looked at his sleeping wife and child, and bade them an unspoken farewell. He left the palace and travelled to the park. Here he cut his hair and beard, changed his royal garments for that of a mendicant, and started his journey to find meaning to life.

Quest for enlightenment

The great legend of the Buddha tells of how he travelled from the land of Sakya to Rajagaha, the capital of the neighbouring kingdom of Magadha that stretched along the Ganges valley (see figure 1.2). Gautama travelled from place to place looking for a spiritual guide. The Buddhist scriptures name two teachers: Alara Kalama and Uddaka Ramaputta. From the first he learned to achieve the advanced levels of meditation. When he had learned all he could from that guru he travelled on to another, but he failed to find the complete release that he was looking for. He became convinced that true enlightenment was not to be found within Brahmanism. It is as a result of this quest that he was also given the title Sakyamuni (Pali: *Sakyamuni*, meaning "sage of the Sakyas").

Gautama therefore turned to the extreme bodily asceticism advocated by some gurus, as seen among the Jains. According to the Pali texts, he spent six years as an ascetic, practising increasing degrees of austerities. He sat on a bed of thorns, refused to wash his body, and reduced his diet to only one or two beans a day. His body became so thin that his arms and legs became like canes. It is possible that some practitioners experienced hallucinations brought on by such deprivations. However, Gautama did not find the answer to his spiritual quest, and when almost dead from exhaustion, he was convinced that asceticism was not the way. He therefore began to take food again. Five ascetics who had gathered around him in the hope of sharing in his enlightenment left him in disgust. Gautama, once his strength was renewed, returned to his search. Sitting beneath a large fig-tree, which later came to be called the *bodhi* tree (meaning "enlightenment"), he resolved not to move until supreme enlightenment had been attained.

Night fell! He entered upon a process of meditation that took him through the various levels of contemplation. The various accounts of that night tell of many significant experiences, including the great temptation of Mara, the Evil One. Mara sent his three daughters, Discontent, Delight and Desire, to seduce the Buddha-to-be. In one temptation, Mara came as Death to attack him with a great thunderstorm, but the sage remained unmoved.

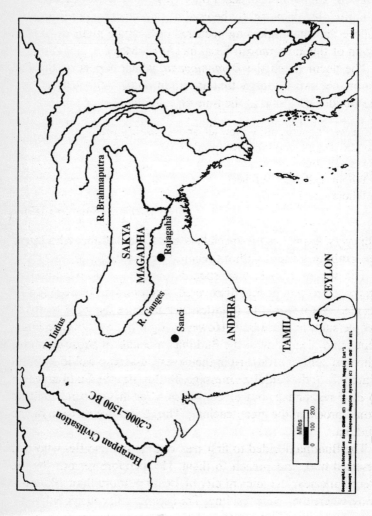

Figure 1.2   Map of the Indian subcontinent about fifth century BC

Finally, Gautama came to a realisation of the supreme truth. In that state of freedom arose the consciousness that rebirth had been destroyed and the higher life fulfilled. When dawn came a Supreme Buddha sat beneath the tree. From this time, the title of "the Buddha" may rightly be used of Gautama. Most Buddhists believe that the awakening occurred on a single night of the full moon of the lunar month Vesakha (April–May).

The poem called the *Dhammapada*, which is part of the Pali canon, consists of verses that are traditionally held as describing the Buddha's feelings at the time of enlightenment.

> I have conquered all; I know all, and my life is pure.
> I have left all, and I am free from craving.
> I myself found the way.
> Whom shall I call Teacher?
> Whom shall I teach?

(Dhammapada verse 353)

This verse expresses the special status of the Buddha, who found the truth for himself without reliance on any guru.

The next four weeks were spent in the area, in deep meditation on the truths that he had discovered. According to the legends, he decided that it would be pointless to announce the great truths to people sunk in ignorance. However, a god is said to have intervened and pleaded with the Buddha on behalf of those creatures who had "only a little dust in their eyes", and who would respond gratefully to the Buddha's message. To this plea the Buddha is said to have responded, out of compassion for all creatures, that he would proclaim the great teaching. Thus began the mission of the Buddha.

The Buddha decided to first seek out the five ascetics who had deserted him, and preach to them. He therefore set out for the Deer Park near the ancient city of Benares, more than 100 miles away, where they were residing. The ascetics still considered him a failure from the ascetic path and agreed among themselves not to greet him with the usual respect. However, when he arrived, his demeanour was so awe-inspiring that they involuntarily rose from their seats and paid him the respect due to a teacher. They were not readily convinced of his enlightenment but, one by one, they realised the importance of his teaching and received ordination from him.

According to ancient records, it was to these disciples that the Buddha preached his first sermon, the *Dharmacakrapravartana Sutta,* or "Discourse Setting in Motion the Wheel of Truth". This is believed to have consisted of a brief statement of the Middle Way, the Four Noble Truths, and the Noble Eightfold Path. Further conversions resulted, including that of Yasa, a rich young man of Benares; soon after, 54 of his friends followed his example. There were then 60 enlightened beings in the world, besides the Buddha himself. These disciples were the kernel of the new movement and it was they who spread the teaching throughout the region of the Ganges valley.

The wandering life

From this point it is difficult to make any clear chronology of the Buddha's life. He is said to have initially gone to preach at the region of Uruvela, where he is said to have converted 1,000 fire-worshipping ascetics. Many stories are told of this period but most would agree that due allowance must be made for exaggeration. The conversion of groups of other sects appears to have been a special feature of his early ministry that almost disappeared later.

The Buddha's teaching ministry extended for 45 years, from the first sermon in the Deer Park when he was 35 to his passing at the age of 80. During this time, the content of his teaching remained the same but his method of teaching was adapted to his audience. He is therefore attributed with the use of many parables to suit the need of the hearer. Shrona Kotivinsha was the son of a rich man who was converted in Rajagirha; he practised meditation with such effort that blood came from his feet. When in despair, he came to the Buddha, and the Buddha helped him by using the analogy of a lute. "If its strings are stretched too tight, or if on the other hand they are too slack, the lute will never give the proper sound. In the same way if the spiritual enthusiasm is too intense, or if the practice is too slack, one will be far from realization."[8]

The Buddha himself appeared to have continued his wandering life, with the result that this teaching quickly gained many followers, especially in the kingdoms of Kosala, Magadha and Anga. The capital of Magadha was the flourishing town of Rajagaha. Today, the remains of the city are divided into the old and new sections. Neither section has any trace of a royal palace that was supposed to be the dwelling of its king, Bimbisara, but the area remains an important centre for Jains with the ancient Sonbhandar caves near the town. Beyond the north gate are remains of the Bamboo Forest Park (Venuvana Vihara) where the Buddha is said to have stayed many times.[9]

> King Bimbisara of Magadha thought to himself, "This Bamboo Park is not remote from village nor too near; it is convenient of access so that any who wish can easily reach it; in the day there is little disturbance, and at night little sound; it is suitable for meditation. Let me present this Bamboo Park for the Buddha and for the assembly of ascetics." (*Vinaya*: *Mahavagga*)

Another important site is Vulture Peak (Gridhra-kuta) on the southern slope of the hills just visible from the town. It gets its name from a flat outcrop of black rock flecked with white that sticks out from the outline of the hill and looks like the feathers of a vulture. It was from here that the Buddha is said to have given important sermons.

Soon there were so many converts that people began objecting and saying that the Buddha had made parents childless, and wives to become widows.

Parinirvana

Three *sutras* contain accounts of the Buddha's last days. When he was 80 years old he went on one of his preaching trips to an obscure town by the name of Kusinara. On his journey he dined at the home of a goldsmith named Cunda; soon after, he developed food poisoning. Despite his serious condition, he continued his journey until he could walk no more. He lay down under the shade of a tree. The dying Buddha asked the assembled disciples three times if they had any last doubts or questions. All kept silent. His last exhortation to them was, "Conditioned things are perishable by nature. Diligently seek realisation." He then commenced meditation and quickly ascended through to the fourth stage, from which he passed to *parinirvana*. The death of Gautama is taken by Buddhists of the Theravada tradition as year one.

According to legend, earthquakes and thunder marked the moment of death. Some monks burst into lamentations, until the leading teachers reminded them that in so doing they were not in keeping with the teaching of the Buddha. On the following day, people from the village of Kusinara came and held a wake for the Buddha. When they asked Ananda, his cousin and favourite disciple, how his remains should be treated, he told them that it should be in the fashion of a king of kings. The body was cremated and a *stupa* built to contain the relics. The Buddha left his body to the laity; in the ashes were found relics that looked like gem stones. Even today, after a body of a holy monk is cremated, people will look for crystals in the ashes. These are considered by many devotees to multiply of themselves.

He had told Ananda that his time had come to enter *nirvana*, when his earthly existence would end. He had also previously told Ananda that through magic powers, he could stay alive until the end of this current natural cycle (*kalpa*). However, his loyal but bumbling friend Ananda failed to request him to do so. Mara (the Evil One) approached Sakyamuni to tell him it was time for him to finally attain *nirvana*. The Buddha agreed and, after three months, entered *parinirvana*. These stories betray the problems of later generations in answering the question as to why the Buddha failed to avert his own death. Control of one's life span is a yogic power reported by ascetics in India even today.

When the Buddha was asked what would happen after his death, he said that it was not good for his disciples to know. Buddhist cosmology asserts that all that exists is subject to *karma* and thus to be free from *karma* one must have ceased to exist. Once the Buddha passed away, he therefore must have ceased to exist, and had no future involvement in the cosmos. To his disciples the Buddha left the *Dharma,* the body of his teaching.

Interpreting the life

The story of the Buddha's life is a cornerstone of the Buddhist religion, and his life became a model for others to follow. Modern members of the Theravada tradition emphasise that the Buddha was "just a man", but this is usually to contrast him with Jesus Christ, presented by Christians as the "Son of God". Once the Buddha attained enlightenment, he could no longer be thought of as a human, because he had perfected and transcended human nature. The Buddha found, in an ignorant and suffering world, a comprehensive vision that allowed a means of escape. The story of Gautama's enlightenment portrays an embodiment of this teaching. To his followers, he is portrayed as a warrior in the struggle for self-control and insight. His battle was to achieve spiritual growth and ultimately enlightenment.

The life of the Buddha exemplifies the threefold structure of the Buddhist path. First is the period of indulgence, when Gautama lived in luxury. As a young prince he had everything that anyone could desire. Everyone is born into a family and society that conditions one's thinking. This stage is often represented by the palace.

The second stage came when Gautama first encountered old age, sickness and death. These made him realise the impermanence of the world in which he lived. At the age of 29 he set out to seek spiritual reality and commenced the practice of self-discipline that was to lead to enlightenment. His life shows how a person must come to terms with his, or her, heritage. There is a need to come to terms with it and to counteract it, otherwise there can be no spiritual growth and maturity.

The third stage followed his enlightenment, when the Buddha returned to the world to share these new spiritual realities with his disciples. For 45 years he taught the *Dharma*, before finally facing death with calm and composure.

By "the Buddha", or "Enlightened One", is meant not only the historical Sakyamuni. His Buddhahood was not simply the result of a few years' meditation but the product of hundreds of previous lives. The Buddha is said to have remembered many of these reincarnations and related them to his disciples. These accounts are recorded in the *Jataka* texts, of which the Sri Lankan tradition tells of 547 previous lives. Some of these are popular folk stories known throughout India. However, what these stories show is the progress of a person from being an ordinary person to eventually become the Buddha. During these lives Gautama is said to have met no fewer than 24 past Buddhas; inspired by each of them, he vows to achieve enlightenment.[10]

Usually, the *Jataka* stories illustrate the perfections required of a person seeking to become a Buddha. One of the most popular stories in Asia is that of Prince Visvantara, who is commonly thought to have been the reincarnation immediately prior to that of Sakyamuni Buddha. From a very young age the prince displayed a generous nature. Even as a boy, he would declare that he would give away anything he could to anyone who asked him. One day when he was out riding on his white elephant, he met some people from a country suffering from a terrible drought. They asked if they could have the white elephant, as it was considered auspicious and would bring rain to the land. Visvantara gave it to them without hesitation.

When he returned home, the people of his own city were angry with him for giving away such an auspicious animal. They exiled him to Mount Vanka but before leaving, he gave away all the possessions of the palace, including servants, horses and money. He then left the city, riding in his chariot together with his wife and two children. On his way, he met someone who asked for his horses and chariot. He once again gave them away without hesitation. As they walked along, they eventually came to stay in a small hut at a forest hermitage. While his wife was out gathering firewood, a man passed by and asked for his children as slaves. Once again he gave them away without hesitation. When his wife returned she was distraught but eventually accepted the loss. Then another wanderer asked for his wife; once again he gave her away. He lived the rest of his life alone in the forest.

The story is popular not only for its poignancy but as an illustration of generosity. In this story, renunciation is achieved by giving away all of one's possessions, even to the extent of wife and children. For lay people, generosity is one of the most significant perfections to which they can aspire.

The religious movement that has grown and influenced so many through history has been stimulated by an ideal – a quest for enlightenment. Each tradition has built an image of the Buddha for its own path to attainment, but the fundamental teaching of all is that here was a living being who overcame the world. As the Buddha said:

> As a lotus flower is born in water, grows in water, and rises out of water to stand above it unsoiled, so I, born in the world, raised in the world, having overcome the world, live unsoiled by the world.[11]

Christians first looking at Buddhism seek to compare the figure of the Buddha with that of Christ. Both Christianity and Buddhism are religions founded by a figure of history, but the role of the Buddha for Buddhists is quite unlike the role of Jesus for Christians. The historicity of the person of Jesus Christ is essential for salvation within Christian teaching, and this is the reason that this subject has been so vigorously debated in Christian circles. For Christians, Christ is the source of salvation, "the Way, the Truth and the Life". In contrast, the Buddha attained liberation himself through the discovery of the teaching – the *Dharma*. This may be likened to some ancient overgrown path that was rediscovered by the Buddha. The role of the Buddha for the Buddhist is therefore the one who shows the way. As Williams writes:

> What follows from all this is that the corresponding absolutely central role of Jesus for Christians is performed for the Buddhists *not* by the Buddha, but by the *Dharma*. The proper Buddhist place to start the study of Buddhism, therefore, is not the life-story of the Buddha at all but through outlining straight away the Dharma, the practice of which leads to liberation without further ado.[12]

It is not the Buddha who brings enlightenment to his followers; enlightenment comes from following the *Dharma*. It is for this reason that the renowned Buddhist scholar, Lamotte, contrasts the person of the Buddha with Jesus Christ: "[Christ] is not only the author of the gospel teaching, but is Himself the life, the truth, the way: He is one with the truth and the life, and is Himself salvation."[13] The Buddha in contrast claimed no more than to have discovered and preached the *Dharma,* defining himself as the sign that shows the path to follow.

Suggestions for interfaith discussions

The two great symbols of Buddhism and Christianity are the *bodhi* tree and the cross. How do these symbols reveal the aims and character of the Lord Buddha and the Lord Jesus Christ?

Webwise 1 – The Buddha

DharmaNet

www.dharmanet.org

DharmaNet is one of the major Buddhist sites and has a significant collection of material, as well as providing links to many online Buddhist resources. This service is co-ordinated by DharmaNet International and is funded through donations. Its self-confessed aim is to help Buddhists and other interested individuals to find *Dharma* teachings and teachers, to help support *Dharma* centres of all traditions, to promote dialogue and communication, and to help build a vital and co-operative online Buddhist community.

BuddhaNet

www.buddhanet.net

BuddhaNet™ originated with the vision to link the growing worldwide community of Buddhists into an online cyber-*sangha*. In this way, it aims to bring together the ancient Buddhist tradition and the information superhighway to create an electronic meeting place. BuddhaNet is a not-for-profit organisation affiliated with the Buddha Dharma Education Association Inc., which was established as a Vipassana Meditation Centre in 1993 in Sydney by Venerable Pannyavaro, an Australian meditation monk. BuddhaNet is a non-sectarian organisation, offering its services to all Buddhist traditions.

Life of the Buddha

After reading this chapter you may like to look at some accounts of the life of the Buddha. Take particular note of similarities and differences.

1. The website BuddhaNet has an e-book in Adobe Acrobat
   format of the life of the Buddha found at: http://www.buddha
   net.net/pdf_file/lifebuddha.pdf
2. An account of the life of the Buddha drawn from the Pali canon
   is provided on: http://www.accesstoinsight.org/ptf/ buddha.html
   This presents an account that is generally accepted among
   Theravada Buddhists, found in Sri Lanka, Thailand and other
   areas of south-east Asia.
3. This account is taken from *The Buddha and His Teaching*,
   written by Venerable Narada and published by the Cultural
   Conservation Trust: http://www.serve.com/cmtan/ LifeBuddha/
   buddha.htm

Jataka stories

The *Jataka* stories of previous lives of the Buddha are very
popular among Asian Buddhists. You may like to read some of
these at the following sites:

1. Mahindarama Sunday Pali School http://www.geocities.com/
   Athens/Delphi/9241/jataka.htm
2. Wai Pa Buddharangsee http://watthai.net/talon/jataka/ jataka.
   htm

Notes

1. Lamotte, E., *The Spirit of Ancient Buddhism* (Venice: San
   Giorgio Maggiore, 1988), p. 15.
2. Burnett, D., *The Spirit of Hinduism* (Tunbridge Wells:
   Monarch, 1992).
3. Armstrong, K., *Buddha* (London: Phoenix, 2000), p. xxiv.
4. Strong, J. S., *The Buddha: A Short Biography* (Oxford:
   Oneworld, 2001), pp. 4–5.
5. Williams, P., *Buddhist Thought* (London: Routledge, 2000),
   pp. 23–24.
6. *Digha Nikaya* 14.
7. Strong, *op. cit.*, p. 42.
8. Leggett, T., "The Buddha's teaching and ministry", *The
   Middle Way* 75 (2001), p. 224.

9. *Ibid.* pp. 222–233.
10. Strong, *op. cit.*, pp. 20–21.
11. *Anguttara Nikaya* II, 38–39.
12. Williams, *op. cit.*, pp. 22–23.
13. Lamotte, E. *op, cit.*, p. 12.

CHAPTER TWO

THE MIDDLE WAY

What you can learn from this chapter

- the core teaching of the Buddha known as "The Four Noble Truths"
- the distinctive Buddhist understanding of human nature and the human predicament
- the Buddhist understanding of the origin of suffering
- the Buddhist understanding of *nirvana* as the end of suffering
- the way by which one may achieve *nirvana*

At one time the Buddha dwelt in a Deer Park near Benares. There he addressed his five first disciples:

"There are two extremes which are not to be practised.

"What are these two?

"That which is joined to the passions and luxury, which is low, vulgar, common, ignoble and useless. And that which is joined to self-torture, which is painful, ignoble and useless. Avoiding the extremes of sensuality and self-torture, the knowledge of the Middle Way brings insight, calm, enlightenment and Nirvana. What is the Middle Way, by which the Buddha has gained enlightenment, and which produces insight and knowledge, and which tends to calm, to the higher knowledge and enlightenment and Nirvana? It is the Noble Eightfold Way. This is the Middle Path." (*Samyutta 5, 420*)

How can one describe the colour of a flower? In what terms can one express the quality of beautiful music? Experiences can only be described in metaphors and illustrations. The essence of the *Dharma,* or teaching, consists of a mental and spiritual realisation that has come to be known in English as "enlightenment". As the English word suggests, "enlightenment" is an illumination in which things become visible and take on a new form. Thus, enlightenment may be defined as seeing things as they are. It is the discovery of the true nature of reality. The Buddha compared the experience of enlightenment to that of a person who has come out safely from a dangerous jungle, or has been released from prison. It is like the intense feeling of relief and joy when a heavy burden is lifted. It is the freedom from the great veil of assumptions that blind the human mind.

While the actual enlightenment experience is essential to the *Dharma*, this does not mean that the *Dharma* lacks doctrine. The Buddha presented a carefully argued, logical analysis of the human condition, but it is an analysis radically different from Western philosophy because of its totally different assumptions. Western scholars have struggled to find words within European languages that adequately express the ideas conveyed in the Buddhist texts. It is often best to retain the original terms and seek to learn their meaning. As discussed in the previous chapter, the philosophy proposed by the Buddha was based upon the world view of contemporary Indian society, but he introduced some radical innovations.

The study of the *Dharma* appears initially to consist of a few basic philosophical concepts, but these open up layer upon layer with growing elaboration. Western readers are faced with new words and many formulas that stretch their minds as they struggle with an understanding of the *Dharma*. The only way to enter into a study of this great religious tradition is with the philosophy taught by the Buddha, but an intellectual understanding is only the beginning. Sakyamuni Buddha himself likened the *Dharma* to a raft by which a person seeks to cross a dangerous river. The traveller will cling to the raft while struggling in the water, but when he has safely arrived at the other side, he will discard the raft before continuing his journey.[1] The Buddha stressed that the *Dharma* is not merely for understanding but for use. The *Dharma* has traditionally been presented as the Four Noble Truths and the

Middle Way. Most Western scholars consider that it is unlikely that the Buddha initially gave such structured teaching, but this was gradually formulated by his followers into the more concise structure found in the Pali canon. The early teaching is most clearly seen in the Buddha's first sermon in the Deer Park where he wins the allegiance of five ascetics. All traditions agree on what the Buddha actually said, although they may disagree on what he actually meant.

The first Noble Truth of suffering (*dukkha*)

The ultimate question to which Sakyamuni sought an answer related to the first three "sightings" that he had witnessed as a young man. How does one explain sickness, ageing and death in the world? Christians will recognise this as the same question with which the writer of the book of Job wrestles, or the author of Ecclesiastes. The Buddha's answer, however, is fundamentally different from that found in the Old Testament. His answer was that there is an essential sorrow that permeates the universe, such that suffering is found in every aspect of existence. This is the first Noble Truth, called in Pali *dukkha* (Sanskrit: *duhkha*). Suffering results from the fundamental character of existence – all things are transient. All things change, and the life of every being ends in death. It is this characteristic of change that is the inherent nature of sorrow. Although one may have happiness for a moment, conditions will soon change, and the happiness will be no longer. This view is based upon a particular understanding of the nature of living beings that needs to be explored.

The three signs of being

The Buddha taught that all things, whether subjective or objective, have three general characteristics often called the "three marks of existence": impermanence (*anicca*), suffering (*dukkha*), and non-self (*anatta*). Impermanence is to be understood in the sense that everything changes. The rate of change differs but all living beings eventually age and die. The human body lasts on average for about 70 years and during this time continually changes its form. It emerges as a newborn baby and quickly grows into a child, a youth, an adult, before becoming an old man, and a corpse. Similarly, according to the Buddha, human ideas and desires are no less changeable.

The consequence of impermanence is that there is a perpetual feeling of insecurity and frustration. Things are snatched away from us before they can be fully enjoyed. We yearn for some state of security and lasting happiness but it is never achieved. There is a basic unsatisfactory quality about life.

The third sign is the concept of *anatta* ("non-self"), which is of special significance in the Buddhist teaching; it is this teaching that differentiates Buddhism from other Eastern religions and especially Hinduism. In the time of the Buddha, the individual self was postulated to be the same as the universal self, and the spiritual quest was largely the realisation of this identity. The Buddha held that this belief in a permanent self (or *atman*) is one of the most deceitful delusions because it produces attachment to the self.[2] He argued that the belief in a permanent self is due to an erroneous conception of a unity behind the elements that comprise the individual. There is no permanent self (*atman*) as such, only a stream of perishing physical and mental phenomena.

The river Ganges has often been a popular illustration of this effect. A man observes a ball of foam being swept along by the Ganges. He knows that the foam is not solid but empty and insubstantial. Even so, it has the appearance of something real. It is "like a ball of foam, feeling is like a bubble of water, perception is like a mirage, volition is like the trunk of a banana tree and consciousness is like a ghost" (Samyutta III, 140–142). The Buddha took a tiny ball of dung between his fingers and said to a monk: "The belief in the existence of a permanent, stable, eternal and unchanging Self, be it as tiny as this ball of dung, would ruin the religious life which culminates in the perfect destruction of suffering" (Samyutta III, 144).

The five aggregates

The Buddha pointed out that the present "self" consists only of ever-changing elements called *skandhas* ("aggregates", "groups", "heaps"), which make up all living beings. The first category is material, and the others are mental.

1. Form (*rupa*) – material shape. This refers to the material aspect of existence, whether in the outer world or in the body of a living being. Form is said to be made up of the four great elements: earth, water, fire, and wind. Associated with these base elements are four so-called subtle properties, namely solidity, fluidity, heat, and motion. Thus, for example, if you burn yourself, it is not the fire, but heat, that you experience.

2. Feelings (*vedana*). These are the sensations that we experience with objects; they can be pleasant, unpleasant or neutral.

3. Perception (*samjna*). Human beings formulate ideas out of sensations and this allows the conceptualisation of the physical object. Without perception a person might be conscious but would be unable to know what he, or she, was conscious of. This function consists of referring the particular feeling to its appropriate basis and recognising the sensation as real or imaginary.

4. Volition (*samskara*). From the ideas formulated in the mind, judgements are made upon which actions are consequently made. For example, toothache is remembered and recognised again next time. This word must not be confused with *samsara,* which lacks the middle "k" and means the sequence of repeated rebirths.

5. Consciousness (*vijnana*) is the central faculty of the mind, possibly most easily understood as intellect. It arises upon the basis of sense data and, because of the erroneous idea that "I" am, there is a grasping after those sense impressions thought desirable to "me" and a rejection of those thought undesirable. Everything has consciousness but it may be limited, as an animal has less than a human. Without consciousness there is no *samskara.*

The denial of the existence of a permanent self raises the question: What is the nature of a being? The Buddha replied that it is only when the five *skandhas* are together that one can speak of a "being". A well-known illustration of this teaching is that of the chariot, which is quoted here from the Pali text, "Questions of King Milinda".

"If you have come on a chariot, then please explain to me what a chariot is. Is the pole the chariot?"

"No, reverend Sir!"

"Is then the axle the chariot?'

"No, reverend Sir!"

"Is it then the wheels, or the framework, or the flag-staff, or the yoke, or the reins, or the goad-stick?"

"No, reverend Sir!"

"Then is it the combination of pole, axle, wheels, framework, flag-staff, yoke, reins, and goad which is the chariot?"

"No, reverend Sir!"

"Then is this chariot outside the combination of the pole, axle, wheels, framework, flag-staff, yoke, reins, and goad?"

"No, reverend Sir!"

"Then, ask as I may, I can discover no chariot at all. Just a mere sound is the chariot. But what is the real chariot? Your Majesty has told a lie, has spoken falsehood! There is really no chariot!"[3]

None of the items is itself the chariot; the chariot only exists if they all come together. Likewise, the soul (the person) does not exist as such – it is only a name given to a collection of changing formations.

Rebirth

The Buddha spoke of different types of rebirth. In each rebirth, one is born and dies, to be reborn elsewhere in accordance with one's *karma*. The endless cycle of birth, rebirth and redeath is *samsara*. One may be reborn in various "destinies":

1. hungry ghosts, hell-beings (*naraka*)
2. animals (*tiryagyoni*)
3. ghosts (*preta*)
4. humans
5. demi-gods (*asura*)
6. gods (*devas*)

(*Devas* and demi-gods are sometimes considered as a single category.)

"Hungry ghosts" are described as creatures continually tormented by hunger because of their tiny heads set upon huge bellies. These creatures play an important role in folk beliefs, as will be considered later. The first three forms of rebirth qualify as bad "destinies", in that their existence is more suffering than pleasure. In the human form, the two are balanced. For the gods, happiness is greater than sorrow, but they too are subject to transmigration because in Indian thought *samsara* has no exceptions. Rebirth as a human is considered the most desirable, because it is only humans who can achieve *nirvana*.

These six states should not be seen only as future destinies. They are also states of existence one can have in daily life. One is also reborn from moment to moment in this life. Sensuous indulgence is giving expression to the state of "hungry ghost", and one will be reborn.

The frequent charge made of Buddhism is that by continually declaring that life is all suffering, it is a pessimistic philosophy. This is not fully correct. Buddhism is realistic and recognises that life does contain experiences of pleasure. Early texts continually praise the blessings of the life of the householder. He can enjoy the company of the wise, look after his family, do good deeds, and practise religion. The good deeds performed in previous lives produce *karma* that will bring enjoyment in this life. However, the Buddha taught that all such happiness is but for a short time and will eventually end. This form of happiness is a lower grade of happiness and can distract one from the quest for the ultimate reality.

The *devas,* for example, were said to have listened to the message of the Buddha. *Devas* are frequently called "gods" but, more correctly, they are intelligent spiritual beings that do not have material bodies. They are not eternal and are subject to the law of *karma* like all living beings. Although they enjoyed the great sermon of the Buddha they were not enlightened, because they were so caught up with the delights of their world that they did not seek the ultimate truth that existence is suffering.

The second Noble Truth of the origin of suffering (*tanha*)

The second Noble Truth identifies the origin of suffering (*dukkha*) as *tanha,* which literally means "thirst". *Tanha* is the craving for gratification.

The first sermon identifies three types of craving. The first is the craving for sensual pleasure, which is awakened and given form by attractive objects and pleasing ideas. The second is the craving for existence; this is associated with the conviction that existence lasts forever. The third craving is for non-existence – to get rid of unpleasant situations, things and people. Ultimately, this is the impulse for suicide, the rejection of one's whole present life situation. Such a craving, ironically, helps cause a further rebirth whose situation is as bad or worse than the present.

These cravings lead in various ways to suffering. They lead to frustration resulting from a failure to achieve lasting satisfaction in a changing world. Cravings motivate people to feverish activity that have *karmic* effects leading to further rebirths and suffering. They also lead to quarrels, strife and conflict between groups and individuals. For example, I walk down a street on the side where the sun shines but, in a little while, I feel too hot. I cross to the shady side and there I feel too cool. I sit in the comfort of a chair and in a short while I want to stand. When I have stood long enough, I want to sit again. Putting it in modern terms, one can say that I buy a new car but, almost immediately, I am wanting a better one. As a Japanese monk said to me, "I suffer though I don't know it."

Dependent origination

The phenomena of existence, with notions of the *skandha,* the bases of consciousness and the elements, originate in craving. Their appearance and reappearance are ruled by the principle described by the doctrine of "dependent origination" (*pratityasa-mutpada*), translated by some writers as "conditioned arising". This is a central teaching of Buddhist thought. Sariputta, one of the Buddha's chief disciples, said, "Whoever sees Dependent Origination sees dharma, whoever sees dharma sees Dependent Origination" (*Majjhima Nikaya* 1,191).

This doctrine says that all things, mental and physical, arise and exist because of certain conditions, and cease when those conditions are removed. Nothing except *nirvana* is independent and non-conditioned. It is assumed that all things without exception are causally related. It covers the entire physical world, as well as the human body and psyche.

The Buddha never indulged in speculation as to the origin of the world, stating merely that for lack of evidence it cannot be known. He conceived of the world as being in a continuous state of evolution and dissolution. This assumption causes the philosophy to be totally distinct from that of Christianity, where creation is seen to have its origin and meaning within God. In Christianity one can argue that A was caused by B, and B was caused by C, and C was caused by D, and so on, back to the "First Cause", who must have created something out of nothing. However, the Buddha rejected a linear system of causation and assumed that the line of causation is a circle (see figure 2.1).

The teaching is usually presented in a standard formula of

Figure 2.1 The Wheel of Becoming, illustrating the formula of dependent origination

twelve links, each factor affecting another. They form a series of conditioned and conditioning links called *nidanas*:

1. spiritual ignorance
2. constructing activities
3. (discriminative) consciousness
4. mind-body
5. six base senses
6. sensory stimulation
7. feeling
8. craving
9. grasping
10. existence
11. birth
12. ageing, death, sorrow . . .

The primary aim of the twelvefold causation is to express the stream of human life from one existence to another. In other words, effects follow from causes naturally. The Buddha considered he had discovered the inner turnings of the universe and the possibility of liberation. The discovery was clearly a liberating concept for the Buddha – an enlightenment.

The details of most of the process are, however, not so obvious. One theory held by later Buddhist traditions has the twelve links spreading over three lifetimes. The first two links of the process pertain to the previous life. Ignorance in the past gives rise to wrong intentions that bring about the third link, consciousness in the present life. Consciousness here comes about in the mother's womb and is the first stage of the rebirth process. The mind-body is conditioned by the consciousness and so experiences sensory stimulation, feelings, craving, grasping, existence and death. Links 11 and 12 refer to a forthcoming life.

The Buddha did not teach that the "reborn" being is the *same* as the being who died. Neither did he say that it was different from the one who died in the sense that two people are different. The reborn being is linked to the being that died by a causal process. If person X dies and the reborn being is Y, then Y is not the same as X, but is a result of the actions of X, whether they were morally wholesome or not. At death, the causal factors in some way result in the occurrence of another reborn being that we have called Y. At death, the bundle of *skandhas* reconfigure and another configuration takes place. Thus, we cannot say that Y is the same as X or is totally different from it either. Instead of the two options of the eternal nature of the soul or its annihilation, the Buddha proposed dependent origination.

The twelvefold formulation for dependent origination is usually described with the origin of all *dukkha* being spiritual ignorance. However, this should not be seen as an absolute beginning. It is merely a relative point on the spiral of existence that is eternal. In describing the components of a circle, one has to start at some point. The Buddha started with ignorance, and the oral tradition continued to do so.

This contrasts markedly with Christian teaching where the human problem is sin – the wilful rebellion against the Creator God. In this case, it is a linear cause-and-effect relationship, in which God is the "First Cause" of all existence. This is a dogmatic assumption of the Judaeo-Christian tradition expressed in the first chapter of the Bible as, "In the beginning God created the heavens and the earth" (Genesis 1:1). Sin is considered to affect all of human nature, including the mind. Reason alone cannot therefore lead to salvation, and so the biblical emphasis is upon salvation through faith in the person and work of Jesus Christ.

The third Noble Truth of the cessation of suffering (*nirvana*)

Lamotte writes, "Buddhists are assailed by a terror of desire."[4] This is because desire carries one on in the infernal cycle of existence. The third Noble Truth affirms that there is a state of detachment from material things, and a cessation of desire when all craving ceases. This is *nirvana* (Pali: *nibbana*). If the first two Noble Truths are exclusively concerned with the world of becoming, the third Truth is the state to be achieved.

By putting the formula of dependent origination in reverse order, it can be seen that the cessation of *dukkha* comes about by an ending of spiritual ignorance. The key to release consists of non-grasping insight – enlightenment. To be able to achieve such enlightenment there is an inherent assumption that the mind must in essence be pure. The Buddha recognised that the mind contained many impure tendencies but, at the most fundamental level, he concluded that the human mind was essentially pure and bright. It was the latent effects of previous lives that affected even a newborn child. Only in deep meditation is the essential purity of the mind experienced, and here is the possibility of achieving *nirvana.*

What is *nirvana?* Some have maintained that while the Buddha described the path in great detail, he remained silent regarding the goal. This is only partly true. In negative terms, *nirvana* is whatever the world is not. The word literally means "extinction", such as with the quenching of a fire. The fires would refer both to the causes of *dukkha* and *dukkha* itself. When one has destroyed these "fires" they cannot be reborn, and one has attained *nirvana.*

Nirvana may be described in many ways.

1. *nirvana* is destruction of desire and the basic passions, which are craving, hatred and delusion. The destruction of the passions neutralises actions and prevents them from yielding any result.
2. *nirvana* is the disappearance of the five *skandhas* and therefore the end of painful rebirths.
3. *nirvana* is the end of suffering but this should not be equated with the Christian view of paradise. *Nirvana* is outside space and time, and is actually nowhere.
4. *nirvana* is supreme happiness. However, since by definition, feeling is absent from it, what causes the bliss of *nirvana* is the very absence of bliss.
5. *nirvana* is unconditioned, free from change.

What is *nirvana?* King Milinda asked the holy monk to be more tangible so that he could grasp the meaning. He asked for an illustration, and the monk spoke of the lotus. As the lotus is unstained by water, so is *nirvana* unstained by all the defilements. As cool water allays feverish heat, so also *nirvana* is cool and allays the fever of all the passions. Moreover, as water removes the thirst of men and beasts who are exhausted, parched, thirsty, and overpowered by heat, so also *nirvana* removes the craving for sensuous enjoyments, the craving for further becoming, the craving for the cessation of becoming.[5]

Another illustration comes from the text of *Dhammapada*:

> Health is the greatest gift, contentment is the greatest wealth, trust is the best relationship. *Nirvana* is the highest happiness. (*Dhammapada*, 204)

Arhat

Nirvana has two aspects, namely that which relates to the present life and that which relates to the future.[6] In this world, *nirvana* may be likened to saintliness; writers often use the word "saint" for those who are considered to have achieved the state and are known as *arhats*. One who has reached the state of *nirvana* is fully aware of things but responds to whatever happens without selfish desire or self-indulgence. It is the state of perfect serenity in the midst of life's turmoil, without fear of death, or sensuous desires. It is a life that transcends the needs, sufferings and fears of the ordinary life. The *arhat* is one who has seen through the delusion of a permanent self.

The word *arhat* literally means "worthy", as in worthy of great respect. This person is one who has fully completed spiritual training, is fully endowed with all factors of the Path, and has quenched the fires of defilement. The calm actions of the *arhat* no longer create karmic results that lead to rebirths.

> Calm is his mind, calm is his speech, calm is his behaviour who, rightly knowing, is wholly freed, perfectly peaceful and equipoised. (*Dhammapada*, 96)

The balanced detachment of the *arhat*'s mind is such that while he may experience physical pain, no mental anguish can occur. This is because he does not identify with the pain as personal but merely as a non-self, passing phenomenon. Even in the face of death, the *arhat* is unruffled.

Although *arhats* are free of craving and fear, they have not become emotional androids. They have distinct characters and are noted for specific abilities such as teaching, ascetic lifestyle and psychic powers. In popular Buddhism in southern Asia, *arhats* have become cult figures endowed with magical properties. Devoted lay persons seek them out for boons and wear protective amulets bearing their image. The monasteries become centres of pilgrimage during and after their lifetimes. The classic study of the *arhat* in the Theravada tradition is Horner's book, *The Early Buddhist Theory of Man Perfected.*[7] The title of the book captures the essence of the whole concept of the *arhat* – the perfected human.

Nirvana

Nirvana after life occurs at the death of the *arhat* when the *skandhas* disintegrate. This is the future and fullest expression and is known as the *parinirvana* ("full *nirvana*"). The *arhat* is often likened to a flame that has gone out for lack of fuel, yet it should not be understood as annihilation. The Buddha never told his disciples about the nature of the state of *nirvana* after death but instead conveyed its nature in this life through his own existence. In a famous story in the Pali canon, the disciple Malunkyaputta asks the Buddha a series of metaphysical questions as to the Buddha's state after death. The Buddha responds with a question: If a man is struck by a poisoned arrow, will he worry about the origin and nature of the arrow, or rather pull it out? In brief, the early Buddhist texts primarily approach *nirvana* as a practical solution to the essential problem of human suffering.

The fourth Noble Truth of the path that leads to the end of suffering (*magga*)

The fourth Noble Truth deals with the path (*magga*) that leads to *nirvana*; this is the "Middle Path" proclaimed in Sakyamuni's first sermon. It is the way of moderation in which the bodily appetites are fed sufficiently for health rather than subject to physical and mental austerities. The Middle Path is not simply a way of moderation but a comprehensive system that engages the whole person. The Eightfold Path, as it is known in the West, is often understood by Buddhist monks by a shorter formula, the "Threefold Training" (see figure 2.2). This is namely, wisdom (right views and intention),

The Eightfold Path	The Threefold Training
1. Right Views	Wisdom (*prajna*)
2. Right Intention	
3. Right Speech	Morality (*sila*)
4. Right Action	
5. Right Livelihood	
6. Right Effort	Concentration (*samadhi*)
7. Right Mindfulness	
8. Right Concentration	

Figure 2.2   The Eightfold Path

morality (right speech, action and livelihood), and concentration (right effort, mindfulness and concentration).

The Buddha accepted the prevailing views concerning *karma* but he also added a significant point. He taught that not only the deed but also the intention or will behind the deed is important. *Karma* is only generated when intention is present. This is why the Buddha attached so much importance to the discipline of the mind. The Buddhist definition of *karma* is will plus bodily action; this has a bearing on morality.

Morality (*sila*) consists of a conscious determination to abstain from misconduct of the body, of speech, and of mind. Sins of the body are murder, theft and lust. Sins of speech are lying, boasting and idle talk. Sins of the mind are covetousness, prejudice and wrong philosophical ideas. These are similar to the Christian Ten Commandments with the absence of duty towards God. The general aim of Buddhist morality is to avoid any action that might harm some other being.

Concentration (*samadhi*) is the fixing of the mind on one point. This is achieved through specific techniques that were commonly known to Indian mendicants of the period. Sakyamuni probably learned them from his two teachers. They do not require mortification of the body but the cultivation of psychic skills. I will return to a more detailed discussion of meditation in chapter 7.

Wisdom (*prajna*) is most important because it is the means by which the mind is freed from impurities. This is not knowledge of facts, nor a gnosis of vague ideas and emotionally held views. It is a clear vision that embraces the Noble Truths and realises the characteristics of things – impermanence, suffering and impersonality – as well as the peace of *nirvana*. The Buddha distinguished three kinds of wisdom, according to whether their origin is from scriptures (or oral traditions), from reasoning, or from contemplation. The first form of wisdom is a simple act of faith in the words of the teacher. The simple believer is like a man who does not know how to swim and so crosses a river by use of a lifebelt. The second kind of wisdom is from reasoning; Sakyamuni often called his disciples to think for themselves. This superior form of wisdom is like an inexperienced swimmer who crosses the river partly swimming and partly holding onto the lifebelt. The third kind is the wisdom that comes from meditation; it is the direct vision of the emptiness of phenomena. It is accessible to *arhats* who have destroyed their passions and purified their minds. They are like good swimmers who cross the river through their own skills.

*　　*　　*

As with Christianity, the human predicament is at the heart of Buddhist teaching. The Wisdom literature of the Old Testament uses the Hebrew word *hebel* (usually translated into English as "vanity") in a way that has similar connotations with the Buddhist term *dukkha*, implying the unsatisfactoriness of life. The writer of Ecclesiastes, like the Buddha, sees desire as the root of the human predicament. The fundamental difference is that Buddhism seeks to eliminate the cause of *dukkha* through the practice of the Middle Way, whereas the Wisdom literature recognises the divine. In the frequent use of the expression "under the sun" the Wisdom literature shows the restricted scope of the intellectual inquiry and therefore the need, by faith, to take the transcendent into consideration in the quest for meaning. It is God who is the giver of good gifts; life will never be meaningful until he is known.

Buddhists do not believe in the existence of God. They do recognise the existence of "gods" (*devas*) but these are only part of the cycle of death and rebirth. Buddhists would argue that *Dharma* makes God, as understood by the Christian, unnecessary. However, as Paul Williams, a former Buddhist, has pointed out, "there is a gap in the Buddhist explanation of things."[8] Beyond the question of the First Cause is the question: "Why is there something rather than nothing?" Why is there a universe in which the causation detected by the Buddha operates? One answer may be to say, "Why not?" The question asks why it is the case that there is something rather than nothing at all. The existence of anything demands an explanation. Christianity would answer that the explanation is God, but the Buddhist has no answer.

With the preaching of his first sermon Sakyamuni "set in motion" the wheel (lore) of *Dharma*: the Four Noble Truths and the Eightfold Path. This teaching has been succinctly expressed by Eliade as "from the terror of the eternal return to the bliss of the inexpressible".[9] With time, modification of the basic teaching was to occur, but the elegance of the essential philosophy has appealed to many throughout history. At the conclusion of the sermon, it is said that the eldest of the five disciples perceived the truth of the Buddha's teaching, and the Buddha immediately ordained him as a monk. The four others soon followed and were ordained. The sermon of the Four Noble Truths led directly to the formation of the Buddhist community – the *sangha*.

Suggestions for interfaith discussions

The law of karma provides the basis of Buddhist moral order – good deeds produce happiness; bad deeds produce suffering. How can such an order be sustained without a Creator to bestow order and morality?

Webwise 2 – The Middle Way

Dharma the cat

http://www.dharmathecat.com
This is one of the most popular Buddhist sites because it is a fun site with a serious message. Cartoons are used to blend humour and spirituality. On the rocky path to *nirvana*, a novice monk learns many lessons from his cat Dharma and a mouse hell-bent on cheese. Simon & Schuster has published *Philosophy With Fur by Dharma The Cat* in Australia and New Zealand. The site has many interesting sections including an interfaith forum.

The four Noble Truths

http://www.buddhanet.net/4noble.htm
The Four Noble Truths is a clear description of the *Dharma* by Ajahn Sumedho. He is an American who was ordained in Thailand in 1966 and trained there for ten years under the famous Thai teacher, Ajahn Chah. He is currently Abbot of Amaravati Centre, Hemel Hempstead, UK. You will find this popular presentation is found on many sites and represents the Theravada tradition.

Dhammapada

http://www.buddhanet.net/pdf_file/scrndhamma.pdf
The *Dhammapada* is the most widely read Buddhist scripture in the Theravada tradition. This version is available in pdf format, which means that you must have Adobe Acrobat. This can be downloaded free from:
http://www.adobe.com/products/acrobat/readstep 2.html

Notes

1. *Majjhima-nikaya* 1, 134.
2. Sanskrit, like many European languages, gave the negative of the word by adding "a", so the Sanskrit term *anatman* is equivalent to the Pali term *anatta.*
3. Conze, E., *Buddhist Scripture* (Harmondsworth: Penguin, 1988), pp. 148–149.

4. Lamotte, E., *The Spirit of Ancient Buddhism* (Venice: San Giorgio Maggiore, 1961), p. 18.
5. Conze, *op. cit.*, p. 157.
6. *Itivuttaka*, 38–39.
7. Horner, I., *The Early Buddhist Theory of Man Perfected* (London: Routledge, 1936).
8. Williams, P., *The Unexpected Way: On Converting from Buddhism to Catholicism* (Edinburgh: Continuum, 2002), p. 31.
9. Eliade, M. *A History of Religious Ideas* (Chicago: University of Chicago Press, 1982), vol. 2, p. 91.

CHAPTER THREE

COMMUNITY OF THE RENOUNCERS

What you can learn from this chapter

- how the community of monks (the *Sangha*) was formed
- the missionary nature of Buddhism
- the content of the Buddhist canon – the *Tipitaka*
- common practices within the monastic community
- the issue of women in the *Sangha*

The household life is full of hindrances; it is a path of the dust of passion. The life of him who has renounced worldly things is free as the air. How difficult it is for that man who dwells at home to live the higher life in all its fullness and purity and perfection. So let me cut off my hair and beard, clothe myself in saffron-coloured robes, and go forth from Home to the Homeless state.[1]

The Buddha was one of many of his time who renounced the world and sought a spiritual path distinct from the rituals of the Brahmin priests. The teaching of the Buddha quickly gathered a growing number of "renouncers" who felt called from the daily life they knew. Society therefore became divided into two sections: renouncers (monks, or *bhikkhus*) and lay people. The renouncers formed a new and distinct community within the larger existing society and this became known as the *sangha*. This monastic community has been a characteristic of most Buddhist societies over the centuries and is the subject for this chapter.

The founding of the *Sangha*

According to the Pali canon, the monastic community was first established in Benares when, following his enlightenment, the Buddha went to his former disciples and taught them the *Dharma* through the famous sermon in the Deer Park. These five men received the *Dharma* and became enlightened like the Buddha. Tradition tells the story of the conversion of the Buddha's two chief disciples, Sariputta and Moggalana. They were great friends who were both striving for enlightenment. They promised one another that whoever attained it would tell the other. One day Sariputta met one of the five original disciples and was immediately struck by his serenity; he asked who was his teacher. The disciple said that he had only recently come to follow his master and could quote only the first two stanzas of the verse summarising the Buddha's doctrine of causality. Sariputta immediately grasped the truth and was won over to the Buddha's teaching. He then told his friend and as they approached the Buddha, he immediately declared that they would be his chief disciples.

Others joined the movement and, when it had grown somewhat, Gautama charged them with a mission that transformed this local religious movement into a potential world religion. Those from the Christian tradition will not fail to note the similarities of this command with the "Great Commission" of the Lord Jesus Christ.

Although there are similarities, there are some marked differences. First, whereas, in Matthew the mission command is founded on the authority of Jesus, in the Buddhist text it is based not only on the liberation of the Buddha himself but also on the similar liberation of his followers. It is because the *bhikkhus* have achieved enlightenment that they can now proclaim the *Dharma*. Second, although both commands include a summons to teach, the Christian tradition commands the disciples to teach all that Jesus commanded them, while the Buddhist command is to teach the *Dharma*. Third, as Carrithers remarks, the *bhikkhus* "were no Protestant evangelists creating a church of laymen, for they were to propound the absolutely perfect and wholly pure life of celibate mendicancy".[2] Even though renunciation was the heart of the message, the *bhikkhu* missionaries were dependent on the food and support of the local people as they travelled along the trade routes of the region.

Mahavagga 1.10–11

The Lord said to the *Bhikkhus*, "I am delivered, O *Bhikkhus* from all fetters human and divine. You, O *Bhikkhus*, are delivered from all fetters, human and divine."

"Go ye now, monks, and wander for the gain of the many, for the happiness of the many, out of compassion for the world, for the good, for the gain, and for the welfare of gods and men. Let not two of you go the same way. Preach, monks, the Dharma which is lovely in the beginning, lovely in the middle, lovely at the end, in the spirit and in the letter; proclaim a consummate, perfect, and pure life of holiness. There are beings whose mental eyes are covered by scarcely any dust, but if the Dharma is not preached to them, they cannot attain salvation."[3]

"And I will go also, O *Bhikkhus*, to Urvela to Senanigama, in order to preach the Dharma."

Matthew 28:16–20

Then Jesus came to them and said, "All authority in heaven and on earth has been given to me."

"Therefore go and make disciples of all nations, baptising them in the name of the Father and of the Son and of the Holy Spirit, and teaching them to obey everything I have commanded you."

"And surely I am with you always, to the very end of the age."

The word *sangha* was a common Pali word meaning "multitude" or "assembly". In Theravada Buddhism it has become more of a technical term that refers to a religious community in two similar senses. First, the "*Sangha* of the four directions" refers to Buddhists everywhere – all who have taken refuge in the Three Gems. It is similar to the Christian use of "church universal". The second and more common use is that for the monastic order whose members are called *bhikkhus* (males) or *bhikkhunis* (females) and novices.

Indian society of the fifth century BC recognised a difference between the householder and the homeless wanderer. The *bhikk-*

hus lived by receiving alms but they were differentiated from ordinary beggars by the sacramental character of the act. The *bhikkhus* were not begging just as a means of subsistence but as an outward token that they had renounced the world and its goods and were looking to receive a bare living through public charity. This is exactly what the Buddha had done when he left his wife and child to seek a meaning to suffering. These people were recognised by the begging bowls as visible symbols of their quest for the *Dharma*. When two wanderers met casually on the wayside two questions would be asked: "Who is your master? What is the *Dharma* you have adopted?"

The Theravada tradition says that for 20 years after the establishment of the *Sangha*, there was neither rule nor offence. But as the years went by, the *Sangha* grew in number and some joined whose motives were not of the purest. A *bhikkhu* named Sudinna, a native of Kalanda village near Vesali, had sexual intercourse with his ex-wife. This was in essence against the teaching of the Middle Path in that it was a practice of indulgence. In the light of such a grave offence, the Buddha convened an assembly of the *bhikkhus*. The Buddha, using his supernormal powers, reflected on what rules earlier Buddhas would lay down under certain conditions and adopted similar regulations to meet the situation that had arisen in his time. In this way, there emerged a code of conduct for the monks.

Soon after the *parinirvana* of the Buddha, a council of the *Sangha* was held in Rajagaha, the capital city of Magadha; this was given under royal patronage. The date of the council was a few weeks after the *parinirvana* during the rainy season which, according to the Theravada tradition, would make the date as July–August 483 BC. The leading monk of that time, Mahakasyapa, was asked to convene the council and select the representatives with the purpose of consolidating the teaching of the Buddha. According to legend, he invited 499 monks who had achieved enlightenment, plus Sakyamuni's attendant and favourite companion, Ananda. Some sources say that at this time Ananda had not achieved enlightenment because he had been so busy serving his master he had no time for meditation. In due course, Ananda is reported to have attained *nirvana*. Ananda played a major part at the conference because his close association with Sakyamuni meant that he could well remember the teachings; these were later to be transcribed into the canon known as the *Tipitaka* (Sanskrit: *Tripitaka*).

Most Western scholars consider it unlikely that such a well-structured and ordered canon would have been produced within a few months of the Buddha's *parinirvana*. It is more likely that the remembered teachings of the Buddha were preserved and transmitted orally for many years by groups of monks specialised in memorising and chanting portions of the tradition. The oral tradition was finally written down in Sri Lanka sometime in the first century BC. Even afterwards, when writing was more common, the tradition was still memorised and the text only used to aid memorisation. The Buddhist canon deriving from this early period consists of three sections, called "baskets", and hence the name *Tipitaka* ("The Three Baskets"). They consist of:

1. *Vinaya* – collection of rules for monks.
2. *Sutras* – sermons given by the Buddha.
3. *Abhidharma* – systematic teaching of the Buddha.

These texts provide valuable information on the early life of the *Sangha*. Although they are quite voluminous in themselves, later Buddhist traditions have produced an ever-growing body of commentaries and canonical works. Figure 3.1 provides an outline of the Pali canon including the content of the *Tipitaka*.[4]

The *Vinaya Pitaka*

The *Vinaya* is a set of rules of discipline laid down for regulating the monastic life of the monks and nuns. They deal with transgressions of discipline and consist of a rule, either positive or negative in character. For example, "I allow you, *bhikkhus,* to do this or to refrain from doing that." The offences for which penalties are laid down are often classified under seven categories, depending upon their nature. The most important set of rules is the *Patimokkha*, consisting of 227 rules that apply to the *bhikkus*, and a few extra rules for women members of the order. The *Sangha* meets to recite the rules of the *Patimokkha* twice every month to ensure that the

A CANONICAL (*Tipitaka*)

I *Vinaya Pitaka*: "Basket (*pitaka*) of Rules" for the orders of monks
1 *Patimokkha*: 227 rules and expositions
2 *Khandhakas*: teaching
3 *Parivara*: a synopsis of 1 and 2

II *Sutta Pitaka*: "Basket of Threads", i.e. a collection of connected sayings
1 *Digha Nikaya*: Long Collection
2 *Majjhima Nikaya*: Middle-length Collection
3 *Sanyutta Nikaya*: Connected Collection
4 *Anguttara Nikaya*: Further Parts
5 *Khuddaka Nikaya*: Short Collection
   a. *Khuddakapatha*: short sayings
   b. *Dhammapada*: verses on *Dhamma*
   c. *Udana*: verse of uplift
   d. *Itivuttaka*: short sayings
   e. *Sutta-Nipata*: the "bunch of threads"
   f. *Vimanavatthu*: "mansion" stories
   g. *Petavatthu*: stories of "those gone before"
   h. *Thera-theri-gatha*: verses of the elder monks
   i. *Jataka*: stories of previous lives of the Buddha
   j. *Niddesa*: exposition
   k. *Patisambhidamagga*: "way of analysis"
   l. *Apadana*: text by or about the Buddhas
   m. *Buddhavansa*: "the lineage of a Buddha"
   n. *Cariya-pitaka*: "basket of deeds"

III *Abhidharma Pitaka*: "Basket of Supplementary Teaching"
1 *Dhammasangai*: compendium of mental experiences
2 *Vibhanga*: dividing, inquiring into subjects
3 *Dhatukatha*: talks on elements
4 *Puggalapannatti*: designation of types of people
5 *Kathavatthu*: bases of teaching
6 *Yamaka*: the "pairs book"
7 *Patthana*: cause and effect

B POST-CANONICAL
1 *Milindapando*: "Questions of King Milinda"
2 *Nettipakarana*: "Book of Guidance"
3 *Petakpadesa*: "*Pitaka* reference"
4 *Visuddhimagga*: "Path of Purity"
5 *Mahavansa*: "Great Chronicle"
6 *Culavansa*: Sequel to the "Great Chronicle"
7 Other lesser works

All the above have been published by the Pali Text Society except the *Jataka* and *Milindapando*. The best introductory text is *Guide to the Tipitaka* (Bangkok: White Lotus, 1993).

Figure 3.1 Pali literature

monks are following them. Horner, in her classic work on the *Vinaya* literature, writes of this practice:

> This recitation served the double purpose of keeping the rules fresh in the minds of the monks and nuns, and of giving each member of the monastic community the opportunity, while the rules are being repeated or recited, to avow any offences that he or she had committed.[5]

For each breach of the rules, appropriate punitive measures are indicated. The rules are classified into groups of relative importance. The most important are the four *parajikas* ("offences") that lead to loss of status as a monk.

1. To abstain from sensuous misconduct

The first rule is celibacy, which was a common religious practice among the renouncers at the time of Sakyamuni. Within the original *Sangha* the aim was to remove everything that impeded inner progress. Monks and nuns trying to achieve selflessness must be detached from all sources of sensual pleasure. In addition, sexual relations entail social responsibilities, and the attendant worries were an obstacle to mental concentration. For this reason the Buddha was strict about the complete prohibition of sexual relations.

> If a monk who has accepted the Discipline, who has not rejected the Discipline and has not pronounced himself unable to continue (with the religious life), has sexual intercourse, even with an animal, he commits an offence entailing defeat. That monk is one who is defeated; he is not in communion. (*Vinaya* 3:23)

However, as the *Sangha* grew in number, questions began to emerge as to how far one could go and still be a monk. Does celibacy include masturbation, homosexuality, non-penetration, or having sex with a monkey? The *Vinaya* contains a full range of examples given to describe the limits of behaviour of a monk. All such sensuous behaviour is condemned as digression from the path of selflessness.

2. To abstain from taking what is not given

The second rule is total honesty and the rejection of deliberate theft. This is wider than the law "Thou shalt not steal" and relates to motives more like "Thou shalt not covet". Theft comes from craving to possess and therefore is annulled. The *Vinaya* tells many stories of monks whose motives were not as lofty as they should have been. For example, the story is told of two monks who wanted a pot of honey belonging to another monk. The honey, however, was on a table that belonged to them, so they carried the table away without touching the pot of honey.

3. To abstain from taking life

The third rule is the avoidance of any form of killing, not just taking human life. This precept implies pacifism; hunting, warfare and butchering are traditionally abhorrent to Buddhists. The *Vinaya* is subject to much debate as to what this actually meant. For example, what if a monk gives a woman a medicine to cause her to have an abortion? Is that killing? Again, what if a monk helps a person to commit suicide – is that killing? What if a man intends to kill a man but by accident kills another? When once discussing this topic with a group of Buddhist monks, the monks of the Theravada tradition were adamant that the answer was "No!" What was important was that the man did not deliberately intend to kill the individual. Today, this precept raises major issues for Buddhists as to what is "right livelihood" in the modern world.

4. To abstain from false speech

The fourth rule was the avoidance of false proclamation of supernatural faculties; hypocrisy is an apt description here. Whenever a monk claims an attainment he does not really possess, he should be put out of the *Sangha*. From the stories in the *Tipitaka,* this problem seemed to have occurred during a famine when monks claimed greater attainments in order to get more food.

The implication of this ethical teaching is that thinking about doing something bad is not wrong in itself, provided you do not actually do it. Evil thoughts do not impinge on your personality. If you do it accidentally it is not significant, because it is the intention that is important. Further, the Buddha said that there was nothing wrong with marriage and sex but that a monk should not then continue to pretend to hold to his vows. A monk must return to his teacher and take back his vows, and then he can take a wife.

In addition to the four important *parajikas*, there are the 13 *sanghadisesa* rules required for formal participation in the *Sangha*. The following are prohibited:

1. emission of semen
2. contact with women
3. blasphemy against women
4. flirting with women
5. go-between monks (making arrangements)
6, 7. excessively large living huts
8. false charges against another monk
9. defamation of character
10. causing schism within the *Sangha*
11. opposition to the *Sangha*
12. obstinate monks who refuse discipline of the *Sangha*
13. bringing the *Sangha* into disrepute by bad behaviour among laity

If a monk transgresses these rules and wishes to remain in the *Sangha* he must confess them to the *Sangha*. The *Sangha* determines the offence and orders a penance (usually probation for a month). After fulfilling the penance, the monk then asks the *Sangha* to reinstate him to full association again.

The next set of rules in the *Vinaya* are the two *aniyatas* offences, which are of uncertain category as to whether they are *parajika* or *sanghadisesa* offences:

a. sitting down privately with a woman in a secluded place
b. sitting down privately with a woman at such a distance that she and the monk cannot be heard

There then follow the thirty *nissaggiya*, or "minor" offences. These are rules laid down to curb greed for possessions but, because they are so old, it is often difficult to know what they originally meant.

Fifteen rules relate to monks' robes: no more than three robes should be worn by a monk. A monk may accept robes only at the beginning of the rainy season and then only from members of his own family. He should only have one begging bowl and receive no silver or gold.

Then there are the 92 *pacittiyas* offences, which are classified into nine categories. These include rules stipulating that monks are:

> not allowed to sleep in the same room as a woman or a member of the laity
> not allowed to drink alcohol
> not allowed to amuse themselves (play) in public
> not allowed to frighten another monk
> not allowed to listen to the conversation of other monks
> not allowed to eat after noon
> required to take two baths a month

Monks must confess an offence to another monk; this usually occurs at the public confession of the *Sangha* that occurs twice a month. At this time the whole *Patimokkha* is read and, after every rule, monks stand up to confess any failing. This is all based on personal honesty. Then follow the 75 *sekhiyas* (rules for good conduct) and the 7 *adhikaranas* (legal procedures).

The reason for this extended discussion of the first part of the *Vinaya* is not to weary the reader but to illustrate the concern of the monk with purity of life in his endeavour for enlightenment. The *Vinaya* shows that the early Buddhist *Sangha* was essentially a discipline of life rather than a religious priesthood.

The second and third baskets

The second basket is the *Sutta Pitaka*, the "Basket of Threads", which is a collection of many of the discourses of the Buddha delivered on various occasions, and a few given by his leading disciples. It is a massive literary work running into many dozens of volumes and divided into five separate collections. No Buddhist sits down and reads through the Pali canon as a Christian would study the Bible. There are different types of literature with different uses in Buddhist life. The parables of the Buddha are often retold by the monks and the most widely read sections are the *Dhammapada,* the *Sutta-Nipata* and the *Jataka.*

The *Dhammapada* has, in the Pali version, 423 verses divided into 26 chapters. It is an anthology of Buddhist devotion and practice, which brings together verses in popular use or gathered from different sources. Radhakrishnan in his translation and commentary writes:

> Though it may not contain the very words of the Buddha, it does embody the spirit of the Buddha's teaching, summoning men to a process of strenuous mental and moral effort. *Dhamma* is discipline, law, religion; *pada* is path, means, way, base; *Dhammapada* is then the base or the foundation of the religion.[6]

The text is widely read by Buddhists.

The *Sutta-Nipata* consists of discourses of the Buddha or his leading disciples to both monks and lay followers. The collection of *suttas* is presented in an unsystematised form, non-academic, but giving an exhortation to lead a balanced, ethical life.[7]

The *Jataka* stories, some 500 of them, recount the previous incarnations of the Buddha. These stories are colourful and dramatic and for this reason are popular in folk beliefs. These were mentioned in chapter 1.

The third basket, the *Abhidharma,* is another extensive set of texts, probably compiled much later than the previous two "baskets". Tradition attributes the nucleus of this work to the teaching which the Buddha gave to his mother Deva and others, continuously for three months. Some Buddhist scholars therefore place great importance upon the *Abhidharma*, and consider it to be the higher teaching of the Buddha. For example, Narada Maha Thera writes:

> The *Dhamma*, embodied in the *Sutta Pitaka*, is the conventional teaching and the *Abhidhamma* is the ultimate teaching. In the *Abhidhamma* both mind and matter, which constitute this complex machinery of man, are microscopically analysed. Chief events connected with the process of birth and death are explained in detail. Intricate points of

the *Dhamma* are clarified. The Path of Emancipation is set forth in clear terms.[8]

Monastic life

The *Vinaya* provides some fascinating insight into the life and organisation of the early *Sangha*.

Ordination

Ordination in the early *Sangha* was performed in various ways. In the first period of the Buddha's preaching, admission into the *Sangha* took place with the Gautama simply saying, "*Ehi*, come! Come follow the *Dharma* and put an end to suffering." Afterwards, conditions and ceremonies were progressively introduced because of the great number and diversity of the candidates. The Buddha's own father came to him to express the concern of society at the many converts who were leaving their social responsibilities to join the *Sangha*.

Because some unsuitable people were wanting to join the order, the Buddha appears to have laid down increasingly more stringent rules of ordination. For example, ten monks had to be present in order to ordain a new monk, and five monks in an isolated area. Specific people were excluded from ordination, such as transvestites, those with contagious diseases, those branded as criminals, prisoners, and lay members in the king's service. Later, slaves running away from their masters were discouraged from joining the *Sangha*. Children had to be over fourteen years old to be ordained without parental consent but small boys were allowed to stay at monasteries as novices.

The robes

The monk had four resources: robe, lodges, food, and medicine. The robe was one of the most important symbols of the life of the renouncer. There are numerous references to the subject in the *Vinaya* which seem to have been established at a definite stage in the evolution of the community.

According to the *Mahavagga*, during the first 20 years, the Buddha and his disciples wore a garment made of rags. In other renouncer sects the ascetics wore garments of grass, tree bark or skins, while some remained completely naked.[9] The *Sangha* did not want to imitate the way of dress of other ascetics so adopted a costume made up of rags that they had collected. Then, after 20 years, there was a marked change in the discipline.

The *Mahavagga* tells the story of how, when the Buddha was ill, he was treated by the royal physician. The doctor later gave to the Buddha a length of cloth for him to make a robe. The Buddha accepted the fabric and addressed the monks in the following words: "Monks, I allow you to accept pieces of material given by lay people and to wear robes given by lay followers, or to continue wearing rag-robes."[10] Following this, the dress of monks and nuns began to be governed by rules. The monk's costume was to comprise of three robes: one with a lining, to be worn as an outer cloak, one without a lining, to be worn as a toga, and one used as underclothing. The robes were not to be made from a single piece, but had to be made of pieces sewn together in a way similar to the earlier rag-robes.[11]

Lodges

Wanderers had to reckon with the monsoon conditions that halted the annual movement. It was therefore customary for all sects of wanderers to seek shelter for the rainy season. The Jain and Brahmanical wanderers had no regulations prescribing how the community should live together during the rains, but the Buddhist ideal became one of fellow monks congregating together in retreats known as *vassa*. The *bhikkhus* would naturally make their *vassa* settlements in localities where alms were available. In practice, two kinds of *vassa* came into existence. The first, *avasa*, were in the countryside and were set out, built and maintained by the monks themselves. The second, *arama*, were in or near towns and were situated within their own private enclosures and looked after by a wealthy lay patron. The monk-built *avasa* were temporary structures liable to be robbed and dismantled after the monks had left them at the end of the rainy season. This contrasted with the *arama* that were preserved by the patron and elaborated over a period of time. The name *arama* denotes a pleasure-ground, usually an orchard or garden of a wealthy citizen. When it was given to the monks, it became named *sangharama*. Among the structural needs that arose was for a meeting hall for communal gatherings.

Only three *aramas* have been traced by archaeologists, of which the most impressive was that of Jetavanarama.[12] According to legend, Anathapindada was a wealthy banker of the city of Savatthi and had come to Rajagaha on business. He was so impressed by the person of the Buddha that he invited the Buddha and his followers to spend the next rainy season at Savatthi. Anathapindada was delighted when the Buddha agreed, and went to find a suitable place for the monks to reside. He decided Prince Jeta's pleasure-garden would be ideal but when he asked the prince, he did not want to sell the land. The prince therefore quoted a fantastic price of as much gold as would cover the park. Nevertheless, Anathapindada agreed and brought the gold out of his store in wagon loads. He then provided the site with all the amenities a monk-settlement required. The story is often recounted as an illustration of a devoted lay person.[13] The Jetavana site was continually occupied for almost a thousand years and was identified in 1863 by the British archaeologist Cunningham as being located in present day Maheth, Uttar Pradesh.

Food

Monks and nuns were not allowed to work for a living or to grow their own food. Even if they chanced upon some food, they were not allowed to eat it. They could only eat that which was given to them; in this way they were completely dependent on others, just like little children. There were therefore only two ways of obtaining food: they could walk from house to house receiving food or be invited to eat by lay followers. Lay people did not see Buddhist monks as beggars nor vagrants. They were "renouncers" who had dedicated themselves to the spiritual quest. Many members came from rich families and had renounced the life of luxury, so lay people gave them food with respect and regarded it as their duty to provide for them.

When the monks were given something, they were not to look into the person's face, nor to try and find out if the donor was a man or a woman. They were to wear their robes correctly when on their begging rounds and were to control their senses and practise mindfulness.[14] Monks and nuns were only allowed to eat once a day, before noon.

Medicine

In the *Vinaya* the health of monks and nuns was given a high priority; for this reason they were allowed to consume medical foods. One day the Buddha saw some emaciated and sickly-looking monks, and told them:

> Monks, there are five kinds of food, ghee [clarified melted butter], fresh butter, sesame oil, honey and molasses, which everyone regards as medicines. Although they are nutritious they do not count as real meals. I permit you to accept these five medicines and to consume them, during "the right time" (*Vinaya* 1:199) .

A few days later, the Buddha amended the restriction and, since then, monks and nuns have been allowed to take medicine at any time.

Women in the early *Sangha*

There were many women who showed great interest in the teaching of the Buddha and supported the new religious movement. Some women wished to join the Buddha's community as nuns but the Buddha declined their request. His aunt and foster mother, Maha Pajapati Gotami, asked that an order of nuns be established but the Buddha refused. Finally, through the intervention of Ananda, who himself asked three times and was refused, the Buddha granted their request.[15]

There has been much discussion as to why the Buddha declined their requests for so long. It is clear that the Buddha anticipated that problems might arise for nuns in the course of their everyday lives. For example, a young nun was raped in the forest. For this reason nuns were not allowed to travel or dwell in the forests on their own.[16]

The new community had to conform to the norms of society in

northern India at that time and so the Buddha imposed eight rules for women members. These were:

1. A nun must always greet a monk with deference, rising from her seat and showing him proper respect.
2. A nun was forbidden to spend the rainy season retreat in a district where there was no monk.
3. Twice a month a nun was to ask the monks to preach the *Dharma*.
4. At the end of the rainy season, a nun was to ask both the order of nuns and the order of monks if they had seen or heard her behave wrongly.
5. A nun who had committed a serious offence had to undergo a temporary probation.
6. A nun could only be ordained at the agreement of both orders of monks and nuns, after following the six precepts for two years.
7. A nun was on no account to revile or abuse a monk.
8. A nun could not give admonition or advice to a monk.

Although the office of the nun was clearly inferior to that of the monk, the Buddha was definite in his teaching that a woman could achieve enlightenment. Near the end of his life, the Buddha was asked by a wandering mendicant whether there were any nuns who had reached the perfect state. The Buddha replied:

> Not merely a hundred, nor two, nor three, four or five hundred, but far more are those nuns, my disciples, who by the elimination of defilements have here and now realised by direct knowledge the freedom of mind and wisdom that is without defilements, and who abide (in that realisation).[17]

The order of nuns was parallel to that of the order of monks but was organised independently for the nuns' communal life. They possessed a complete code of discipline; ten years after her ordination, a nun was called "elder". Nuns continued in the Theravada tradition until at least the tenth century AD, when in Sri Lanka they disappeared. A few nuns continued in other southeast Asian countries but their numbers are small.

Householders (laity)

The Buddha was primarily occupied with the pure ideal of utter renunciation and it was on those who would follow him that he focused his teaching. However, there were many who wished to remain in family life as believers. To them the Buddha taught the merit of giving and the merits of keeping certain precepts by which they would be reborn after death to a happy life.

According to the Buddha, the life followed by the laity was inferior to that of the monks because they could not attain *nirvana* directly. Their aspiration was merely one of a happy rebirth and the paradises of the gods. There were three virtues required of the laity: faith, morality and generosity. Faith (*sraddha*) is not a reasoned adherence to a clearly defined body of revealed truth but a disposition that imparts serenity of mind and restrains emotions. The Buddhist faith does not oblige the adherents to reject their ancestral beliefs nor even reject their observances. Each person is allowed to worship the traditional deities of the area and caste and, in addition, he or she acknowledges the "Triple Jewel". The Buddha never denounced the multitude of gods of the Hindu pantheon but regarded them as caught up in *samsara* and so useless in the quest for ultimate liberation.

The second virtue of the laity was morality (*sila*). The individual was to commit himself to five precepts of abstinence. These are, first, to abstain from taking the life of any living being; second, from taking what is not given by the owner; third, from sexual misconduct; fourth, from false speech; and finally, abstinence from intoxicating drinks and drugs. The third virtue of the laity was generosity (*dana*), which was generally considered the most important. The texts have lists of meritorious donations given by individuals according to their means.

*   *   *

The Buddhist *Sangha* was originally a community committed to the *Dharma* of the Buddha. The *Tipitaka* effectively transformed the sect into a religious order that met periodically to confirm their unity through the recitation of the *Patimokkha*. Buddhism was therefore essentially a discipline rather than a religion. The Buddha founded an order with a rule of life, not a temple with a priesthood and system of worship. Monks are therefore not mediators between god(s) and humans, as is the role of the priest. Buddhist monks generally regard themselves as having a dual function: to strive for their own enlightenment and to preserve the *Dharma.*

The aim of these early Buddhist monks was therefore a very personal one, to achieve one's own enlightenment. Today, this remains an important element in the Theravada tradition of Buddhism found throughout much of south-east Asia. As a leading Japanese Buddhist scholar said to me, "In Theravada tradition, you go like a rhinoceros. You go by yourself, not with others." If one fails in the rules of the *Vinaya,* it is oneself alone that is affected, so mercy has no part in the early tradition of Buddhism.

Suggestions for interfaith discussions: church and *Sangha*

The buddha taught a way of liberation dependent upon self-sufficiency. His compassion was a natural overflow of his fully enlightened state but he had no need of others. In contrast, the Christian idea of God is love. The Christian, even when alone, is with the community of the church. It is useful to consider the differences and similarities between the monastic order (*Sangha*) and the church.

Webwise 3 – Community of the Renouncers

Pali Text Society

http://www.palitext.demon.co.uk
The Society was founded in 1881 by T.W. Rhys Davids "to foster and promote the study of Pali texts". It publishes Pali texts in roman characters, translations in English and ancillary works including dictionaries, concordances, books for students of Pali and a journal. Most of the classical texts and commentaries have now been edited and many works translated into English.

Tipitaka

http://www.accesstoinsight.org/canon
The *Tipitaka*, or Pali canon, is the collection of primary Pali language texts which form the doctrinal foundation of Theravada Buddhism. The *Tipitaka* and the ancient commentaries together constitute the complete body of classical Theravada texts.

Read the rules for the monks listed in the *Patimokkha* at:

http://www.sacred-texts.com/bud/sbe13
or
http://www.accesstoinsight.org/canon/vinaya/bhikkhu-pati-intro.html Here the texts are those translated from the Pali by T. W. Rhys Davids and Hermann Oldenberg.

Or:
http://www.vipassana.com
Vipassana.com is an independent site promoting the practice of Buddhist meditation as found in the Theravada tradition. Its aim is to "offer resources to help nurture and sustain a fulfilling and effective meditation practice that is consistent with the Buddha's teachings".

Ordination of women

http://lhamo.tripod.com/4ordin.htm
Women Active in Buddhism (WaiB) has an extensive site providing information about the ordination of women in various Buddhist traditions. It has links to many support groups for ordained women and other resources.

A selection of some of the most common sutras

http://hjem.get2net.dk/civet-cat/theravada-writings.htm#suttas
This site presents the teaching of Ajan Chah who advocated the Forest tradition that was influential on many Western seekers.

Notes

1. *Digha Nikaya* 1, 62
2. Carrithers, M., *The Buddha* (Oxford: OUP, 1983), pp. 83–4.

3. *Mahavagga* I.11.1–2, "The Book of Discipline" vol. IV, translated by I. B. Horner (London, 1951).
4. Penenchio, M., *Guide to the Tripitaka: Introduction to the Buddhist Canon* (Bangkok: White Lotus, 1993).
5. Horner, I. B., *The Book of the Discipline* (London: Luzac, 1936–1966), vol. 1, xii.
6. Radhakrishnan, S., *The Dhammapada* (Delhi: OUP, 1974), p. 1.
7. Saddhatissa, H., *The Sutta-Nipata* (London: Curzon Press, 1985).
8. Narada Maha Thera, *The Manual of the Abhidharma* (Colombo: Vajirarama, 1956), p. iii.
9. *Vinaya* 1:282.
10. *Mahavagga* 1:280.
11. Wijayaratna, M., *Buddhist Monastic Life* (Cambridge: CUP, 1990), pp. 30–37.
12. Leggett, T., "The Buddha's teaching and ministry", *The Middle Way* 75 (2001), p. 231–233.
13. Dutt, S., *Buddhist Monks and Monasteries of India* (London: George Allen & Unwin, 1962), pp. 63–64.
14. *Vinaya* 2:215–216.
15. *Vinaya* 2:253–256.
16. *Vinaya* 3:35.
17. *Mahavagga* 1:490.

CHAPTER FOUR

COUNCILS AND CONTROVERSIES

What you can learn from this chapter

- the history of the early Buddhist councils in India
- the nature of these controversies and how they led to various divisions
- the emergence of the innovative Mahasanghika tradition.
- the teaching of the early schools of Buddhism (500 BC–1 AD).

Shortly before his *parinirvana,* the Buddha advised Ananda regarding the future of the *Sangha* with the following words:

> If, Ananda, it occurs to you: "The doctrine is such that it is rendered teacherless; we are without teachers", you should not consider it so. Ananda, whatever doctrine I have taught and discipline I have instituted, that will be your teacher after my death.[1]

The Buddha did not appoint a central authority to succeed him and decide matters of belief and practice. His teaching was essentially one of individual endeavour to achieve enlightenment. This reluctance of the Buddha to appoint future leadership, and his request that the *Dharma* (doctrine) and the *Vinaya* (discipline) be their guide, concentrated the attention of the movement on determining the nature of the *Dharma* and discipline.

Although the religious philosophy of the Buddha was both elegant and comprehensive, it failed to address certain issues.

These were sometimes topics that the Buddha refused to speak about, such as his own nature in *nirvana*. He continually argued that his primary concern was to encourage his disciples to practise the path that he taught. Speculation in other matters was therefore unnecessary and a digression from the real purpose, which was to gain enlightenment. His teaching was pragmatic, with the aim of conquering death. However, this did not stop speculation, which resulted from the later developments of the philosophy that had been taught by the Buddha.

These areas became the centres of debate and sometimes led to the emergence of alternative schools of philosophy. These did not necessarily result in acrimonious divisions; often, adherents of different schools lived in the same monasteries. The main features of the recorded history of the early Buddhist movement concern the meetings of three councils of the *Sangha* and the later debate recorded only in the Theravada tradition. Before discussing these councils it is worthwhile first to give a general schema of the major canonical councils and the issues involved.

Location	Date	Principal participants	Religious issue(s)
Rajagaha	483 BC	500 *arhats*	Recitation of *Dharma* and *Vinaya*
Vaisali	383 BC	700 monks	Controversy over ten illicit practices
Pataliputra	247 BC	King Asoka	Debate on orthodoxy and defining of Pali canon
Gandhara	c. 100 AD	King Kaniska and 499 scholars	Composition of *Mahavibhasa*

The First Council (Rajahaga)

In the previous chapter, mention was made of the First Council, at which the recitation of the traditional content of the *Tipitaka* was first made. This gathering was held in Rajagaha a few months after the *parinirvana* which, according to the most popular reckoning, would be 483 BC. Rajagaha was the capital of King Bimbisara, ruler of the state of Magadha, and a chief royal patron of the Buddha. The meeting was held during the rainy season; the king and the community provided the necessary food and shelter for the convocation.

Many divergent accounts of the gathering have been passed on but the oldest Pali tradition says that the monk Mahakapasypa selected 499 *arhats* to perform the recital and insisted the Buddha's attendant, Ananda, be present, even though he had not had time to meditate to achieve enlightenment. However, he had accompanied the Buddha for more than 20 years and remembered his teaching best. Tradition says that Mahakapasypa first asked questions of Upali, a dedicated disciple of the Buddha and also his barber. He recited the entire *Vinaya*. Ananda then recited the *Sutta-Pitaka* – the second "basket" of the *Tipitaka*. The individual said to have recited the *Abhidharma* depends on the particular traditions consulted, but Ananda or Mahakasypa are commonly attributed with the task.

After the recitation, Ananda revealed that shortly before his death, the Buddha declared that, if they wanted to, his disciples could dispense with the less important precepts. The *Sangha* immediately asked which were the minor rules but Ananda had to admit that he had never thought of asking the Buddha. The council then spent time discussing which rules the Buddha could have meant and finally concluded that they had best adhere to them all.

Although Ananda's close relationship with the Buddha was of advantage in the knowledge of his teaching, it did raise many criticisms of Ananda himself. In the stories, Ananda is portrayed as a sincere but rather bumbling individual. Some of the criticisms are far from obvious.

First, Ananda was accused of stepping over the cloth of the Buddha during the rainy season. This is difficult to explain but seems to imply a lack of respect for the Enlightened One.

Second, Ananda was accused of allowing women to honour the body of the Buddha by weeping over the body. It could have been that he had shown the women the 32 special marks on his body and this would have meant revealing the sexual organs. Alternatively, this could have referred to the debate as to how one treats a corpse. In the thinking of the period, the "soul" needed to be released from the body by hitting the head. When a person has reached the enlightened state of *arhatship* the release of the "soul" appears no longer needed. The Buddha also is said to have given his body to the laity with the distribution of relics.

Third, it was said that the Buddha had the ability to stay in the world if he so chose. Ananda then was accused of not asking the Buddha to stay in the world.

Fourth, Ananda was also accused of helping women to join the *Sangha*. According to tradition, he had made a strong representation to the Buddha on behalf of the women, as mentioned in chapter 3. He asked the Buddha the key question, "Are women able to become *arhats*?", to which the Buddha said that they were. This led to the obvious following question, "So why can they not join the *Sangha*?" The Buddha, according to tradition, replied that if women were allowed to join the *Sangha* the deterioration of the *Dharma* would come within 500 years. Ananda did not consider that he had done anything wrong but, for the sake of unity of the *Sangha*, he made confession to the convocation.

As the convocation was about to close, a travelling monk named Purana arrived at Rajagaha with 500 *arhats*. According to the Pali tradition, he was invited to join the proceedings but declined the invitation saying that he remembered the *Dharma* and *Vinaya* precisely as spoken by the Buddha. In so doing, Purana was establishing an alternative tradition that threw doubt on the authority of the whole convocation, which was the main reason for the gathering.

Although the Buddhist schools attribute the compilation of the *Tipitaka* to this council, historical facts appear more complex. Most Western scholars consider that the dramatic events of the First Council have been elaborated over the centuries. The meeting was probably a gathering of a few of the Buddha's disciples after his death to discuss the future of the movement in the religious climate of India. It is also more likely that the various sayings of the Buddha were initially transmitted orally and gradually took on a more structured form.

The Second Council (Vaisali)

The Second Council is generally accepted by historians to have taken place 100 or 110 years after the Buddha's *parinirvana*, in the city of Vaisali (27 miles north of Patna). The account of this meeting is known in both the Theravada and Mahayana tradition but the details of the meeting vary. The Pali tradition tells of how the monk Yasas visited the monks at Vaisali and accused them of certain misconduct. This included having a large copper pot filled with water into which lay people were asked to throw money. Yasas was offered a share of the money but protested that this was not in accordance with the *Vinaya*. For this he was punished by the local monks, whereupon he convinced the laity that the monks were in error. He was then expelled by the monks at Vaisali. Both parties enlisted support and the whole movement was faced with a serious split.

According to the Pali tradition, 700 monks gathered for the Second Council. It was agreed that four monks should be appointed from either side to judge the issue; the respected monk Revata was selected to preside over the meeting. Sarvagaman, an elder monk who had been the close disciple of Ananda, was questioned on ten points concerning the interpretation of the monastic code. These were as follows:

1. Were monks allowed to preserve salt in a horn for future use during shortages? According to the *Vinaya,* monks were not allowed to store food – but was salt food? Salt certainly made food taste better.
2. Were monks permitted to eat food after noon? The *Vinaya* said monks were not allowed to eat food once the shadow of a tree was more than "two fingers wide".
3. After a monk had finished eating a meal in one village, was he allowed to go to another village to eat?
4. Who should be present at the twice-monthly recitation of the *Tipitaka*? Could this be only part of the local *Sangha*?
5. Who should be present in confirming a rule of the local *Sangha*? It appears that some monks wanting to pass a particular motion would wait until any monks who would object were absent from the *Sangha*.

6. Could monks make their own additions to the teaching of the *Vinaya*? It appears as though leaders of the local *Sanghas* began making their own innovations, rather than simply following the *Vinaya*.
7. Could a monk drink unchurned milk after noon? Although most monks were not eating after noon, they were free to drink as they wished. Unchurned milk was somewhere between milk and curds, so was this drinking or eating?
8. The *Vinaya* did not allow the drinking of intoxicating liquors, but could a monk drink unfermented wine?
9. Monks were allowed few possessions, one of which was a sleeping mat, which they could renew every six months. The monks at Vaisali seem to have been decorating their mats with a border. Was this allowed?
10. Were monks allowed to receive silver and gold?

The convocation concluded that the monks at Vaisali were wrong on all ten accounts in being too liberal in their interpretation and practice of the code. The main Pali tradition tells that they were reconciled and that the meeting ended with the recitation of the *Vinaya*. This situation appears to have been essentially about the limits of the rule of the *Vinaya*, as local *Sanghas* faced new and different situations. Monks were trying to adapt the common practices to meet particular local needs. Thus, the notion of a universal *Sangha* with a common code was under threat.

Legend tells that the Buddha had foretold that 18 schools would emerge within the movement; often, writers have arranged the various sects into such a scheme. Irrespective of the actual number of groups, they can be classified as conservatives and reformers. The conservatives sought to hold rigorously to the traditional teaching of the Buddha and were therefore called Sthavira, or "elders, traditionalists". In contrast, the reformers claimed to develop the *Dharma* initiated by the Buddha, and extend it in its application. These monks were to become known as the Mahasanghika, or "great *Sangha*". The schism between the Mahasanghikas and the Sthaviras appears to have arisen about 340 BC and was occasioned by a dispute concerning the status of the *arhats* (see figure 4.1). By the time of the consecration of King

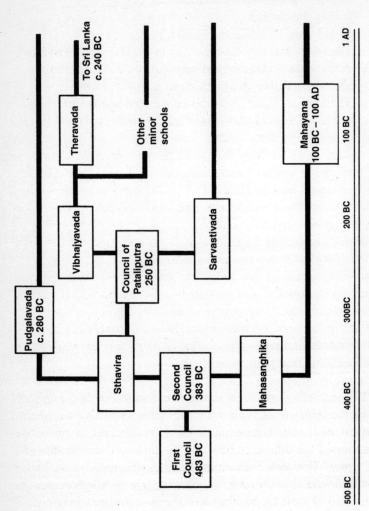

Figure 4.1 Major Buddhist sects in India, 500 BC–1 AD

Asoka in c. 270 BC, the Buddhist sectarian movement was well advanced.

The Council of Pataliputra

Some 40 years later, the sectarian tensions had increased to breaking point and a non-canonical council was held at Pataliputra. Traditions vary widely as to the details and date of this gathering. The events at Pataliputra are especially linked with a monk named Mahadeva, who openly cast doubt on the *arhat*. He is said to have propounded five points:

1. *Arhats* are subject to sexual temptation. For example, they may be seduced by a goddess in their sleep and experience seminal emission. The criticism here is not one against their holiness but against their self-control.
2. *Arhats* have a residual ignorance in that they do not have infinite knowledge.
3. *Arhats* are subject to doubts. For example, when on a journey they can doubt if they are travelling on the right road just like other persons.
4. *Arhats* are dependent on information from others.
5. *Arhats* can sometimes cry out in despair when they realise that life is wretched.

This raises two important issues. The first relates to the insularity of the *arhat* way of life in which the *arhat* seeks his own enlightenment with total disregard to the laity. Second, it raises the question of the difference between the nature of the Buddha and the *arhat*. Although Sakyamuni Buddha originally spoke of his first followers as entering into the same state of enlightenment as himself, with time the attributes of the Buddha grew in comparison to those of living *arhats*. The Buddha discovered the path that the *arhat* follows.

The Third Canonical Council was held 236 years after the *parinirvana*, during the time of King Asoka, about 250 BC. At this time Buddhism was contending with a serious internal crisis, some monks claiming that within the monastery at Pataliputra were some people who were not pure monks. The tension grew such that the emperor convened a council at his capital, Pataliputra. The conference was directed by the brother of King Asoka who was a well-respected monk called Moggaliputtatissa. The monks were asked, "Which doctrine do you follow?" The Buddha often said that he followed the *Vibhajy*, the "doctrine of distinction". Those monks who did not reply with the words "*Vibhajy-vada*" were thrown out of the monastery. The Pali tradition says that 60,000 monks were thrown out by Moggaliputtatissa, who then convened the remaining monks to recite the *Vinaya*. King Asoka's support for the Theravada school was to have a great influence on the future development of Buddhism, as we shall see in the following chapter. It is necessary now to consider the main teachings of the various schools that emerged during this period.

Mahasanghika, or "Great *Sangha*"

Five main areas of development were expressed by the Mahasanghika, the most important of which related to the nature of the Buddha.

The person of the Buddha

Sakyamuni assumed a Brahmanic cosmology that admitted a multitude of gods and a continuity of the universe within vast periods of expansion and decline (*kalpas*). Sakyamuni, because of his enlightenment, claimed supremacy over the *Vedic* gods. This is best illustrated in the story of his encounter with the great god Brahma, in which the Buddha claimed superiority through his greater insight. In so doing, the Buddha brought the Hindu gods within the orb of Brahmanic cosmology and into subjection to the law of *karma*. The gods were therefore little different to other living beings. Although they were more elevated, their state of bliss actually hindered them from achieving *nirvana*.

The question therefore emerged within the *Sangha* about whether there were other Buddhas in the cosmos. Sakyamuni assumed that he was part of a continuity of Buddhas, each associated with a *kalpa* of the universe. In Indian cosmology a *kalpa* was considered to be a vast period of time associated with the growth and decay of the cosmos as a whole. Sakyamuni was the Buddha of this present *kalpa* and the first to achieve enlightenment. In doing so, he set the wheel of *Dharma* in motion for this *kalpa*, which allowed other human beings to enter the path to enlightenment. Other *kalpas* would have their own Buddhas.

Early Buddhist thought accepted a great and elaborate cosmology that contrasted with the narrow earth-centred cosmology of many Western traditions. In the Pali texts for example, reference is made to tens of thousands of parallel universes. The question then arises about whether there is a Buddha for each of these universes. The Mahasanghika elevated the view of the Buddha to such a degree that he was perceived not merely as a human being but as a transcendental being above all gods.

In the discussion of the *Dharma* it was mentioned that the teaching of the Four Noble Truths is supported by the doctrine of "dependent origination". In other words, they are conditioned, resulting from particular sets of causes, and will arise and disappear as the set of causes changes. This is the state of *samskrta* that is ruled by the law of *karma*. The Buddha placed everything that exists into this category, including the gods, as we have mentioned. In comparison, there is the state of *asamskrta*, the "unconditioned", essentially known as *nirvana*. The Buddha, through his achievement of enlightenment, placed himself within *nirvana* and therefore beyond all other beings, including the gods. He is therefore the greatest – the ultimate.

As early Buddhist scholars reflected on this matter, questions arose as to the nature of the Buddha. Does the Buddha sleep or dream? At these times one is not in full control of one's thoughts and, as the Buddha is always in control, it must be assumed that he never sleeps. Does the Buddha speak? The *Dharma* permeates the whole cosmos, and people understand according to their ability. The sound of the *Dharma* reverberates throughout the universe, even today. Gradually, the *Dharma* will dwindle and be lost from the world. Speculation suggested that when the *Dharma* has totally dwindled, the next Buddha will eventually come.

The developing ideas within the Mahasanghika were to grow into full bloom in the theory of the "three bodies of the Buddha".

This will be discussed in the following chapter, when the main Mahayana school is considered.

The nature of the arhats

If the nature of the Buddha was so exalted, the question emerged as to the nature of those human beings whom the Buddha himself had regarded as having achieved enlightenment. What was the distinction between these *arhats* and the Buddha himself? He was certainly the first to achieve enlightenment but, through achieving enlightenment, were not all humans able to move from *samskrta* to *asamskrta* and thus *nirvana*? It was clear to many within the *Sangha* that those who claimed to be *arhats*, and were generally recognised as such, had weaknesses. This was shown in the five propositions of Mahadeva which challenged the perfection of the *arhats*. For example, *arhats* were considered still subject to eject semen while asleep and were not all-knowing, as seen in the fact that they did not know everybody's name.

This does not appear to be a general "downgrading" of the status of *arhats* but applies to an earlier form of *arhat*. This first type of *arhat*, it was implied, had achieved only a limited level in the meditative state and lacked the higher knowledge. Later *arhats* had achieved this higher state and were using it for the benefit of the people.

The nature of the human being

The question of the nature of the *arhat* then raised issues about the inherent nature of the human mind. As was discussed in chapter 3, consciousness (*vijnana*) is one of the five *skandhas* characteristic of all living beings. It is through becoming aware of the inherent spiritual ignorance that an individual begins the path to enlightenment. Wisdom (*prajna*) is the most important means by which the mind is freed from impurities. But is the mind inherently impure? The Mahasanghika group thought that the mind was inherently pure but badly stained by wrong ideas and notions resulting from society. Although even a newborn infant was considered stained, within this pollution there was an essential purity of nature. The Mahasanghika tradition therefore has a positive view of human nature.

This early discussion is an attempt to deal with issues inherent to all religions. How does one explain the failure of human beings while recognising the inherent desire to do that which is "good"? Within Christianity, the answer assumes that because of the rebellion of humanity against the will of God, described as the Fall, human beings are in a state of sin. This was described by the Reformed theologians as "total depravity". By this they did not mean that humanity was 100% evil but that every part of the human make-up has been affected by sin. Therefore, a human being cannot do anything with perfection; all is influenced by sin. This Christian view therefore contrasts with the positive view of humanity that emerged within early Buddhism.

The state between death and rebirth

Sakyamuni assumed the contemporary teaching of the Brahmins concerning the nature of *karma*, although, as we have seen, he did modify the basic teaching. He refused to speak much about the nature of reincarnation but questions continued to arise about the nature of the state immediately after death. When a person dies, is there a period before rebirth, or is there an immediate rebirth? The two options each demand answers to various questions; these are illustrated by the two traditions.

The Mahasanghika did not accept any theory of an intermediate state between death and birth. They believed that there was an immediate reassembly of five *skandhas* to form another being resulting from the *karma* of previous lives.

In contrast, the Sthavira accepted the view that there was an intermediate state called *antarabhava*. What then is the nature of this state and how long may one reside in it before rebirth? The Sthavira thought that the intermediate being flies around to find a child that is about to be born and enters the new being. Numerous other questions arise, which were widely discussed in early Buddhism. What happens if the intermediate entity does not find a child about to be born? Does it continue to fly around? In Sri Lanka today, the general view is that the intermediate being flies around for seven days before it finds a child and is born. If it fails to find a child the first time, it will continue to do so, seven times seven. If on the last time it fails, then the intermediate being dies.

The nature of the Sangha

As was discussed in the previous chapter, the teaching of the Buddha divided people into two sets of opposites: men and women, monks and lay. Especially in the time of Asoka, lay patrons had an increasingly important role in the support and expansion of the religion. The Sthavira held to the view that the *Sangha* consisted essentially of the monks who were committed to the practice of the *Dharma*, and so lay people were excluded from the meeting and decisions of the *Sangha*. In contrast, the Mahasanghika recognised the involvement of the laity; some of the lay members had an active part in the decisions of the community.

Sthaviras

The Sthaviras were soon to divide into three schools of thought: Sarvastivadas, Pudgalavadas, and Vibhajyavadas (see figure 4.1). Within the Sthaviras, the Sarvastivadas became the most significant school in the northern part of the Indian subcontinent. The school flourished under the patronage of King Kaniska I, who ruled in the late first or early second century AD. Kaniska sponsored a council, probably held at Gandhara, to consider the doctrines of the Sarvastivada school. Invitations were sent to all the learned Buddhists of the time, from whom 499 were finally chosen to attend the conference. This is sometimes known as the "Fourth Council". During the conference they produced a new version of the *Vinaya,* which was committed to writing at the conference, and a great commentary, known as the *Mahavibhasa*, on the *Abhidharma* text.

The *Abhidharma* undertakes a philosophical development on two main issues. First, it refines the *skandha* analysis to give to all things a fine-grained inherent character known as *dharmas,* which may be regarded as the basic elements of existence. The similarity of this model to the atomic theory of matter was quickly grasped by many Western scholars.

The Sarvastivada tradition recognises 75 *dharmas* consisting of two categories. The first type is *samskrita* meaning "compounded" and "conditioned". These 72 *dharmas* cover all things that exist. These *dharmas* were classified according to the five *skandha*s pattern, as illustrated in figure 4.2.

dharmas	skandhas
11	rupa (matter)
1	vedana (sensation)
1	samjna (perception)
58	samskara (volition)
1	vijnana (consciousness)

Figure 4.2   Sarvastivada classification of dharmas

The second type is *asamskrita*, referring to the three "uncompounded" or "unconditioned" elements. These are essentially two kinds of *nirvana*. The notion of two forms of *nirvana* comes from the analysis that when the Buddha became enlightened, he then attained *nirvana* but his body continued; only later did he enter his *parinirvana*. There must therefore be two forms of *nirvana* to account for this happening. The Theravada tradition rejects this view and holds to only one form of *asamskrita dharma,* which is *nirvana.*

The second contribution of the *Abhidharma* is a refinement of the doctrine of dependent origination. This is done by showing how particular *dharmas* are interrelated by one or more of 24 kinds of conditional relationships. Each *dharma* has its own distinct nature and they are bound together in a person by a *dharma* known as *prapti* ("possession").

Pudgalavadas

The Pudgalavadas deviated from the Sarvastivadas over the notion of the "person", or *pudgala*. As Edward Conze writes, "The *Pudgalavadas* represented the reaction of common-sense against the improbabilities of the *dharma* theory in its more uncompromising forms."[2] The Pudgalavadas challenged the assumption that denied the reality of the *atman* and claimed that besides the impersonal *dharmas*, there is still a "person".

They taught that the "person" is a reality in the ultimate sense, which provides a common link for the successive rebirths up to Buddhahood. They were, however, careful to define the relationship of the "person" to the *skandhas* in such a way as not to contradict the essential teaching of the Buddha concerning nonself. The person is neither identical with the *skandhas* nor is he in the *skandhas* nor outside them. The "person" provided a kind of structural unity for the psycho-physical elements that were carried forward with *karma*.

> We claim that there is a Person; but we do not say that he is an entity. Nor do we believe that he exists merely as a designation for the *skandhas*. What we say is that the word "Person" denotes a kind of structural unity that is found in correlation with the *skandhas* of one individual, i.e. with those elements which are actually present, internal to him, and appropriated by him.[3]

Although the Pudgalavadas were criticised by all other Buddhist schools, they had a remarkable influence in India. Under the patronage of Emperor Harsa in the seventh century AD, a quarter of Indian monks belonged to this school.

Vibhajyavadas

The third school within the Sthavira tradition emerged in about 244 BC. The dispute related to the ontological teaching of Katyayaniputra, who taught that not only present events are real, but so are past and future events real. This surprising view can be understood if one considers the monk's basic practice of meditation. While in meditation, the experiences around an individual at that particular moment are no more and no less important than past experiences or future experiences.

It was the task of the monk in meditation to impress on his mind his distaste for the material world. He would do this by taking an event, or *dharma,* and consider its transience in the way it comes, becomes and goes. The question would then arise about the possible reality of the past and future as well as the present. If only the present exists, this raises the issue of its duration, which is only an instant. This would mean that nothing exists for any length of time, and one must conclude that it is annihilated and re-created from instant to instant.

Katayayaniputra argued that not only does this stretch the bounds of common sense but it raises questions about the doctrine of *karma*. If past actions have ceased to exist immediately after taking place, how can they have effect many years later? This would mean that something that no longer exists has an effect at a time that it no longer exists. Similarly, the knowledge of past and future objects, as attested by memory and prediction, would be impossible, since no knowledge is possible without an actual object in the mind. He therefore proposed a pan-realist model that avoided the problem but which introduced many others.

The elegant philosophy of Sakyamuni Buddha attracted the admiration of many followers in the early centuries following his *parinirvana* but it left many unanswered questions. Many philosophers have tried to provide answers by speculating in ways that the Buddha refused to do. Theories became more elaborate and diverse. Even so, each development stimulated new vitality and growth within the northern states of India. It was, however, as the result of the adoption of Buddhism by King Asoka that Buddhism was to become a world religion.

Suggestions for interfaith discussions

How did early Buddhism seek to address the question of the failure of human beings while recognising the inherent desire to do "good"? How does Christianity seek to answer this question?

Webwise 4 – Councils and Controversies

Rajagaha website

http://www.geocities.com/Athens/9449/holysite2.htm
A series of photographs of the four holy Buddhist sites in north India.

Disciples of the Buddha

http://www.buddhanet.net/e-learning/history/disciples.htm
Here are brief life stories of some of the Buddha's earliest and most famous disciples including Ananda and Sariputra.

Arhats (lohan)

http://www.buddhanet.net/e-learning/history/lohan_h.htm
In Theravada Buddhism, the *arhat* (Chinese *lohan*) is one who has followed the Eightfold Path and has achieved deliverance from

this earthly existence. He has reached "the other shore" and is saved for all eternity. *Lohans* are well-known for their great wisdom, courage and supernatural power. Due to their abilities to ward off evil, *lohans* have become guardian angels of the Buddhist temple; there in the main hall, standing guard, are the ever-present, indomitable-looking 18 *lohan* figures, sometimes accompanied by 500 or more lesser *lohans*. According to tradition, there were originally only 16 *lohans*. Two were added to the list by the Chinese in the T'ang dynasty.

History of Theravada

http://www.accesstoinsight.org/history.html

The Access to Insight site contains much useful information including this brief history of the early centuries of Buddhism.

Notes

1. *Digha-nikaya* 2:154.
2. Conze, E., *A Short History of Buddhism* (Oxford: Oneworld, 1993), p. 31.
3. *Abhidarmakosha* IX, 232–234.

CHAPTER FIVE

ASOKA AND THE EXPANSION OF BUDDHISM

What you can learn from this chapter

- the conversion of King Asoka to Buddhism
- the way Asoka promoted Buddhism as the state religion
- the significance of relics and the emergence of popular devotion of the Buddha
- Buddhist missions to Gandhara

During the first two centuries after the *parinirvana* of the Buddha, his followers formulated the canon of scriptures and became a small but recognised religious tradition. However, the movement did not spread beyond the bounds of the Magadha and Kosala states in the central region of the Ganges valley. The primary reason for this restriction was the frontier wars fought as the Magadha kingdom continued its expansion. Within the kingdom itself, domestic struggles were common and it was a regular practice for the royal heirs to kill the reigning monarch in order to gain the throne more quickly.

The Greeks and the Mauryas

In contrast, north-west India had for two centuries been under the influence of the Achaemenid dynasty of Persia. Suddenly, in the matter of a few weeks in 327 BC, that empire collapsed as Alexander the Great swept across Persia into the regions of Kapisa, Gandhara, Punjab and Sind. Although the Greeks had known something of

India before the invasion, now for the first time they came into close contact. The Greeks admired the skill of the Indian soldiers and the austerity of the naked ascetics but, as a whole, the contact had little lasting effect. After 311 BC, the north-western states were subject to the authority of the Greek king of Asia Minor, Seleucus I Nicator, founder of the Seleucid dynasty. The north-west region of India was essentially a political vacuum that was open to conquest.

During the period 324–304 BC, a bold and unscrupulous warrior of the Maurya family led a revolt against the king of Magadha.[1] Candragupta established himself as king of Magadha and soon led a large army to liberate the Punjab from Macedonian rule. When Seleucus I crossed the Indus to reconquer the region, he was soundly defeated by Candragupta and readily accepted a new frontier boundary. The result was that a great new Indian state was established, reaching from Magadha in the east to the Punjab in the west. Candragupta was a follower of the Brahmanical customs for most of his life but it appears that near the end of his life, he accepted the Jain religion. He is said to have retired to a monastery and to have died through religious suicide in the manner of the Jain saints.[2]

Buddhism, like many of the other religious movements of the period, could have disappeared if it had not been adopted by a powerful new protector in the person of Asoka, a nephew of Candragupta. Asoka's father Bindusara had conquered the Deccan plateau but it was Asoka who brought the empire to its peak. From his capital at Pataliputra (modern Patna) King Asoka ruled an empire that covered two thirds of the Indian subcontinent. For the first time in history, virtually the entire Indian subcontinent was politically unified, with only the southernmost tip of the peninsula outside his rule. His 40-year reign, 272–232 BC, established for the first time in Indian history a period of peace and relative prosperity (see figure 5.1).

The legend of King Asoka

Stories of King Asoka are found in Sanskrit, Pali, Chinese, Tibetan, Japanese, Thai, Sinhalese and many other Asian languages. It is necessary here only to summarise the contents of what

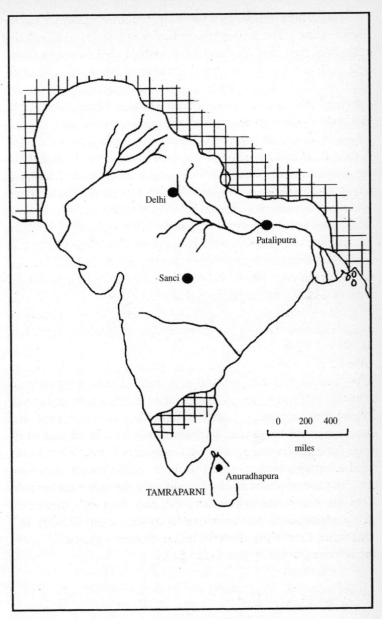

Figure 5.1   The empire of King Asoka

is perhaps the oldest text about Asoka available in Sanskrit – the *Asokavadana*.[3] The legend is supported by a series of significant edicts engraved on rocks and pillars that record his exploits and opinions. In the thirteenth edict is contained a remarkable statement of his remorse and conversion to the teachings of the Buddha. The first of these edicts was discovered in the 19th century and deciphered by James Prinsep in 1873 but, even so, many problems still remain concerning the inscriptions.

According to legendary biographies, Asoka was disliked by his father from birth because of his ugliness; his skin was rough and harsh, and his face deformed. However, a fortune-teller predicted that he would accede to the throne. This he achieved by conniving and finally by murdering his stepbrother (the legitimate heir). He quickly became known to his subjects as *Canda Asoka* ("Asoka the Fierce") due to his impetuous temper. He oppressed the people by building a state prison, known as "Asoka's hell", where individuals were randomly tortured and put to death.

Scholars have generally argued that these stories have been exaggerated to magnify the degree of his change but all of these events are known to have occurred. In 206 BC he conquered the country of Kalinga; in this campaign he saw about 100,000 innocent people killed and 150,000 deported. The story tells of how even this ruthless king was distressed at these scenes and came to believe that war was wrong. For more than a year, Asoka lived near a Buddhist order and performed religious austerities. In the tenth year of his reign, the rock edicts say, he became "enlightened", but the phrase is such that it could also mean that he went on a pilgrimage to the place of the Buddha's enlightenment. Even so, what is clear is that there was a marked change in the character and outlook of King Asoka. The rock edicts that he constructed are very different from the great inscriptions of Darius I, for instance, which date from a similar period. Those of Darius glorify the emperor and catalogue his many victories.

One story told about the king's conversion tells that he was one day looking out of the window of his palace when he saw a monk walking while meditating on the "beauty of the *Dharma*". Drawn by the compelling vision of his spiritual virtue, the king sent for the monk. When the monk entered the palace he unselfconsciously handed the king his begging bowl and, seeing no other monk present, seated himself on the king's throne. The monk proceeded to preach about diligence, so converting the king to the teachings of the Buddha. Not only does the story tell of the conversion of Asoka but it establishes the principle that even the most junior monk has precedence over the highest lay man – the king. The importance of the relationship between *Sangha* and state will be returned to later, with the spread of the Theravada tradition throughout many south Asian countries.

In the tradition of Indian kings, Asoka supported all religions, although he expressed publicly his commitment to the teachings of the Buddha. After his conversion, he started to feed the monks on a vast scale and showed a new concern for the welfare of his subjects. He inaugurated public works, such as the building of wells, provided medical aid for both people and animals, and encouraged the support of the old and the orphaned. While Asoka kept his army as a deterrent to invasion, he gave up the policy of widespread conquests. Asoka gave Buddhism a central place in his empire, much as the emperor Constantine did for Christianity.

The lavish patronage bestowed by the king had an unintended consequence for the *Sangha* in tempting many to take the role of a monk. The rise of nominality caused great difficulties for the true monks, who could in no way co-operate with them. Although Asoka remained a lay follower, he was eager for the purity of the *Sangha*. Buddhist texts claim that he carried out a massive purification of the *Sangha* at Pataliputra, expelling many corrupt monks. In due course, Asoka's younger brother, his son Mahinda and his daughter Sanghamitta entered the *Sangha*; later they became missionaries to Sri Lanka.

Asoka's Rock Edict

The Beloved of the Gods, Compassionate King (*Piye-dasi*) in the ninth year of his reign conquered the Kalinga. One hundred and fifty thousand persons were thence carried away captive, one hundred thousand were slain, and many times that number perished.

Ever since the annexation of the Kalingas, the Beloved of the Gods has zealously protected the Law of Piety (*Dharma*), has been devoted to that law and has proclaimed its precepts.

The Beloved of the Gods feels remorse on account of the conquest of the Kalingas, because during the subjugation of a previous unconquered country, slaughters, death and the taking away captive of the people necessarily occur, whereat the Beloved of the Gods feels profound sorrow and regret.

There is another reason for the Beloved of the Gods feeling still more regret, namely that in such a country dwell Brahmans and ascetics, men of different sects, and households who all practise obedience to elders, obedience to father and mother, obedience to teachers, proper treatment of friends, acquaintances, comrades, relatives, slaves and servants, with fidelity and devotion. To such people dwelling in that country happened violence, slaughter, and separation from those they love . . .

The only true conquest is that effected through the Law of Piety (*Dharma*), which avails both for this world and the next. Let all the pleasures of my sons be the pleasures of exertion which avails both for this world and the next.

"*Dharma* of Asoka"

Conscious of his duties as monarch, Asoka aimed to secure the well-being of all his subjects; therefore he wrote his views in a form of political and religious thesis known as the "*Dharma* of Asoka". On royal decree this thesis was copied and spread throughout the empire and was written in the famous rock edicts. The "*Dharma* of Asoka" was not the same as the teaching of the Buddha. Asoka himself made a distinction between the *sad-dharma* ("good law") preached by Sakyamuni and his own *Dharma*, which was a system he wanted put into effect to pay his debt towards all living creatures. For example, in the "*Dharma* of Asoka" there is no reference to the Four Noble Truths nor the doctrine of *nirvana* nor even the path that leads there. His *Dharma* stands above the different religions of his state without trying to absorb them. It was to be accepted by all, monks and laity, Indians and foreigners.

A fundamental principle of his beliefs was that all people were essentially equal and should all observe the *Dharma*, including himself. It may be summarised as avoidance of sin and seeking to do good. All people were encouraged to have compassion for all living beings, speak the truth, act with forbearance and patience, and help those in need. Asoka instituted great social development projects. Medicinal plants were cultivated and planted along the roads for the use of the sick. Wells were dug, and rest-stops built for travellers.

Asoka was specially diligent in his conduct of government affairs. He believed that the monarch's chief responsibility was to the people of the country and he wished to make people happy in this world and the next. Asoka spread his views on the *Dharma* in two ways, through regulations concerning the *Dharma* and through quiet contemplation of the *Saddharma*. Through such contemplation the people would attain a deeper understanding of the prohibitions on taking life and then apply it to their own lives. By the 26th year of his reign, Asoka had declared amnesties for prisoners 25 times. He stressed the virtues of kindness, generosity, truthfulness, obedience to parents, and justice.

The importance of non-violence was repeatedly stated in Asoka's edicts. His respect for life was based on the belief that all beings had feelings. Needless killing was prohibited and laws were passed against the killing of pregnant and nursing animals. Asoka gave up the sport of hunting and embarked on *Dharma* tours around the country, visiting the major pilgrimage sites. The amount of meat that was provided in the palace was greatly reduced; this was in part responsible for the growth of vegetarianism in India. On these pilgrimages, Asoka visited scholars to give them alms and encouraged them to teach the people the *Dharma*.

The king was a lay man like any other of the laity and as such gave respect to the monks for their moral superiority. In other words, the monks reigned over the political realm both as exemplars and preachers. The institution of kingship, and the position of any particular king, was therefore legitimated by his relation to the *Sangha* expressed in the ceremonies of kingship. The king's duty was to protect the *Sangha* and provide support for the mon-asteries; the monks in turn generally helped the kings retain local support for their rule. This close relationship between *Sangha* and state became an important model for other Buddhist states but it had its disadvantages in that it tended to infuse a nationalistic spirit into Buddhism. King Asoka is represented as one of India's most enlightened rulers and is held up as the ideal Buddhist monarch.

The relics and popular devotion

Asoka's endorsement of Buddhism greatly popularised the relig-ion among the people of the empire. Buddhism was effectively transformed from being a minor religious movement alongside many others in the Indian states to become a world religion. An important element of the popularisation of Buddhism was the building of *stupas*. These seem to have been based upon the pre-Buddhist burial mounds for monarchs, warriors and saints. The *stupas* became important in Buddhism because of the relics they contained and, in some cases, their location at significant sites in the Buddha's life. Four sites are considered of particular impor-tance: the place of his birth, enlightenment, first sermon, and *par-inirvana* (death). After the Buddha's *parinirvana*, his body was cremated according to local custom and the relics were buried under a pile of earth, which was later covered with bricks.

The story is told of how King Asoka opened the existing *stupas* and divided the relics and then sent them to be the focus of some 84,000 *stupas* both inside and outside his empire. Having been part of the body of an enlightened being, relics were considered to be infused with something of the power of an enlightened mind. They are therefore thought to bring blessing to those who express devotion in their vicinity.

One of the oldest and best-preserved *stupas* in India is at Sanci in central India; it dates from the first century AD (see figure 5.2). It was built over an earlier *stupa* embellished by King Asoka. The Sanci *stupa* has the typical dome referred to in early texts as the *kumbha* or "pot", which is the outermost container of the relic. This is entered by four gates set at a crossroads. A circular path

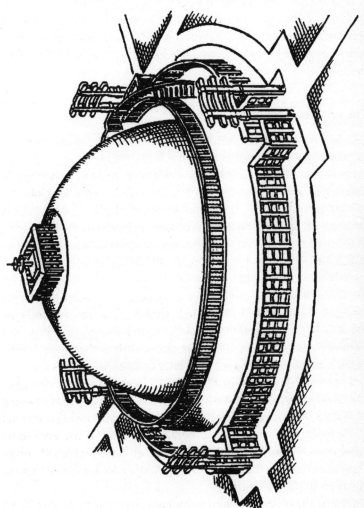

Figure 5.2   The stupa at Sanci

rings the dome for the circumambulation of the devotees. Over the dome is a parasol a traditional symbol of royalty in India. Later, the *stupas* became increasingly ornate as they were adopted by artisans of other countries. *Stupas* are now often known as "pagodas", probably a corruption of *dagaba*, or "relic-container".

Devotion

From these early times, acts of devotion have been an important element in the lives of most Buddhists. The term *saddha* in Pali (*sraddha* in Sanskrit) is often given the meaning "faith" in dictionaries, but a fuller definition would be trust, confidence, faithfulness and respect. Buddhist devotion is focused by use of various artefacts such as images. In the home, it can be expressed as a simple high shelf with various images and pictures. In temples, there is always some form of shrine room where images are housed. Offerings of incense, oil lamps, candles, food and clothing are common. Paying respect by act or gesture, especially prostration and chanting, are believed to give merit.

Theravada Buddhism recognises three kinds of object of worship: relics of a Buddha or *arhat*, relics of use, and symbols that remind one of the Buddha or *Dharma*. Archaeology shows that images of the Buddha did not occur in the early history of Buddhism, probably because the Buddha as a personality was deemed to have passed outside history altogether at his *parinirvana* (death). In these early years, his presence was symbolised by such motifs as his footprints marked with the "wheel of the law", the begging bowl, or the *bodhi* tree.

The representations of the Buddha in human form probably originated in northern India between the first century BC and the first century AD. They rapidly became popular, as it seems that the laity wanted a personified image with whom they could relate. These images show the Buddha wearing the robe and mantle of a monk, with his head encircled with a halo. The 32 auspicious marks that designate a Buddha were quickly incorporated with the circular tuft of hair on his forehead, the bump in his skull that looks like a bun of hair, the distended earlobes, the webbed fingers, and the golden colour of his skin. The body language of the images became highly significant, with the seated posture being common and also the use of various hand gestures.

By the fifth century, representation of the Buddha was common throughout the Buddhist world. Images presented him standing, seated or reclining. Images ranged from small to those of vast proportions made out of stone, cast bronze, clay and even chiselled in cliff faces. Throughout the history of Buddhism, iconography reflected the changing concepts of the Buddha.

Gods and divinities

Buddhism had little difficulty accommodating to the many local beliefs about gods, spirits and ghosts. There are many references to the gods (*devas* or "shining ones") in the sermons of Sakyamuni Buddha and of their acclamation of the truth he preached. Buddhism was essentially a philosophy by which committed individuals could seek release from the world of *karma* and illusion; the existence (or not) of gods and spirits was irrelevant and ignored. However, for the laity, the spirits remained a significant feature as they sought to cope with the everyday problems of life. Buddhist texts refer extensively to the various encounters between the Buddha and Mara the tempter. Mara's temptations extend to the contemporary lives of monks, nuns and lay people in order to lure them from the path.

There has been much debate among scholars as to the precise relationship between Buddhism and local cults. Some writers see a supernatural hierarchy, with the Buddha at the summit, and the gods and spirits reduced to the sphere of *karma*. Other scholars have tended to contrast the "great tradition" of Buddhist teaching with the "little tradition" and spirit cults. Some have seen the existence of such local cults to be a corruption of the original teaching of the Buddha.

Often, for the villagers, the roles of the gods have become subservient to that of the Buddha, and this is told in myth and ritual. In central Thailand there is a well-known story of the Buddha's descent from heaven. According to the story, the Buddha's mother died seven days after his birth and so was deprived of hearing the *Dharma* from the lips of her own son.

The Buddha, in compassion for her, ascended in three steps to reach Indra's heaven to which his mother had been transported, and there preached to her and the gods for three months. Indra then devised three ladders to facilitate the Buddha's return to earth. The centre ladder was made of seven precious substances – gold, silver, coral, ruby, emerald and other gems. The Buddha descended on this. To its right was a ladder of gold on which Indra descended, blowing the conch and accompanied by his retinue of gods. To its left was a ladder of silver by which Brahma and the other Brahma gods descended, holding an umbrella over the Buddha. The three ladders appeared to the people of the earth as three rainbows.[4]

Tambiah and Obeysekera have questioned the dichotomy of the "great" and "little" tradition, because the lay members of society do not have such a division.[5, 6] Ordinary villagers have an integrated perception within the context of their daily life as they cope with their basic needs. De Silva lists the following five facts about *devas* (gods) which relate to the Buddhist scheme:

> *Devas* are not immortal.
> *Devas* must first be born as men before they attain *nirvana* since there is too much sensuous enjoyment in the *devaloka*.
> *Devas* can only help with material benefits, not with spiritual favours.
> The *deva* worlds are not places of eternal bliss but places of temporary refuge.
> All *devas* are subject to the Buddha who has gone beyond them into enlightenment.[7]

Buddhist festivals have become superimposed on local religion. In Thailand, for example, people of different social groups may come from great distances to patronise a temple. However, the cult of the guardian spirits of the village is essentially of a local character related to the land and the community. The lay people are concerned with the rites of passage, and especially death. Thai villagers distinguish between normal and abnormal death, because it is considered to have an effect on the fate of the soul. The corpse of someone who has died abnormally is buried quickly, so that the earth may contain the dangerous powers. The monks are then invited to conduct rites that invest the deceased with merit and grant protection to the living. The monks have therefore come to relate to the particular beliefs and fears of the ordinary people in Thailand.

Missionary outreach

As mentioned previously, Asoka's generosity to the *Sangha* appears to have attracted a growing number of novices to the order, but some came from the false motive of receiving an easy living. Some monks began to teach their own deviant doctrine, and the more diligent monks refused to associate with them. Asoka tried in vain to restore harmony to the community and eventually called a council at his capital at Pataliputra in an attempt to remove the differences. This was the Third Council according to the Pali tradition, and was discussed in the previous chapter.

At the end of the council, Moggaliputra sent out groups of missionaries to all parts of India to preach the true *Dharma*. These missions seem to have been successful in converting many people in the areas of north-east India, the east coast of India and the Himalayan regions. Stories are told of monks being sent to the successors of Alexander the Great in Egypt, Cyrene and Epirus.

The Gandhara province included north-western India between the Khyber pass and the Indus river and the region of the Kabul valley in Afghanistan. In the sixth to fourth centuries BC Gandhara was dominated by the Achaemenid dynasty of Iran. The successors of Alexander the Great maintained themselves in Bactria and Gandhara from 322 BC to about 50 BC. However, as early as the second century BC, these Greek dynasties were already overrun by peoples of both nomadic and Parthian–Iranian origin. Rejoined to India under the Maurya dynasty, the Gandhara province became the object of missionary activity during the reign of the emperor Asoka.

Gandharan art is often referred to as the Graeco-Roman Buddhist school. The founding of the school has been credited to the Kushan emperor Kaniska (c. 129–160 AD), because of his patronage to Buddhism and his great artistic development. The character of Gandharan art is determined by the commercial relations between the Kushan and the Roman empires. The many

archaeological discoveries of Alexandrian and Syrian workman-
ship at Taxila in the Punjab and Begram in the Kabul valley testify
to the cultural and diplomatic connections with the Graeco-
Roman West. Many artefacts, in particular sculptures, have survived and are now dispersed in major museums throughout the
world. Some of the largest of the rock carvings were destroyed by
the Taliban in March 2001.

The Gandhara school is credited with the first representation of
the Buddha in human form, rather than as a symbol. Perhaps the
school intended to create a human *Bodhisattva*, a representation
of Prince Siddhartha, the Buddha Sakyamuni while still a
Bodhisattva. All early *Bodhisattvas* are shown wearing turbans,
jewellery, and muslin skirts, a costume that was an adaptation of
the actual dress of Kushan and Indian nobles. The jewellery of
these royal statues was a duplication of Hellenistic and Samatian
gold, created by Western artisans. A definite borrowing from
Roman art was the method of representing the story of the
Buddha's legend in a series of separate episodes and panels. Other
examples of this borrowing are the earliest Gandhara Buddhas,
where Sakyamuni is portrayed with the head of the Greek god
Apollo and arrayed in a Roman toga.

Gandhara was also a source of intellectual activity; many manuscripts written on birch bark scrolls have been discovered from the
first century BC to the second century AD. Many such scrolls have
been discovered buried in clay pots and these have been painstakingly restored by the British Museum.[8] They were not a complete
canon like that of the Pali tradition but appear to be random selec-
tions translated from the oral tradition by Gandharan scholars.

In the first century AD the Kushans, a tribe of Scythian stock
from north China made themselves masters of Gandhara. Their
rule, however, was interrupted by the invasion of the Persian king
Shapur I in 242 AD; the Buddhist civilisation of Gandhara was
finally completely destroyed by the White Huns, the Hephthalites,
in the sixth century. The Chinese traveller, Sung Yen, visited the
region in 520 AD and reported that the Huns had overrun the
country. A few years later, he reported that the Huns had virtually
expiated Buddhism, had destroyed monasteries and had killed
most of the population in Gandhara. A century later, when the

famous Chinese pilgrim Hsuan-Tsang travelled through north-west India, he found Gandhara in a ruined, depopulated state.

Buddhism was, however, to have a longer presence in Sri Lanka, as will be discussed in the next chapter.

*   *   *

A legend of King Asoka tells how his dream had always been to distribute 100 million gold pieces to the *Sangha*. Towards the end of his life he realised that he had only given 96 million and so he resolved to complete his donation. Unfortunately, he became ill and his heir Sampadin took advantage of the situation to take possession of the throne and property of the monarch. Nevertheless, Asoka sent his personal furniture to the *Sangha,* down to his last silver plate. He was reduced to poverty and yet, according to the legend, donated the last thing that he had, a myrobalan fruit. He ordered that this should be taken to the *Sangha.*

Before dying, Asoka made a will, in which he left his whole empire to the *Sangha.* After his death, Sampadin, his heir, was obliged to redeem the empire for the sum of 4 million pieces of gold. Thus, Asoka is said to have realised his ambition to offer the enormous amount of 100 million pieces of gold to the *Sangha.* Whether one discounts the story as being no more than a later elaboration, the remarkable change in his life and his social concern means that even the non-Buddhist must respect such a great ruler. It is not surprising that King Asoka became the model of the ideal Buddhist king for later monarchs throughout south-east Asia.

Although Asoka's patronage did much to spread Buddhism, there are disadvantages when a religion becomes the established religion of a state. The formal structures can lose the inner spirit, and people join the religion for social reasons. Soon after his death, Asoka's empire was to split up once again into smaller states.

Suggestions for interfaith discussions

Both Buddhism and Christianity are missionary religions. How do they compare and contrast in their motivation and methods?

Webwise 5 – Asoka and the Expansion of Buddhism

Gandhara artefacts for sale

http://www.gandhara.com.au
Most of Afghanistan's architectural heritage was plundered during the anarchy that plagued Afghanistan after the withdrawal of Russian forces in 1989.

Recording and preserving Gandhara's cultural heritage

http://www.mcdonald.cam.ac.uk/IARC/cwoc/issue3/Gandhara.htm
Culture without Context provides a newsletter of the research centre run by Ihsan Ali and Robin Coningham for the study of the illicit trade in antiques.

Bamiyan tragedy

http://www.sibv.org/bv21.htm
On Monday 12 March 2001, the Director General of UNESCO, Koichiro Matsuura, said in a statement released at the UN cultural organisation's Paris headquarters that the UN envoy to Afghanistan had confirmed that the ancient Buddha statues at Bamiyan had been destroyed by the ruling Taliban militia.

Notes

1. Basham, A. L., *The Wonder that was India* (London: Sidwick & Jackson, 1988), pp. 48–51.
2. Basham, *ibid.*, p. 51.
3. Strong, J. S., *The Legend of King Asoka* (Princeton: Princeton Paperbacks, 1989).
4. Tambiah, S. J., *Buddhism and the Spirit Cults in North-East Thailand* (Cambridge: CUP, 1970), p. 61.
5. Tambiah, *ibid.*
6. Obeysekera, G., "The great tradition and the little in the perspective of Singhalese Buddhism", *Journal of Asian Studies,* (1963) 22 pp. 138–153.
7. De Silva, L. A., *Buddhism: Beliefs and Practices* (Colombo: Wesley Press, 1974), p. 141.

8. Salomon, R., *Ancient Buddhist Scrolls from Gandhara: The British Library Kharosthi Fragments* (London: British Library, 1999).

CHAPTER SIX

THE THERAVADA TRADITION IN SOUTH-EAST ASIA

What you can learn from this chapter

- the history of the Buddhist mission to Sri Lanka
- the expansion of Theravada Buddhism into south-east Asia
- the formation of Buddhist states
- the distinctive forms of Theravada festivals

During the reign of King Asoka, the new missionary initiative spread the *Dharma* beyond the regions of his great empire. According to tradition, the island of Ceylon (now Sri Lanka) accepted the new religion readily. It was to become an important centre for the propagation of the Theravada tradition.

Sri Lanka

The story of how Buddhism came to Sri Lanka is told in the Pali chronicles of Ceylon, namely the "Island Chronicle" (*Dipavamsa*) and the "Great Chronicle" (*Mahavamsa*) and the writings of the great scholar Buddhaghosa, written in the latter half of the fifth century AD. Although this was 800 years after the events described, the oral transmission appears to have been passed on with meticulous care. Tradition tells the story that at the accession of Devanampiya Tissa (307–267 BC), a great quantity of precious stones was discovered in the island, and the king decided to send some to King Asoka with whom he was a friend, although they had never met. Asoka accepted the gifts and responded by sending to Tissa all the gifts for an Indian consecration. The list given in the chronicles includes a fan, a diadem, a sword, a parasol, shoes, a turban, ear ornaments, chains, a set of garments, red-coloured earth, water from the Ganges, and 100 wagons of mountain rice. With these things, Asoka sent Tissa the gift of the *Dharma* (Pali: *Dhamma*), saying, "I have taken refuge in the Buddha, the *Dhamma* and the *Sangha*. I have declared myself a lay disciple in the discipline of the Shakyan. Seek then even thou, O best of men, converting thy mind with believing heart, refuge in these best of gems!" He continued by saying to the envoys, "Consecrate my friend yet again as king."[1]

On the arrival of the envoys back in Ceylon, the gifts were eagerly received and Tissa was consecrated according to Asoka's request. The second stage of the story was the arrival of some of the members of the Indian *Sangha* to the island. This group was lead by Mahinda, Asoka's son by his first wife. He first met King Tissa while the king was out hunting and then and there, he began to preach to him the discourse known as "The Discourse of the Simile of the Elephant's Footprint". This sermon covers a range of topics about the life and teaching of the Buddha. At the end of the discourse, King Tissa and his companions declared their intentions to take refuge in the Buddha, the *Dharma* and the *Sangha*. The next day Mahinda was invited to expound the *Dharma* to the women of the royal household, and many of them on that day became "stream-enterers" (i.e. embarked on the Buddhist life).

The king provided the missionaries with a park on the outskirts of the capital city of Anuradhapura in which to reside (see figure 5.1). According to the Pali chronicles, the king later stated his intention to build a *stupa* and requested some relic of the Buddha for the building. The legends tell of how such a relic was provided by means of a mystical flight from north India to the Himalayas, where the great gods were visited, and from there to Sri Lanka. It is also claimed that Emperor Asoka took a cutting from the sacred *bodhi* tree under which the Buddha attained enlightenment and sent it to Sri Lanka. Irrespective of the historical accuracy of the stories, what is interesting is that from earliest times, the building of a *stupa* was considered a necessary aspect of Buddhist life and practice. After much other building, the king asked the missionaries if Buddhism could now be considered as established on the island. Mahinda replied that it was established but that it would not take root until a Sri Lankan, born of Sri Lankan parents, took the robes in Sri Lanka, learned the discipline in Sri Lanka, and recited it in Sri Lanka. In other words there is no Buddhism without the *Sangha,* and no *Sangha* without the *Dharma.* Many Buddhist historians have also added that there is no Sri Lanka without Buddhism.

By the end of Mahinda's life, some 48 years after his arrival on the island, the pattern of the Asokan Buddhist state had been reproduced. This pattern became a model for many of the kings of Sri Lanka who built monasteries and supported the *Sangha,* often at great cost. A first century AD king is said to have offered himself, his queen, his two sons, his state elephant and his state horse to the *Sangha,* despite remonstrations from the monks. He then redeemed the offerings with great gifts.

Late in the first century BC, civil wars and the Tamil invasion led to a terrible famine. This probably stimulated a sense of crisis, as the Buddha had said that if the order of nuns was founded, the *Sangha* would last only 500 years. This would mean that in Theravada chronology the end time would be approaching late in the first century BC. One of the consequences of this was that Buddhist scriptures were committed to writing and not transmitted orally as previously. The *Mahavamsa* states:

> Formerly, clever monks preserved the text of the Canon and its commentaries orally, but then, when they saw the disastrous state of living beings, they came together and had it written down in books, that the doctrine might long survive.[2]

The first recorded division within the Theravada tradition came soon after the war against the Tamil invaders. Late in the first century BC, after the war, King Vattagamani gave a monastery in Anuradhapura to a monk who had assisted him. The *Vinaya* knows no precedent for such a gift to an individual, and the monks of Mahavihara charged the monk with offences and expelled him. The monk, with others, then severed relations with Mahavihara and moved to Abhayagiri.

At that time, a conference of monks debated the question whether learning or practice was the basis of the Buddhist tradition. The majority decided that according to the Pali canon, it was learning and the preservation of the scriptures, because without it there would be no "Insight meditation" (see chapter 7). The *Sangha* therefore formalised the creation of two roles for monks: "book yoke" and "insight yoke". Book yoke was seen as the most important role and concentrated upon learning and preaching, while the insight yoke concentrated upon meditation. Today, the division between the roles is seen in the distinction between "village-dwelling" and "forest-dwelling" monks.[3] Village temples are situated usually on high ground at the edge of the village and provide residence for the monks. "Forest dwelling" is the classic ascetic option that is undertaken either temporarily or for life.

A second split came in the fourth century AD when King Mahasena (277–304 AD) came under the influence of an Indian monk who wanted the monks to convert to the Mahayana tradition. The monks at Mahavihara left the capital in disgust, and the king had their building demolished and the materials given to Abhayagiri. These decisions were soon reversed, the king had the Indian monk assassinated, and he built a new monastery called Jetavana. History then repeated itself as the monk was accused of an offence and expelled; he went and formed his own school at Jetavana. The Abhayagiri tended to be more open to the new Mahayana influences from India than was the Mahavihara. From the fourth till the twelfth centuries there were these three schools in the capital.

It was about this time that another important relic arrived on the island. This was claimed to be the Buddha's left wisdom tooth along with the alms bowl that he is said to have used. The tooth was enshrined in a golden casket and placed in the Temple of the Tooth in Kandy, which has now become an important tourist centre. The tooth has come to symbolise the social identity of the Sinhalese people as Buddhists, in opposition to the Hindu Tamils in the north.

One of the greatest Buddhist scholars of Sri Lanka was the fifth century translator Buddhaghosa, whose role has been equated to that of St Thomas Aquinas in the Roman Catholic traditions.[4]

According to tradition, he was born a Brahmin in India and converted to Theravada Buddhism. He journeyed to Sri Lanka early in the fifth century and appears to have joined the Pali literary project. His first work was the *Visuddimagga* ("The Path to Purity"), often dated about 412 AD.[5] This a compendium of Theravada doctrine arranged in three parts according to the old hierarchy of morality, concentration and wisdom. The work gives full quotations from the canon, and its lively anecdotes give glimpses into the way of life of a monk at that time.

The following works of Buddhaghosa were commentaries on the *Vinaya* and important sermons. Most of his material was written in Pali, rather than the local language of Sinhala. According to Buddhaghosa, Mahinda brought with him commentaries on the Pali canon and translated them into Sinhala; many of the texts were memorised by the monks. However, living languages change and, by the fifth century, the text written down in Sinhala in the first century BC must have been difficult to understand. Since the canon was in Pali, which was the foundation language of monastic education, it appears to have been more convenient to study a dead language to preserve the commentaries accurately. After Buddhaghosa, there was a shift from Sinhala to Pali for religious studies.

The positive effect of the reversion to the classical language was to internationalise the Theravada tradition. Like the Latin-speaking priests of Christian Europe, the monks were able to communicate with others of their tradition, despite local variations in pronunciation of Pali. The result has been that when the *Sangha* has declined in one country, it has been able to renew itself from abroad. The drawback, of course, is that a dead language is unintelligible to the ordinary, uneducated people. The Buddhist monks have always been great translators and there is evidence of the translation of the canon into Sinhala in 400 AD. However, the texts most translated for the laity were the *Jataka* and similar stories. Paintings on the temple walls give an impression of the knowledge held by people concerning Buddhism. The subjects usually concern the lives of the Buddha.

In 1160 a council at Anuradhapura terminated the dissension between the Mahavihara and its rivals. King Prakkamabahu I, who ruled the island from the new capital at Polnnaruwa between 1153 and 1186, set up a single authority structure of the national *Sangha*. To ensure its control he had all ordination ceremonies performed at one time of the year in the capital. Although the chronicles of the times say that he reunited them, it appears more likely that he abolished the Abhayagiri and Jetavana and made all the monks from these schools laity; only the better ones were allowed to become novices in the new, unified *Sangha*. The *Sangha* was headed by a monk known as the *Sangharaja* ("King of the *Sangha*") and ruled by him with two deputies. Such a political organisation for the *Sangha* was something quite new, and it became imitated several times within the Theravada tradition in south-east Asia.

Why did Buddhism spread so successfully in Sri Lanka? Gombrich suggests three major factors that had a great influence. The first factor is "the power and beauty of its thought".[6] Buddhism offered a coherent and universal ethic that provided a significant answer to the issue of suffering. Second, by the time that Buddhism reached Sri Lanka it "encountered no rival ideologies". The people followed their traditional beliefs, which lacked an explicit cosmology or soteriology. Buddhism was able to fill this intellectual and religious gap, while allowing freedom for people to continue with traditional customs and gods if they wished. Third, the positive support of the monarch for the *Sangha* was crucial in determining its acceptance and growth. It was a religion attractive to the growing class of travellers and merchants detached from the local deities of rural communities.

Soon after 1200 AD, there was a collapse of the *Sangha,* not so much due to a failure within Buddhism as within the social system that supported it. Invasions from India weakened the central power, and Muslim pirates ruled over areas of the island. Later in the 16th century, the Portuguese persecuted the *Sangha*, claiming that it encouraged the worship of the sacred tooth. The long occupation of Sri Lanka by Europeans almost resulted in the extinction of the *Sangha* but in 1880 revival began, first stimulated by the Theosophical Society, about which more will be written in chapter 17.

Myanmar

Theravada Buddhism had already spread throughout the region of present-day Myanmar before the Burmese people settled the country.[7] Some of the earlier inhabitants were the Mons, but little is known of their history and culture. There is a legend that King Asoka sent a mission consisting of Theras Sona and Uttara to spread the message of Buddhism to Suvannabhumi ("Land of Gold"), but it is not possible to identify the country with that of the Mons. The Mons do not appear to have been converted to Buddhism until several centuries after Asoka and then only after adopting Hindu cults alongside Buddhism.

The ancestors of the Burmese moved gradually from the north into the fertile Irrawaddy plain from the mountainous country east of Tibet. The Burmese language is actually part of the Tibeto-Burmese group. The earliest Burmese state was that of Pyu which was established in about the third century in the centre of modern Myanmar. It was originally much influenced by north Indian culture and many became adherents of the Vishnu cult of Hinduism, or of the Mahayana and Tantric forms of Buddhism. The rulers of Nan Chao, who were related to the Pyu, conquered the Pyu state in 832 AD; they founded their capital at Pagan in 849 (see figure 6.1). Although they continued to follow their traditional religions, they were much influenced by the Tantric Buddhism that the Pyu had adopted. The priests formed a powerful organisation of monks who called themselves *aris* (meaning "noble") and, although there is little information about their teaching, they are known to have worshipped the Mahayana deities, performed Tantric rituals, and indulged in magic.

The *Aris* absorbed many local customs and, as in other Buddhist countries, the local cults were allowed to survive, provided their objective was purely for this world. Buddhism was concerned with escape from the cycle of life to which such spirits were thought to belong and so, like human beings, they were transitory. The local spirits were called *nats* and were believed to relate to families, villages, regions, and finally to the state. The holy mountain of the *nat* cult is the extinct volcano, Popa, not far from Pagan; it has become the place of pilgrimage. The *nat* cults have

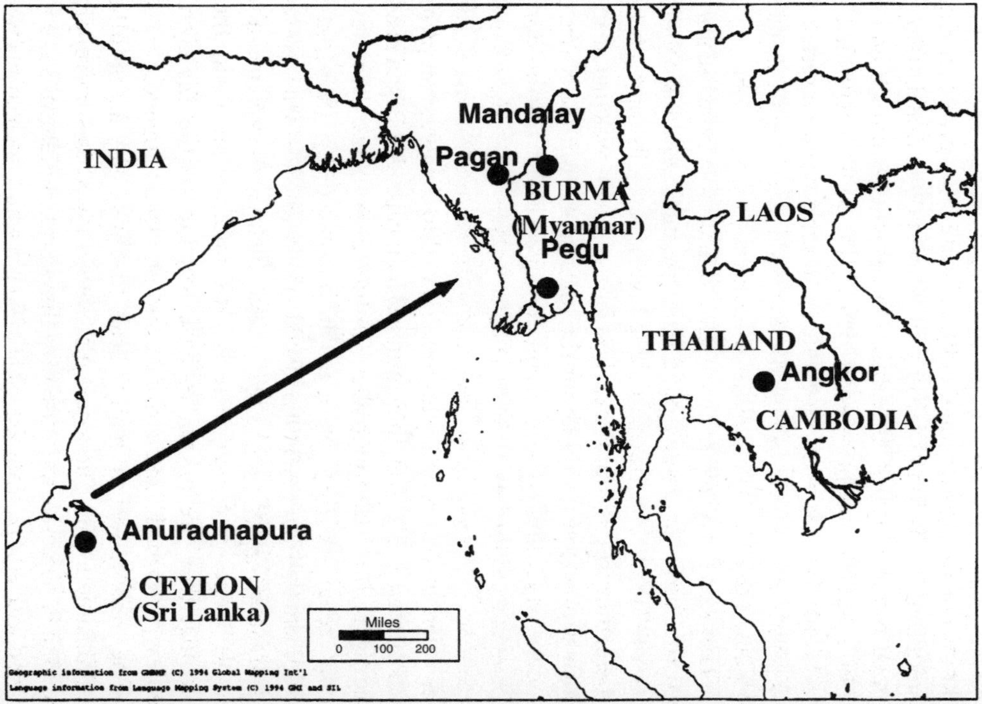
INDIA
Mandalay
Pagan
BURMA
(Myanmar)
Pegu
LAOS
THAILAND
Angkor
CAMBODIA
Anuradhapura
CEYLON
(Sri Lanka)
Miles
0 100 200
Geographic information from GNBNP (C) 1994 Global Mapping Int'l
Language information from Language Mapping System (C) 1994 GMI and SIL

Figure 6.1 *Spread of Theravada Buddhism throughout south-east Asia*

important social functions in that they bind members of a family together, and village communities to their homes. In addition, there were *nats* who were the gods of cities or pagodas. The most important priestly functions in the *nat* cults were carried out by the mother of the family, but there were also professional priest-esses.

Throughout the history of Myanmar, Buddhism and the *nat* cults were able on the whole to co-exist quite peacefully because of their different aims. The objective of the *nat* cults was purely that of material well-being and the aversion of danger, while the true aim of Buddhism remained, in theory at least, the attain-ment of enlightenment. In practice there was mixing and, throughout the history of Myanmar, Buddhist reformers objected to what they considered excessive belief in the spirits by the village people.

Theravada Buddhism was introduced into the state by King Anuruddha (1044–77); this was to mark a turning point in Myanmar's religious history. Burmese chronicles speak about Anuruddha being converted by a Mon monk called Shin Arahan, but there were no copies of the *sutras* in the capital of Pagan. The king asked the Mon king of Thaton for copies of the *sutras* and some relics; on his refusal, Anuruddha attacked and conquered the Mon state. He brought the captive Mon king, his family and many monks and craftsmen to Pagan. This act brought Mon culture and Theravada Buddhism into Burmese society and revi-talised the culture of the whole society. The influence of Tantric Buddhism was finally broken; it quickly declined until it only remained along the borders of the state.

By the end of the twelfth century the *Sangha* in Sri Lanka had gained such a high reputation that the king sent a group of Burmese monks to the island. They studied the Sri Lankan forms and introduced them into Myanmar. The Sri Lankan tradition immediately came into competition with the local Burmese expression and gradually became dominant. The Sri Lankan tra-dition could trace its history back to that originally founded by Mahinda, the son of Asoka, while the origin of the Burmese tra-dition went back to the missionaries Sona and Uttara who had been sent by Asoka. As in Sri Lanka and later in Siam, some groups of monks broke away from the majority and went to live in the forest in order to concentrate upon meditation.

The twelfth century saw a thorough revision of the Pali texts in Myanmar; throughout the following centuries the study of the texts has been pursued eagerly. Aggavamsa wrote the *Saddaniti,* the most important work on Pali grammar, in the twelfth century. It has been the *Abhidharma Pitaka* that has been the centre of greatest study in Myanmar. It is said by south Asian monks that this contrasts with Sri Lanka which has given precedence to the study of the *Vinaya,* and Thailand to that of the *Suttas.* Today, in Myanmar, not only monks but also lay people study the *Abhidharma* and eagerly discuss questions of systematic philosophy. The debate has been applied to the contemporary political situation of the country.

The dynasty of Pagan created some of the most magnificent temples in Myanmar, but many were destroyed by the invasion of the Mongols from China in 1287. The repercussion was the disintegration of the central state. The Mons in the south regained their independence, and the Shan and Thai peoples settled in large areas of the north. The *Sangha* suffered much through the period; many monks contravened the rules of the order and amassed wealth for themselves through the practice of astrology and medicine.

Burmese Buddhism underwent a major reform under King Dhammaceti (1472–92). He first came to the country from the Mons as a monk and helped Queen Shin Sawbu as ruler of Pegu in 1453. When the queen decided to retire to spiritual pursuits, she appointed Dhammaceti as her successor. Dhammaceti left the monastic order to become king but used his new position to work through the reforms. In 1476 he sent a delegation of 22 monks on two ships to Sri Lanka. They were re-ordained in the Sri Lankan tradition in the river Kalyanisima on the west coast of the island. On their return to Pegu, a new ordination hall was constructed called Kalyanisima after the Sinhalese river. The monks were then invited to submit themselves to re-ordination. These formalities were required because the serious transgressions against the monastic rule incurred automatic expulsion from the *Sangha.* The validity of the succession could only be assured if the way of life of the monks belonging to the *Sangha* was morally above reproach.

The kingdom of Pegu was conquered and destroyed by the Burmese in 1539 and again in 1551. However, the reform of the *Sangha* affected all parts of the country and was so successful that all Burmese monks today trace their ordination back to the Kalyanisima tradition.

A serious dispute divided the *Sangha* in the 18th century when a group of monks maintained that covering both shoulders with the robe was in accordance with the original laws. The rest of the monks wanted to cover only one shoulder, which is generally considered to be historically correct. The dispute reached such great proportions that King Bodawapaya intervened in 1784, deciding in favour of covering both shoulders. Until today, this way of wearing the monk's robe is characteristic of Burmese monks. The significance of this story is that it shows the control exercised by the kings through a central monastic administration headed by a *Sangharaja*.

The *Sangharaja* was appointed by the king, on whose death or overthrow the validity of the appointment would end. He was supported by a council of eight to twelve elders who worked in close collaboration with the secular authorities in the supervision of the monastic property and registration of monks. As this system depended on the effectiveness of the state government, it broke down completely with the annexation of Myanmar by the British after 1885. This breakdown was more marked in Sri Lanka as the *Sangha* had lost most of its tradition of self-government.

Although Myanmar is often considered a poor country by Western observers, it has a strong religious presence. Writers consider that Buddhism is stronger in Myanmar than in any other country in south-east Asia. It was said to have over 400,000 monks and 6,000 *viharas* in the later 1990s.[8] Some of the larger monasteries have over 1,000 monks studying the Buddhist scriptures and meditation practice. It also has 75,000 nuns, the largest number of Buddhist nuns of any country.

Thailand

The development of Buddhism among the Thai followed similar patterns as in Myanmar. The Thai migrated southwards from south-western China and gradually moved into the lands dominated by the Mons and Khumers. Here they came in contact with the Theravada and Mahayana forms of Buddhism and also Brahmanism. When Khublai Khan invaded China in 1254, an even greater number of Thai moved south, dominating the Mons and the Khumers and adopting more of their culture. The Thai established two major states in the late thirteenth and fourteenth centuries, Sukhothai and Chiangmai. As in Myanmar, Mon Buddhism had a major influence on the Thai; both states became important Buddhist centres.

In about 1260, the kingdom of Sukhothai became a free state and King Rama Khamheng (1275–1317) made Theravada Buddhism the official religion in the kingdom. His grandson, Lu Thai, invited monks from Sri Lanka to visit the kingdom and strengthen the purity of the Thai *Sangha*. The visit gave a great increase in the scholarship of the Pali scriptures in the kingdom. However, it also gave the Sukhotai kingdom the Sinhalese model of government. Sukhotai was taken over by the Thai kingdom of Ayudhya, which existed from 1350 until 1767. During this time, Cambodia became a dependency of the Thai kings.

By about 1750, Buddhist culture had reached such heights that its reputation was known in Sri Lanka, and King Kirthi Sri sent three missions to Ayudhya. The last mission finally succeeded and was warmly welcomed by King Maha Dhammaraja II (1733–58), who sent a delegation of monks to Sri Lanka. The monks remained in Sri Lanka for three years. In 1753 ordained monks formed the nucleus of the sect known as Siyam Nikaya.

In 1767 the kingdom of Ayudhya was destroyed by Burmese invaders but, later, King Taksin (1767–82) restored Thai independence. He was soon deposed by the first king of the Chakri dynasty, Rama I (1782–1809), who established a new capital at Bangkok. Both these kings reformed the *Sangha* and ordered new collections of the scriptures. The greatest reformer of Thai Buddhism was King Rama III (1851–68) who had been a monk for 27 years before becoming monarch. While still a monk, he had started a reformist movement in the *Sangha* called the Dhammayuttika-Nikaya, and had followed a stricter discipline than the majority of the *Sangha*.

Theravada festivals and rituals

In all societies where the Theravada tradition dominates, the temples hold regular calendar festivals. Especially in the villages, these rituals cover a range of social interests. They establish social harmony; they instruct the laity; they celebrate good harvests and seek to ensure prosperity in the coming year. They generate merit for the devout and provide fun for all.

The average Sri Lankan Buddhist visits the local temple four times a month on *poya* days, which equate to the phases of the moon. The day of the full moon is the most important and is always a national holiday. Worship is individual and usually involves offering flowers, lighting oil lamps and burning incense. *Dharma* sermons are conducted in temples and people come to hear *pirit* – the chanting of protective *sutras*.

Theravada Buddhists celebrate the birth, enlightenment and death of the Buddha in an important three-day festival called Wesak that falls at the full moon in May. Light is a prominent feature of the festival, as may be assumed as it is a celebration of the enlightenment of the Buddha. *Wesak* lights are conspicuous everywhere during the festival, illuminating homes, temples and *bodhi* trees. Homes and streets are decorated, *Wesak* cards are sent, and monks receive gifts from the lay people. Flowers are also prominent, not only for their beauty but to emphasise the transitory nature of life. People visit temples and give gifts to friends and relatives.

Poson, at the full moon in June, is particular to Sri Lanka, as it celebrates the first arrival of Buddhism to the island. The festival of Kathina, meaning "cloth" is celebrated in October or November, depending upon the lunar calendar. It is a joyful ceremony that comes at the end of the rainy season retreat for the monks. Gifts, especially new robes, are offered to the monks in gratitude for their preserving the *Dharma*.

Another three-day festival is the Buddhist New Year held in April, when Buddha images are washed and adorned in robes for the monks. Many lay people adopt the Five Precepts on the last day and many buy captive birds to release them, in order to accrue good *karma*. No one seems to think of the bad *karma* acquired by the one who has so painstakingly spent the time to capture the birds. New Year is also a festival for fun, and water is often sprayed in a great water fight. Traditional dancing, kite-flying and shadow-puppet plays are part of the festivities.

A particular aspect of the Sri Lankan festivals is the carriage of the sacred tooth around the streets of Kandy (Kandy Perahera). Although the beginnings of this celebration are dated back to the reign of King Megavanna (301–331 AD), it was actually in the 18th century during the reign of King Kirthi Sri Rajasinha of Kandy that the festival took its current form. A magnificent tusked elephant, adorned with colourful cloth and carrying on his back the illuminated replica of the casket of the sacred tooth, leads the procession. Then follows a train of elephants, followed by the leaders of the temple and other dignitaries, including the Kandyan dancers.

The only life cycle ceremonies performed in Theravada Buddhism are ordination and funeral ceremonies. There is no Buddhist ceremony for birth or marriage, which are considered purely worldly. In Sri Lanka colonial and missionary influence has brought about a change in the traditional practice; by the mid-1970s monks began to make appearances at weddings, and weddings were even solemnised in temples.[9]

Death is considered a good occasion to help the living consider the brevity of life and reflect on the Buddhist teaching on suffering and impermanence. People in mourning wear white, and white flags can decorate the house and area. The monks are asked to chant the Three Refuges and the Five Precepts, and water is poured as symbolic of transferring merit to the dead person. At fixed intervals after the funeral (one week, three months and on the anniversary), meals are prepared for the monks, as it is believed that merit is transferred to the deceased. The transference of merit to the dead person is intended to improve the state of their rebirth, which seems to contradict the strict teaching on *karma*. Sharing merit is a very old tradition in Buddhism; scholars would say that it is merely a psychological consolation for the bereaved. However, whether the transference of merit is understood as actually working, it is a common attitude among most lay people.

Theravada Buddhism has had little difficulty accommodating to the large number of local beliefs concerning the various gods and spirits. Buddhist teaching sees the universe as a vast complex including many such beings, all circumscribed by the law of *karma*. Many local cults such as those of the *nats* continue to play a major part in the life of villagers. Certain texts from the Pali canon are ritually recited by the monks for protection; special rituals are undertaken at times of sickness, when dedicating a new house or in some time of life transition. The monks pass a thread around the people concerned, and texts are recited with the pouring of water. This is generally understood by lay people as making the evil spirits more kindly disposed to the people.

Even though gods are considered to be part of *samsara*, they do have the power to be able to help with worldly problems. Many of these gods are Hindu gods, especially Vishnu and Skandha who in Sri Lanka is called Kataragama. Buddhist temples often have attached shrines, called *devale,* especially for the Hindu deities. Many lay Buddhists in Sri Lanka visit the great shrine at the town of Kataragama that is dedicated to the god of that name. Here people often come to fulfil their vows to the deity by pushing skewers through their cheeks or by fire-walking.

Astrologers are common and often consulted before making any important decision. While travelling in Sri Lanka, I asked my Buddhist driver about horoscopes and he laughed off the practice as superstition. I then asked him if he ever went to the astrologer. He replied, "Yes, I go every week but that is only to be forewarned of any danger."

Thus, today one finds a rich mixture of belief and ritual throughout these nations of south-east Asia. The monks concentrate upon morality and meditation, and seek to practise and preserve the *Dharma*. For many lay people they are seeking spiritual power to enable them to deal with the everyday problems of a country with a struggling economy.

Suggestions for interfaith discussions

The folk rituals reveal the apparent failure of Theravada Buddhism to address the worldly problems faced by ordinary people. Thus, alongside Theravada doctrine, most people turn to the local and Hindu gods. Does Christianity have a better answer to this apparent religious dualism?

Webwise 6 – The Theravada Tradition in South-East Asia

Photographs of modern Thailand

http://www.terragalleria.com/theravada/country.thailand.html
This site is designed for tourists and teaches much about modern Thai culture. It contains 150 excellent images from nine different sites in central and northern Thailand.

Photographs of modern Myanmar

http://www.terragalleria.com/theravada/country.myanmar.html
This is another site mainly designed to promote tourism but it contains many attractive photographs of the cultural and religious heritage of Myanmar.

Buddha Dharma Education Association and BuddhaNet

http://www.buddhanet.net/e-learning/buddhistworld/theravada.htm
This site has been produced by Theravada Buddhists to teach the Theravada tradition. It is mainly written by John Bullett and, in addition to a brief summary of Theravada teaching, it gives insights into the main Theravada countries of south-east Asia.

Access to Insight: readings in Theravada Buddhism

http://www.accesstoinsight.org
This is one of the most extensive sites on Theravada Buddhism with links to the Pali canon and various library archives.

The ancient city of Anuradhapura

http://www.geocities.com/withanage/Anuradha.htm
This is another tourist website that contains many photographs of ancient Sri Lanka and various rituals.

The Mahavamsa

http://lakdiva.net/mahavamsa
The full text of the Mahavamsa, translated from Pali by Wilhelm Geiger, is presented on this site. It also contains a genealogy of the Sri Lankan kings and a bibliography of Pali words.

Kataragama

http://www.xlweb.com/heritage/skanda/buddhist.htm
Kataragama is a town in southern Sri Lanka that contains a major shrine to the deity Kataragama. This site has been produced by the Kataragama Devotees Trust and contains information about the town and shrine, as well as many photographs.

Notes

1. *Mahavamsa,* XI, 33–36.
2. *Mahavamsa,* XXXIII, 100–101.
3. Gombrich, R., *Theravada Buddhism* (London: Routledge, 1994), pp. 156–157.
4. Gombrich, *ibid.,* p. 154.
5. Buddhaghosa, B., *The Path of Purification* (Singapore: Singapore Buddhist Meditation Centre, 1956).
6. Gombrich, *ibid.,* p. 151.
7. Myanmar changed its name from Burma in 1995.
8. Dhamma, Venerable Dr R., "Buddhism in Myanmar", *The Middle Way* 74 (1999), pp. 114–117.
9. Lamb, C., "Rites of Passage" in Harvey, P. (ed.), *Buddhism* (London: Continuum, 2001), pp. 151–180.

CHAPTER SEVEN

THE CULTIVATION OF WISDOM: MEDITATION

What you can learn from this chapter

- the nature of meditation as the key practice of Buddhism
- the two forms of Theravada meditation – Calm and Insight
- Western attempts to relate to Buddhist meditation

The aim of the Buddha's teaching is to free those who follow it from *dukkha*.

> Mind foreruns all conditions, mind is chief, mind-made are they. If a man speaks or acts with an unskilled mind, because of that, pain pursues him, even as the wheel follows the hoof of the draught-ox. (*Dhammapada* 1.1)

However vividly one tries to describe the architecture, the ceremonial, and activities of the *Sangha,* an important aspect of the life of the Buddhist community is missing – the mental process. Perhaps the closest a non-Buddhist can get to the essence of Buddhism is to watch the faces of monks in meditation, because it is in the control of the mind through meditation that there lies the real life of the monk. Meditation as a means of spiritual discipline is not unique to Buddhism but in its form and centrality to the gaining of liberation it is unique. Wherever Buddhism has been vigorous, meditation has not only been practised by monks and nuns but also by committed lay people.

Each of the Four Noble Truths requires some activity. The first Noble Truth of suffering is to be fully *comprehended.* The second

Truth is that the arising of suffering is to be *abandoned.* The third Truth of escape from suffering is to be *made visible.* The fourth Truth of the path leading to the ceasing of suffering is then *bhavana,* "bringing into being", often rendered as "meditation".

Bhavana is the process of bringing into being the path to liberation, and the training that is necessary for this. The goal can only be achieved by cultivating wisdom (Sanskrit: *prajna*), which directly sees things "as they really are". Learning meditation is a skill akin to learning to play a musical instrument; it requires regular practice and much patience. In meditation, the mind is the instrument which one must learn how to "tune" and "play", but this cannot be forced. Using another metaphor, meditation in the Theravada tradition can be likened to gardening: plants cannot be forced to grow. They must be given the right conditions, so that they develop naturally. For meditation, the right conditions are the application of mind and the specific techniques that are used.

The philosophy of the Buddha emerged at a time when India was experiencing a fervour of religious ideas and speculations. The Aryan migrants had settled into city-states along the Ganges valley, and the society was facing great social dislocation. Some people were seeking to find new meaning through the practice of yogic concentration.

The Pali tradition tells of how Gautama placed himself under the discipleship of two different *gurus* but found their teaching and meditation methods to be inadequate for his ultimate goal; he eventually rejected them. He probably took over certain forms of meditation from these teachers and incorporated them into his own teaching, and these may well have continued to develop throughout his public ministry. Similarly, his teaching was interpreted by his early followers and adapted to their particular needs. Thus, the early scriptures do not present a neat package of teaching on meditation, although there are certain identifiable patterns of practices and teachings. In all these sources, meditation is presented as the only successful means to attain full and final release from the endless round of birth and death.

There were believed to be two approaches to the attainment of knowledge. The first, equivalent to the approach of the modern rationalist, argued that truth is only achieved through the empirical senses and the use of reason. The alternative view was that true knowledge was achieved through yogic concentration that would lead into alternative states of consciousness known as *jhanas*. The Buddha steered a middle course between these two positions and taught that neither reason nor revelation were complete in themselves. According to the Buddha, true knowledge is found through the development of the natural abilities of people and is not something supernatural. He taught that super-sensory perception was a valid means of knowing but warned of the dangers of drawing false conclusions from such perceptions. The first *sutra* of the *Digha Nikaya* (the *Brahmajalasutra*) contains a summary of all the wrong theories that people derive as a result of wrong speculation resulting from states of deep meditation.

In practice, most meditation is done with the legs crossed in a full or half lotus position, seated on a cushion if necessary. The hands are together in the lap, and the back is straight but not stiff. Once a person has become used to the position, it is stable and can be used as a good posture for quieting the mind. Any type of meditation is done under the guidance of a meditation teacher, known in the Theravada tradition as one's "good friend" (*kalyanamitta*). The Buddha said that having such a teacher was the most useful external factor in aiding the purification of the heart.[1] The teacher gets to know his student, gives guidance through difficulties, and guards against inappropriate application of meditation. In return, the student must apply himself or herself to the practice and be open to where the master leads.

Two types of *bhavana* exist, translated into English as "Calm" (*samatha*) and "Insight" (*vipassana*). The most common method is to take Calm as the vehicle (*yana*) and seek to develop the higher states of consciousness. The alternative, Insight, was at one time unusual but in recent years it has become more popular, especially in Myanmar. Today, centres for the practice of Insight meditation are to be found in England, Germany, the USA and India. Almost all of these derive from Myanmar but are not all of the same branch of Burmese meditation.

Calm meditation (*samatha*)

To attain deep insight into the truth of things requires a high degree of mental tranquillity. Right mindfulness (*sati*) is the process of bearing something in mind with clear awareness. It is that awareness that does not merely drift along the surface of things but is a thorough observation.

Mental focus (*samadhi*)

A person's normal experience of "concentration" varies from half-hearted paying attention, to becoming totally absorbed, as in reading a good book. Theravada meditation aims to cultivate the power of concentration until it becomes truly "one-pointed", with total attention set upon a chosen, calming object. In such a state, known as *samadhi* ("concentration" or "collectedness"), the mind becomes free from all distractions and experiences a unified state of inner stillness. In order for meditation to develop appropriately, the techniques must be used in the right way. If an individual attempts to concentrate upon an object but is without proper vigour, he or she will become sleepy. If an individual concentrates without being mindful of the object, he or she can become fixated on the object, which is "wrong concentration".

In the fifth century, Buddhaghosa wrote the *Visuddhimagga,* which has become the classic meditation manual of Theravada Buddhism. In the *sutra* he describes 40 possible objects that enable people of different characters to develop a state of relatively deep calm. These 40 possible objects for meditation are classified in two ways: in terms of the types of person, and level of attainment. Six types of personal character were recognised by Buddhaghosa, and various objects ascribed to counteract negative character traits.[2]

1 Greed	2 Hate	3 Delusion
4 Faith	5 Intelligence	6 Discursiveness

The six types are grouped in this way because those at the top are parallel to the lower three. "Greed seeks out sense desires as objects, while faith seeks out the special qualities of virtue and so on. And greed does not give up what is harmful, while faith does not give up what is beneficial."[3]

It should be pointed out that all people have all these character-istics within them and from time to time one or another will man-ifest itself as dominant. As it is often difficult to analyse oneself correctly, it is often advised that beginners should have a teacher to guide them. For example, a monk who has trouble with lust might be assigned by his teacher to meditate on the "32 parts of the body", which include hair, skin, heart, intestines, sweat and other bodily excrement.[4]

Some objects of meditation reflect the qualities of the Three Jewels: the Buddha, the *Dharma* or the *Sangha*. A popular object is loving-kindness, which consists of developing a warm acceptance towards others. Meditators start with themselves and, after review-ing aspects of themselves, the focus is then shifted to others. Another approach is to focus first on a highly respected person, then a friend, then a person the meditator is indifferent towards, and finally someone he or she dislikes. In all cases, it is stressed, the subject should be a person of the same sex as the meditator. The aim is to break down barriers that make the mind friendly towards only a limited number of beings, and cultivate an all-pervading kindness.

A common form of meditation, especially in Thailand, is that of corpse meditation. A monastery often purchases the body of some unwanted victim of violence to be brought to the monastery. The smell of the decaying corpse is considered to purify the monks as they perform their contemplations around the body. Thailand also produces popular magazines containing photographs of dead bodies. Death is considered one of the three experiences (with disease and old age) that persuades people to abandon the pursuit of mere earthly happiness and search instead for ultimate reality.

The most common form of Calm meditation is "mindfulness of breathing" (*anapanasati*). This is done with the eyes closed and often begins with some method of counting the in-and-out flow of the breath, so as to aid the mind to stay on the process. After a time, the counting is ended and the sensation arising from the flow of breath is given attention. At first the mind appears to wander more in meditation than at other times but, with practice, the mind can remain on the breath for longer periods.

This is well expressed by the contemporary Thai scholar, the Venerable Chowkhun Noraratrajmanit.

> As we have very often heard, the mind is fickle, light and quick, resembling a monkey. In order to subjugate the monkey the trainer requires a strong stake fixed in the ground to tie the monkey with a rope; and to train the mind as well there must be a stake likewise . . . *Sati* (mindfulness) is like a rope to tie the mind to this stake of breathing . . . Also, an uncontrolled mind is like a wild animal. For example, an elephant which is newly caught for taming dashes to and fro trying to wrench himself free; sometimes so violently that the rope cuts into the flesh or to the bone thereby leading to bleeding at the neck or legs. Before when he was in the jungle he did not behave in this violent manner as he was not the subject of any restraint. Nor when he is well-tamed does he behave fiercely, but becomes gentle. In the same way the mind does not show its ferocious nature while enjoying sense objects.[5]

As the meditator learns to work with the mental images, he or she will have to deal with the five hindrances. The first is sensual desire, where the mind reaches out for some more interesting item. Second is ill-will, where there is a negative reaction to the task of meditation. Third is lethargy and drowsiness. Fourth is anxiety, restlessness and worry. The final hindrance is doubt: the fear of commitment where the mind questions whether the task is worth all the effort. Overcoming these hindrances is likened to taming a wild animal. It is at this point that access to full concentration of *jhana* becomes possible.

In the *Samyutta Nikaya* the parable of the hunter is told.[6] A hunter caught six animals: a snake, crocodile, bird, dog, jackal and monkey. He tied each to a stout rope and then tied the six ropes together. When he released the ropes the six animals all pulled in different directions: the snake to a hole, the crocodile to water, the bird to the air, and so on. As they pulled in different directions, they were eventually pulled by whoever was the stronger. This is said to be like the ordinary mind that is continually pulled by the six different sense objects. However, if the six animals had been tied to a stout post, then they would only be able to go around the post until they became weary. Thus, the meditator focusing upon one object will have a restrained mind.

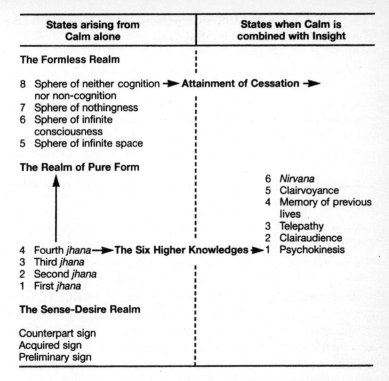

Figure 7.1   States developed using Calm meditation

Levels of concentration

The early texts chart the progress of the mind to deeper levels of concentration. The various levels are known as *jhanas* in Pali (Sanskrit: *dhyanas*) (see figure 7.1).

1. At the first *jhana* the meditator is free from senses of desire (*kama*) and sensual thoughts. The person feels permeated with joy and well-being because of the absence of all external and internal disturbances. However, the mind is still intellectually occupied, operating at the level of analytical thought and deliberately pondering the condition. The Buddha is said to have recounted that as a boy, he once spontaneously experienced the first *jhana* while sitting quietly in the shade watching his father work in a field.

2. At the second *jhana* the intellectual operation and analysis are dispensed with. Joy now comes from concentration and not merely from the absence of disturbance. Here is tranquillity and singleness of mind.

3. The third *jhana* is when joy falls away and tranquillity remains. It commences in the form of warm tingles and culminates in the feeling of all-pervading bliss. Equanimity (*upekha*), mindfulness (*sati*) and clear comprehension (*sampajanna*) remain.

4. In the fourth *jhana* the mind remains in a neutral state, fully mindful and alert, but not moved by intellectualising, pain or pleasure. The mind is here prepared for deeper levels of meditation. After attaining the fourth *jhana*, the mind is considered sufficiently supple to go further. It can now be directed in two directions: to further *jhana* or to "higher knowledge" (*adhinna*).

Formless attainments

The formless realm can be achieved by further use of Calm meditation on its own. There are four levels of mystical trance paralleling the formless realms of rebirth:

1. The sphere of infinite space
2. The sphere of infinite consciousness
3. The sphere of nothingness
4. The sphere of neither cognition nor non-cognition

The spheres are "formless" because the "objects" themselves are simply regarded as having no form. The fifth *jhana* is called *akasanancayatana,* "the dimension of the infinity of space". Here the mind has moved beyond the form and content of specific entities. The infinity of space is transcended and the next *jhana* is entered, "the dimension of nothingness", which, according to tradition, was the deepest level reached by Gautama's teacher Kalama. Beyond this, it is discovered that nothingness is not the ultimate dimension of experience, and the next level reached is the experience of "the dimension of infinite consciousness". Here all empirical phenomena are negated but this experience is still a mental perception. Gautama's other teacher, Uddaka Ramaputta, is said to have penetrated further to "the dimension which is neither perception nor non-perception".

Gautama is said to have broken through this limit as well, reaching an even deeper level, "the cessation of perception and sensation". It is a state in which all perception and experience cease, and a great peace is known. In this state Gautama did not find any ultimate substance but it was still short of *nirvana*. Tradition tells that it was into this state that the Buddha entered before his *parinirvana*, possibly to suppress the natural agonies of dying.

Higher knowledge (*adhinna*)

After the attainment of the fourth *jhana*, the mind is prepared to perceive beyond the range of ordinary sense perception. This will enable the seeker to verify the truth of teachings such as *karma* and the Four Noble Truths. The higher knowledge builds on the fourth *jhana* because it removes distracting sensory experiences but it does not eliminate all perception, as occurs with the higher *jhanas*.

Buddhaghosa recognises five forms of higher knowledge in addition to *nirvana*:[7]

1. Psychokinesis – the ability to exert power over external objects through the will
2. Divine Ear – the ability to perceive sounds far beyond the range of hearing
3. Telepathy – the ability to perceive the thoughts and general state of another
4. Recollection of past lives
5. Clairvoyance – the ability to perceive the arising and passing away of other beings
6. *Nirvana*

The last three perceptions (4–6) were said to have been accomplished by the Buddha shortly before his enlightenment. The Buddha was not interested in the accomplishment of mental feats and tricks but only in cleansing the mind to enable it to see reality. The sixth super-sensory perception was, of course, considered the greater form of insight.

Insight meditation (*vipassana*)

The later developments within Buddhism produced a variety of aims and methods of meditation. The basic techniques of posture and of breath, body and thought control were retained, as were many of the meditational terms. Calm meditation alone, it was claimed, cannot lead to *nirvana,* for while it can temporarily suspend, and thus weaken, attachment, it cannot eliminate it. Calm acts as a preliminary to the practice of Insight meditation, such that it gives the mind the clarity in which things can be seen as they really are. Calm meditation is therefore used to tune the mind and make it a more adequate instrument for insight.

The beginning of the Insight movement was among the monks who chose the relative quietude of the forest life, well before the Burmese were Buddhists. It was King Mindon who in the 19th century welded these forest residents into formal traditions in their own right, which he practised himself. The practice was encouraged by the initiatives of Prime Minister U Nu in the 1950s and since then it has spread beyond Myanmar.

The basis of Insight meditation is known as the "four foundations of mindfulness". Here, rather than focusing on one chosen object, as in Calm meditation, the attention is opened out so that mindfulness carefully observes each passing sensory or mental object. There is a slight detachment, in order to avoid interfering with the natural flow of mental and physical phenomena. The "four foundations" are the spheres in which to develop mindfulness: body, feelings, state of mind, and *dharmas.* As the body is more easily perceived, mindfulness takes this as its first object, in preparation of the more fleeting mental processes. Insight meditation is not done solely in the seated position and can be done as the person moves about. In this the person focuses on the sensations in the feet and leg muscles, and the various phases of movement are mentally noted.

It is during seated meditation that the breath is usually investigated. The mind does not remain solely on the breath but observes

the various physical sensations as they occur, but with "bare attention". It is called this because it involves no thought or comment
about what is perceived. For example, observe what is happening
in your body when you become aware of rumblings in the stomach
caused by hunger. Bare attention is turned to it until it has passed.
Bare attention may then be turned to a stiffness in the neck or a
cramp in the leg. Awareness remains with the pain, adding nothing
to it, until the pain subsides and you are aware of this happening
too. In this way the practitioner come to a greater understanding
of how the body works and where the identity of "I" emerges.
Thus what might be a distraction within Calm meditation can
become an object for Insight.

Once mindfulness of the body is established, attention is turned
to feelings. These are recognised as they come and go, noting
simply whether they are pleasant and unpleasant, from the body
or from the mind. No significance is attached to them; they are
regarded as no more than passing phenomena. Similarly, mindfulness moves on to states of mind, in which emotions and moods are
noted as they arise, and they are allowed to pass. Finally, mindfulness investigates *dharmas* such as the five hindrances. While these
processes are being investigated, the aim is to experientially recognise their shared features, known as the "three marks". These are
their *impermanence,* their *unsatisfactoriness,* and their being *empty
of self*. These insights are not of a conceptual or intellectual nature
but come as flashes of understanding. Once these have occurred
during meditation, they may also arise in the course of the day, as
things are observed with mindfulness.

The stages in the development of Insight are outlined in detail
in the *Visuddhimagga,* which is structured round a scheme of seven
purifications:

1. Calm
2. Insight
3. No person
4. Conditioned arising
5. Defilements of insights
6. Conditioned world
7. "Path-consciousness"

The way of higher knowledge consists in a process of heightened experience. It finally leads to full understanding and is known as "freedom through insight" (*pannavimutti*). The two processes of concentration and insight come together when full enlightenment is attained. In these higher stages it can produce *jhanic*-like results. There is a path-awareness, which is first experienced as a fleeting sensation of the nirvanic essence. The first time this is experienced, the meditator knows that he or she has reached the level of "stream-enterer", with only seven more rebirths awaiting him or her. Then can occur the stages of the "once returner to rebirth", then "non-returner to human birth", and finally "*nirvana* attainer". There is a crowning experience that Buddhaghosa says is possible only for *arhats* who have perfected the mastery of the eight *jhanic* trances. It is the complete cessation of thought and the perception of *nirvanic* bliss that may be maintained for up to seven days.

In southern Buddhism the *arhat* is a rare and lofty, ideal person, who has attained the goal of ending every kind of mental defilement. *Arhats* have done all that is to be done; they are the full embodiment of the *ariya* path – their actions accord fully with the needs of the situation.[8]

Western understanding

"Do Christians meditate?" is a question that I have often been asked by Buddhist monks. Meditation is such an important aspect of their spiritual quest that they assume that it is a necessary requirement in all religious endeavours. The answer must be both "No" and "Yes"! It is obvious from the previous discussion that the Christian tradition has never advocated anything as complex and elaborate as that of the Theravada tradition, and neither has the aim of Christianity been to achieve liberation through self-effort alone. The full methods and aims of Calm and Insight meditation are unique to Buddhism. However, the Bible does use the word "meditate" on many occasions. "He [Isaac] went out to the field one evening to meditate" (Genesis 24:63). In the book of the Psalms, there is a continual affirmation of the writer that he will meditate but, in all cases, the meditation is upon the character and activity of God: "We meditate on your unfailing love"

(Psalm 48:9); ". . . then I will meditate on your wonders" (Psalm 119:27). Christian writers throughout the centuries have spoken of a way of listening to God, of communing with the Creator of heaven and earth.

In an attempt to rediscover meditation within the Western Christian tradition, some have tried to adopt and apply Eastern yogic practices.[9] There is, however, a fundamental difference between Buddhist and Christian meditation. The Buddhist tradition aims at *detachment* from the world of experiences, while the Christian tradition seeks *attachment* to God. A central feature of Christian meditation is that the Bible is regarded as the special revelation of God who created all things. Richard Foster has suggested various methods for use in Christian meditation but stresses the importance of the Bible.

> Like the hub of a wheel, the meditation upon Scripture becomes the central reference point by which all other meditations are kept in proper perspective. The meditation on Scripture is considered by all the masters as the normative foundation for the interior life. Whereas the study of Scripture centres on exegesis, the meditation of Scripture centres on internalising and personalising the passage. The written Word becomes a living word addressed to you.[10]

Buddhist meditation techniques are clearly of a deeper level and character than that known within the Christian tradition, which have never been more than that of a light trance. Theravada techniques allow the practitioner to enter various altered states of consciousness that have increasing degrees of detachment from everyday reality. Christian Suzuko was formerly a teacher of yoga and achieved some of the most advanced levels of meditation before he abandoned its practice. He has attempted to explain to the medical profession what happens during meditation in the following way:

> Western medical science has shown that normally any posture is reported back to the brain, but if a posture is held long enough the body stops reporting back. There is therefore a loss of awareness of the outside world and a dissociated state occurs. A similar reaction occurs when the blood flow is restricted to the brain causing oxygen

starvation. This can be produced by fixed body posture and mental control. The person is no longer aware of external stimuli and is conscious only of their own mental processes. In normal awareness all items are perceived within their context. However, as one develops abilities of concentration on a single item, the meditation awareness becomes narrowed, and the object of focus loses its association with the context. Finally, the element of initial concentration dissolves in awareness, and the person feels identified with the cosmos as a whole. The yoga-sutra actually speaks about the suppression of the operations of the mind causing dissociation. Eastern Meditation contrasts with Judeo-Christian meditation in that the latter draws on rational processes and does not try to suppress them.[11]

Although meditation as a means of spiritual quest is not unique to Buddhism, its irreplaceable centrality to obtaining ultimate salvation is totally distinct. As King summarises in his article on Buddhist meditation, "Basically, meditation is here conceived as a regimen of carefully structured steps of concentration on chosen objects, which concentration is designed to lead in the end to a 'going out' (*nirvana*) from the eternally recurring cycle of birth and death (*samsara*) in which every sentient creature is enmeshed."[12]

Suggestions for interfaith discussions

How does Christian prayer compare with Buddhist meditation? You may like to commence by discussing some common problems such as wandering thoughts.

Webwise 7 – The Cultivation of Wisdom: Meditation

Dhammakaya Buddhist Meditation Institute, Thailand

http://www.concentration.org/intro.html
The founder of the Vijja Dhammakaya approach was the late Venerable Chao Khun Phra Mongkol-Thepmuni, fondly known as Luang Phor. Vijja Dhammakaya employs elements of both *samatha* and *vipassana* meditation. The website gives detailed instructions on how to meditate.

Meditation internet resources

http://www.holisticmed.com/www/meditation.html
A major listing of Internet sites for practitioners of Buddhist meditation.

The World Community for Christian Meditation

http://www.wccm.org/cm01.html
The World Community for Christian Meditation commenced when Dom. John Main, a Benedictine monk, opened the first Christian meditation centre in London in 1975. Since that time, his teaching on contemplative prayer has spread to 50 countries.

Vipassana *meditation*

http://www.dhamma.org
A simple introduction to a Theravada Buddhist meditation technique, as taught by S. N. Goenka.

Notes

1. *Abhidharma* 1.14.
2. Buddhaghosa, B., *The Path of Purification* (Singapore: Singapore Buddhism Meditation Centre, 1956), pp. 102–121 (III, 74–133).
3. *Ibid.*, p. 103 (III, 75).
4. *Ibid.*, pp. 268–283 (VIII, 81–138).
5. Noraratrajmanit, C., *Towards Buddha-Dhamma* (Bangkok: Thai Buddhist Temple, undated).
6. Theo, Ven. Dhammavuddho, "Samma Samadhi, Samatha and Vipassana", *The Middle Way* 77 (2002), pp. 67–80.
7. Buddhaghosa, *op. cit.*, pp. 409–445.
8. Hinnells, J. R., *A Handbook of Living Religions* (Harmondsworth: Penguin, 1991), p. 309.
9. Oechanet, J.-M., *Christian Yoga* (Tunbridge Wells: Search Press, 1984).
10. Foster, R., *Celebration of Discipline: The Path to Spiritual Growth* (London: Hodder & Stoughton, 1983), pp. 25–26.
11. Suzuko, C., "Can yoga be reconciled with Christianity?" in

Watt, J. (ed.), *The Church, Medicine and The New Age* (London: CCHH, 1995), pp. 105–122.

12. King, W., "Buddhist Meditation" in Kitagawa, J. and Cummings, M. (eds.), *Buddhism and Asian History* (New York: MacMillan, 1987), p. 331.

CHAPTER EIGHT

THE RISE OF MAHAYANA BUDDHISM

What you can learn from this chapter

- theories proposed for the origins of Mahayana Buddhism
- the new texts that inspired Mahayana thought
- the distinctive ideal of the *bodhisattva*
- the nature and veneration of the celestial *bodhisattvas*

The monk drew his grey robes about him as he waited for the London bus that would take him to college. His temple in Japan had sent him to Britain as a teacher to the many people who were showing interest in the teachings of the Buddha. Now he was studying at one of London University's leading colleges to gain an MA degree in Buddhist Studies to provide him with an academic qualification. He looked down the road to see if there was any sign of the characteristic red double-decker bus. Suddenly a woman addressed him.

"Excuse me, are you a monk?"

His grey robes and shaven head would in his own country be a clear sign of his status as a monk. He acknowledged the woman politely with just a hint of a smile across his face, telling her that he was a Buddhist monk. She was holding some leaflets, which he saw had something to do with Christianity.

"What did the Buddha teach?" came the next question.

The monk replied simply, "Wisdom and compassion."

The woman seemed stunned by the answer and quickly hurried away. The bus arrived and the monk calmly got on amidst the bustle of the street. Little did the woman realise that she had spoken to a man who had taken the great vow in pursuit of the supreme goal. Although it might take him a thousand rebirths, his aim was to become a future Buddha.

*   *   *

After the death of King Asoka in 232 BC, the Mauryan empire declined rapidly and was finally eliminated by the general Pusyamitra, who founded the Sunga dynasty in 180 BC. The following centuries saw many invasions and social turmoil. From the northwest came a succession of Greek kings and in the south a new rival dynasty was established on the Deccan plateau. By the end of the third century AD, all India east of the Punjab was divided into small kingdoms. The glorious period of the Buddhist empire under Asoka was no more than a memory but it had left a popular legacy of the teaching of the Buddha as one of India's greatest religious masters.

In 320 AD a new empire began to emerge under Candra Gupta. He owed his initial rise to power to his marriage with a princess of the Licchavis people, which united the two states and established control over the regions of Magadha and Kosala. Under his successor, Samudra Gupta (335–376 AD), the great Gupta empire finally emerged. It was under the rule of Candra Gupta II (376–415 AD) that ancient Indian culture reached a high watermark. Later Indian legends tell of his happy and prosperous reign. Even the Chinese Buddhist monk, Fa-hsien, who travelled to India at this time to acquire Buddhist scriptures, noted the peacefulness of India and the rarity of serious crime.

The Buddha had not been exclusive in his teaching of the *Dharma* but had encouraged each of his followers to enter enlightenment and teach the way according to their own perception. It appears that the Buddha was not averse to religious innovation, provided it occurred within the fundamental framework of his basic philosophy of the *Dharma*. In the period from 100 BC until 100 AD, a variety of new writings were produced that built upon the earlier schools of Buddhist thought. These have become known as the Mahayana *sutras*, which gave rise to a wide-ranging movement incorporating many schools.

Origins of Mahayana

Various theories have been put forward for the emergence of Mahayana Buddhism but the origin of the tradition is still not fully understood. One suggestion is proposed by Lamotte, who argues that the Mahayana movement began with groups of lay devotees who administered the *stupas*.[1] After the time of King Asoka, thousands of *stupas* throughout the empire became centres of devotion for pious lay people. As the *stupas* became more important, so did the influence of lay Buddhists. At the same time, the traditional view of the *arhat* ideal was losing its challenge as lay people were more concerned about the practicalities of living in the material world.

This suggestion appears to be supported by an early Mahayana *sutra* called *Pratyutpanna*. In this *sutra* the Buddha speaks to monks and 500 householder *bodhisattvas*, led by a certain Bhadrapala. The text describes how it will be hidden in a cave and rediscovered in the future, during the period of the decay of the *Dharma*. The 500 lay people ask that it should be in their future incarnations that they will rediscover and propagate the text, but the *sutra* does not say whether this will be the case.

The *Pratyutpanna* also says that when the text is discovered, many monks will revile it and will accuse another group of monks with its fabrication. This leads to a second theory, proposed by Williams, which is that the Mahayana tradition arose from sectarian sources who may have developed the ideas of the Mahasanghika school.[2] This teaching was attributed to be the original teaching of the Buddha, which the first disciples were not fully able to comprehend. He therefore accommodated his teaching for them, but now the full depth of the Buddha's teaching was understood. In this way the Sthavira school was undermined and regarded as less developed than the new movement. Hence, the name Mahayana, which comes from the root *maha* meaning "greater, numerous, superior", and *yana* meaning "vehicle". This is carried through in the Chinese name *ta-sheng* and Japanese *daijo*. The Theravada tradition is spoken of somewhat disparagingly as Hinayana. The original meaning of the element *hina* means "discarded", hence the meaning of "inferior" tradition. More objectively, Mahayana can be regarded as more speculative than Theravada and embracing a broader range of practices.

A third theory suggested by Conze is that the new ideas resulted from foreign influences.[3] Mahayana developed in north-west India and south India, the two regions where Buddhism was most exposed to non-Indian influences. In the north the impact of Hellenistic ideas from Iran and the Mediterranean was strong. Conze writes, "This cross-fertilisation incidentally rendered the Buddhism of Mahayana fit for export outside India."[4]

These arguments suggest that there were two types of factors that caused the emergence of Mahayana: social or external, and doctrinal or internal.[5] The external were those cultural influences especially from the north-east, mentioned earlier. Doctrinal issues could have emerged through inspired believers writing new *sutras* drawing upon ideas of the earlier Mahasanghika schools. This would relate to the increasing disillusionment with the *arhat* ideal, and the rise of the Bhakti tradition within Hinduism, as seen in the *Bhagavad Gita*. The devotional images of Krishna must have had an influence within Buddhist thought and the desire for a compassionate deity.[6]

The Mahayana tradition had a major influence and gave new vigour and vitality to Buddhism. A parallel has sometimes been drawn between the Mahayana movement in India and the Protestant Reformation in Europe. Mahayana certainly tended to address the needs of the laity, teaching the enlightenment of all beings, and so a parallel could be drawn to the Protestant teaching of the priesthood of all believers. However, a major difference is that Mahayana was more speculative and supplemented the teaching of the *Vinaya*, whereas Protestants gave emphasis to Scripture alone for their interpretations.

Some Mahayana scriptures

The Theravada canon was closed in the second century BC, within two or three centuries of the Buddha's *parinirvana*. This fixed the oral tradition that was eventually transcribed into the Pali canon that is accepted by all Buddhists. Although the *Tipitaka* fixed the corpus, it did not halt the practice of embellishing the core of the

Dharma with new innovations. These new developments became drafted in the form of new Buddhist literature written in Sanskrit, rather than Pali. The switch from oral to written literature facilitated the dissemination of longer and more complex texts.

Prajnaparamita

The earliest Mahayana scriptures are those that deal with the perfection of wisdom – *prajnaparamita* ("perfection of wisdom"). This school of texts consists of 38 different books, composed in India between 100 BC and 300 AD. In general, the wisdom spoken of in these *sutras* goes beyond the wisdom of everyday life and is often expressed in terms of praise.

> Homage to Thee, Perfect Wisdom,
> Boundless, and transcending thought!
> All Thy limbs are without blemish,
> Faultless those who Thee discern.[7]

The concept of wisdom in these texts is that which comes as the result of deep rigorous thought, and leads to a metaphysical understanding of reality. The central insight of this wisdom is that all things are characterised by *sunyata*, pronounced "shunyata", meaning "emptiness". This term means an emptiness of any inherent content. This will be discussed further in the following chapter that looks at the development of schools of philosophy. The most renowned of the wisdom texts are the *Diamond Sutra* and the *Heart Sutra*, both originating from the fourth century.[8] The *Heart Sutra* begins with the worship of perfect wisdom, personified in the figure of Avalokitesvara.

Sukhavati Sutras

There are two main *Sukhavati Sutras*, the smaller and the larger. They are concerned with the world of Sukhavati ("happy land"), which is one of the "Buddha worlds" other than our own. These *sutras* were first translated into Chinese during the second century AD and probably written originally in Gandhari. They represent the devotional rather than the wisdom teaching of the Mahayana tradition. Sakyamuni Buddha is described as telling his disciples stories of Buddhas of other ages and other worlds. He especially mentions Amitabha.

> Then the Buddha addressed Shariputra, the elder, and said, "Beyond a hundred thousand kotis of Buddha-lands westwards from here, there is a world named Sukhavati. In that world there is a Buddha, Amitabha by name, now dwelling and preaching the law. Shariputra, why is that country named Sukhavati? The living beings in that country have no pains, but receive pleasures only. Therefore, it is called Sukhavati" (*Shorter Sukhavati* verse 2).

In this perfect land everything is easy and any resident is only one step away from *nirvana*.

The Lotus Sutra (Saddharmapudarika)

The most widely known of the Mahayana scriptures is undoubtedly the "Lotus of the Wonderful Law", which Parrinder refers to as the "gospel of half Asia". The exact date of translation is not known nor in what language it was originally written, but we know a Chinese translation was in existence by 255 AD. The so-called *Lotus Sutra* depicts events that take place in a cosmic universe of vast dimensions, reflecting contemporary Indian cosmology. The present world is perceived as being made up of four continents ranged around a great central mountain, Mount Sumeru. India is the southern-most continent where the discourse initially begins. Outside the present world exist countless others, spreading in all directions, some presided over by various Buddhas. All these worlds, like our own, are caught up in a never-ending cycle of formation, continuance, decline and disintegration over vast periods of time.

Like many of the Mahayana *sutras*, the *Lotus* begins with the disciple Ananda speaking the words, "This is what I heard . . ."[9] Ananda describes the occasion when, at Mount Gridhrakuta (Eagle Peak) near the city of Rajagriha, the Buddha preached the *Lotus Sutra*. These opening sentences are in a historical setting but, as Ananda continues to describe the situation, the reader becomes aware that we have moved into a wider cosmic realm. Sakyamuni Buddha is addressing 1,200 *arhats*, 80,000 *bodhisattvas*, and 20,000 gods, including the great Hindu gods Brahma and

Indra. In it the Buddha is portrayed as setting out the "*bodhisattva* ideal", as opposed to the "*arhat* ideal", and declares a higher truth unknown to the *arhats* and only known to the Buddha. The Buddha himself is in the "great vehicle", the Mahayana, and those who pay the simplest act of homage to the Buddha are promised that they will ultimately become enlightened by this devotion. The *sutra* relates that many of the *arhats* withdrew at such revolutionary teaching.

The monks holding to the older Sthavira school considered that the spiritual ideal was the *arhat*, who was a person who had achieved enlightenment. This status required personal meditation and a single-minded determination to break out of illusion, so reaching *nirvana*. The monk therefore appeared remote from the general populace and disinterested in the problems people faced in daily life. The status of *arhatship* required a single-minded determination to achieve one's own enlightenment. In contrast, the Buddha had not been only concerned to achieve his own enlightenment but had, out of compassion, taught the *Dharma* to others. It was this very act that had set the wheel of *Dharma* in motion; he had presented the Eightfold Path for his disciples to follow. A new spiritual ideal began to emerge within the *Sangha* of an *arhat* who did not merely seek his own enlightenment but remained within the world out of compassion for other beings. This was a major reinterpretation of the teaching of early Buddhism. For the *bodhisattva*, enlightenment is not escape but a concern that all other beings may also achieve enlightenment. The word means "a being (*sattva*) who seeks enlightenment (*bodhi*)".

The *bodhisattva*

In the Mahayana doctrine the *bodhisattva* was recast and focused on two separate but overlapping types: one as the ideal to be followed by all living beings and the other as an agent of universal salvation (celestial *bodhisattva*).[10] The basic assumption is that all living beings have the potential to achieve Buddhahood, or that "the gates are open to all". The *bodhisattva* makes a vow not to go to *nirvana* until all beings are delivered. His or her objective is not therefore merely personal liberation, as demonstrated in the ideal of the *arhat* in the Theravada tradition, but a cosmic process based on the twin pillars of wisdom and compassion. In contrast to the Theravada tradition, this way is open to both monks and laity.

The vow

The career of the *bodhisattva* is held to begin when the devotee first aspires to enlightenment; it requires a distinct act of the will, from which the term *bodhicitta* ("thought of enlightenment") derives. It is like a seed that will eventually become an enlightened mind. This intention requires two things. First is an intense concentration at that moment to become a *bodhisattva*, no matter how long it may take and what it may cost. Second is to express the aspiration in a vow.

The vow has two aspects: to attain Buddhahood and to practise the *bodhisattva* morality. This vow is made, not for personal gain, but for the good of others. The intention of doing good for others lies at the heart of this vow. It has profound consequences for the *bodhisattva*. Henceforth, it will be the vow that will be the ultimate controlling factor in one's karmic destiny, although the path of spiritual perfection may take aeons to complete. Even with the great *bodhisattva*s the force of the original vow continues to motivate.

The specific content of the vow will vary. But all will resolve to postpone their own enlightenment indefinitely while endeavouring to save others, and to freely transfer merit to others. The resolve of a *bodhisattva* is compared to that of a warrior wearing armour who is going to the battleground. The *bodhisattva* is thus said to wear the armour of his (or her) vows (*mahasamnadha-smnaddha*). Even as he is leading countless sentient beings to *nirvana*, he knows that no substantial beings exist even as he has no existence as a substantial being. The *bodhisattva*'s spiritual aspiration and determination are the basis for all his practice.

The vow differs from that of a monk, in that the monk's vow is only for this present lifetime. At death he ceases to be a monk. However, the vow of the *bodhisattva* is taken until enlightenment is achieved. It is therefore an unbroken vow that perpetuates itself through countless rebirths, whether these are as a human, animal

or god. The intention is to become a Buddha and bring enlightenment to others.

The duration of the *bodhisattva* career (*carya*) is generally considered to last for three *asamkhyeya*, which is usually translated as
"incalculable" ages. Some say that it would amount to 1×100,
repeated 66 times. Yet others say that the *bodhisattva* has already
experienced three *asamkhyeya* before embarking on the seven ages
of the *bodhisattva*. Some even speak of 33 *asamkhyeya*. However
the time scale is expressed, it should be understood as beyond
human comprehension. Even for the sceptic, the *bodhisattva* vow
must leave one amazed at its scope and scale.

Sakyamuni Buddha, according to tradition, took his vow before
a previous Buddha. This model is followed through with the
bodhisattva vow that should be taken before a living Buddha.
However, very few Buddhas appear in the world and so many
make their vows in the presence of other human *bodhisattvas*. The
vow may even be made in isolation by invoking the "Buddha of
the ten directions" to be your witness. In practice, the vow is
usually made before a recognised *bodhisattva* at a special ceremony; this person makes sure that the vow is sincere and that the
candidate understands the seriousness of the implications. I have
heard the person to whom the vow is made described as a "body-
guard" to ensure that the candidate does not become a vow-
breaker. The *bodhisattva* then gives a promise that in "x" number
of ages the candidate will become a Buddha with name "y", and
will reign in a Buddha land with excellence "z". When the promise
is received the new *bodhisattva* advances his career.

The practice of the bodhisattva

The *bodhisattva* path calls for the practitioner to perfect a series of
virtues called *paramitas* ("perfections"). In early texts there were
six of these, as in the famous *Lotus Sutra*. Later texts such as the
Dasabhumika Sutra of the Yogocara school add an additional
four (see next chapter). The six *paramitas* are the chief factors in
a *bodhisattva*'s discipline, and the additional four are merely sup-
plements.[11]

1. Generosity   *dana*
2. Morality   *sila*
3. Patience   *ksanti*
4. Effort   *virya*
5. Contemplation   *dhyana*
6. Wisdom   *prajna*

plus

7. Skill in means   *upaya*
8. Resolution (the vow)   *dhana*
9. Strength   *bala*
10. Knowledge   *jnana*

The origin of the six chief *paramitas* is probably found in the early Buddhist triad: morality, concentration and wisdom. Buddhist monks are bound by the 227 vows of the *Vinaya* that are known by heart. The *bodhisattva* follows the vows not for himself but for the benefit of others. He will obey the Buddhist morality in whatever way is conducive for the particular state in which he is reborn. Morality involves different forms for different living beings.

The doctrine that all living beings may attain to Buddhahood means that the path of the *bodhisattva* is not exclusive for members of the *Sangha*. Both lay and monastic *bodhisattvas* are mentioned in Mahayana literature. According to some texts, female *bodhisattvas* could miraculously change themselves into men through religious practice. This allowed the realisation of the supreme goal of Buddhahood for women, but not as females. Akira concludes that "such teachings indicate that early Mahayanists appealed to female devotees and practitioners."[12]

Transfer of merit

The first *paramita* is "generosity", and leads to a revolutionary concept of the transfer of merit (*punya*) to others. This has developed into a major teaching within Buddhism, the origin of which remains unclear. Nothing is found about this in the Pali *Tipitaka* apart from a short *sutra* on the *preta* ("ghosts"). The story is told of King Bembisara, a supporter of Sakaymuni, who through his generosity acquired merit. However, one night he became plagued by ghosts who screamed all around the palace. When Sakyamuni came to the palace, the king told him what had happened. The Buddha told him that his past relatives were being punished for their wicked lives and that the king should transfer his merit onto them. Once the merit was transferred, the entity stopped being a *preta*. Another similar story is that of the Buddha who went to the netherworld to release his mother. As will be seen in a later chapter, this story was of great appeal to the Chinese because of its emphasis on parental fidelity.

With regards to the objects that should be given in charity, the *bodhisattva* should give all that he has: his wealth, his limbs, his wife, and his very life. The heroes of the legends record many stories of those who have sacrificed to the very limits. The *Jakakamala* tells the well-known story of a *bodhisattva* who came across a hungry tigress which was weak from giving birth. The *bodhisattva* told his companions to find meat but, fearing that the tigress would eat her own cubs, the *bodhisattva* threw himself in front of her. The tigress was too weak even to attack and kill the *bodhisattva*. He therefore took a sharp bamboo, cut his own throat and fell dead before the tigress.

The act of sharing merit is considered good in itself, if it is without thought of personal gain. If one thinks that by giving, one will acquire merit, then it will not bring any personal benefit. If sharing is generous from a position of compassion, then the giver will acquire more merit. The doctrine is not without its difficulties, as Western scholars have noted. The teaching is essentially contrary to the law of *karma*, which states that any act performed with intention will have consequences in future rebirths. This is totally an individual responsibility and so cannot be transferred to others.

The career of a bodhisattva

The idea of "stages" on the spiritual pilgrimage occurred early in Buddhist philosophy. The early theory of the *bodhisattva* seems to have recognised seven stages. The number of stages seems to have been increased from seven to ten in about 200 AD. The *Disabhumika Sutra*, for example, lists the career as ten stages.[13]

The ten stages (*bhumi*) are patterned upon the life of Sakyamuni and previous Buddhas.

1. *Pradmudita* ("joyful"). Here the *bodhisattva* rejoices in the thought of enlightenment and passes beyond the stages of the common person. He (or she) renounces his home and takes the vows of a monk. He preaches the *Dharma* to the laity and exhorts them to aspire to the higher spiritual life. He is free from pride and arrogance, with the result that he will not be born in a family of low and humble origin.

2. *Vimala* ("pure"). In the second stage he cultivates the virtues of gratitude, forbearance and harmlessness. He devotes himself exclusively to the practice of the perfections.

3. *Prabhakari* ("luminous"). In this stage the *bodhisattva* brings his insight to the world and preaches to the people. He teaches, not for the selfish motive of personal enlightenment, but out of compassion for all living beings.

4. *Arcishmati* ("radiant"). In the fourth *bhumi*, the *bodhisattva* lives in the forest and sacrifices all things. He practises the ten "lights of the doctrine" that purify his disposition.

5. *Studurjaya* ("difficult to conquer"). The *bodhisattva* avoids contact with the laity and nuns but does not exalt himself. He diligently practises the Four Noble Truths.

6. *Abhimukhi* ("face to face"). The *bodhisattva* perfects himself in wisdom, standing face to face with *nirvana*. At this point, the *bodhisattva* has practised all the stages that lead to *arhatship*. He now takes on the distinctive teaching of Mahayana Buddhism concerning the *bodhisattva*.

7. *Duramgama* ("far-going"). The practical stage of the *bodhisattva* is now brought to fruition. He performs all the ten perfections: giving, morality, patience, heroism, meditation, wisdom, skill, the vow, power, and knowledge. He abandons the belief in

the existence of a permanent substantial *atman* and understands that nothing is eternal. Edward Thomas describes the stage in the following words:

> Like a skilled sailor who knows the nature of waves and currents and embarks on a great ship in the ocean but is not defiled by the filthy water, so the *bodhisattva* in the seventh stage has entered the great ship of the Perfections, but he does not yet realise cessation (*nirvana*). He has the knowledge of a Buddha and exercises to the full his task of saving all beings.[14]

8. *Acala* ("immovable"). He is now unmoved by thoughts. He knows that all things are non-existent and, like a person awoken from a dream, realises that the dream was unreal. He can read the thoughts of all creatures and has acquired knowledge far beyond the ordinary. He can see all the Buddha fields. He acquires the sovereignty of the universe and then renounces it. He performs all actions without being attached to anything.

9. *Sadhumati* ("stages of good being"). He acquires the two powers of exegesis and communication. As a preacher of the *Dharma* he develops the analytical knowledge of a *bodhisattva* and preaches to all the universe. He is always reborn in a noble family of a warrior caste or priestly caste and renounces all to seek enlightenment.

10. *Dharmamegha* ("cloud of the *Dharma*"). The *bodhisattva* becomes a Buddha and acquires all the attributes of a perfect Buddha. A vast lotus appears, and the *bodhisattva* sits in it in the concentration called the "knowledge of the omniscient". This stage is dominated by various trances and concentrations. He acquires a radiant body, and works miracles for the benefit of other living beings. When he descends from the Tushita heaven to this world, he is ready to undertake all the prescribed actions of a Buddha in saving living beings.

Dayal writes concerning the last life of a *bodhisattva*:

> In Buddhist philosophy and history, all roads lead to Gautama Buddha. The real and imaginary important incidents of his life have

been regarded as the necessary experiences of all advanced *bodhisatt-vas* in their last lives, during which they attain Enlightenment. All such *bodhisattvas* must be born and live in the same manner. Gautama Buddha's life is regarded as a concrete instance of the general law relating to a *bodhisattva's* last earthly existence, which he at last reaches after three *asankhyeyas* of aeons.[15]

This entails the following:

1. The *bodhisattva* descends from a heaven and selects his own mother. His birth is therefore not the result of *karma*.

2. His reputed father has no connection with his birth; it is a case of reproduction without sexual union. However, this is different from the Christian view of the "virgin birth" in that the *bodhisattva* is a total entity in his own right and does not acquire human characteristics from the mother.

Legend tells the story of Queen Maya dreaming that a white elephant with six tusks entered her body. The future Buddha sat in the womb in a cross-legged position surrounded by a beautiful rectangular canopy that had four pillars. Maya could see the *bodhisattva* seated in her womb and carried the child for ten months (not the usual nine months). The *bodhisattva* was then born from her right side, which remained uninjured.[16]

3. The *bodhisattva* is not soiled by impurities at birth, which is attended by various miracles. His body shows the 32 marks of a Buddha.

4. Even in childhood the future Buddha is highly cultured, excelling in all physical and intellectual activities.

5. He is free from passion but marries to set a good example to the world. His son is born without any sensual indulgence on his part.

6. He practises severe asceticism from similar motives.

7. He meets the evil Mara in combat before attaining enlightenment.

The career of a *bodhisattva* that commenced ages before has thus become completed in a perfect, enlightened Buddha.

Celestial *bodhisattvas*

From the stages in the career of a *bodhisattva*, one can see that Mahayana Buddhism innovated a new class of heavenly *bodhisattvas* into the pantheon. In developed Mahayana, the *bodhisattva* emerges as a mystical aspect of reality that must be distinguished from the aspirant who traverses the ten stages. The *Lotus Sutra* names 23 celestial *bodhisattvas*. Of these, four were to become of great importance: Maitreya, Manjusri, Avalokitesvara, and Mahasthamaprata. There is no evidence that these were historical figures. No *sutra* teaches devotion to a celestial *bodhisattva* until the third century AD, some three centuries after they were first mentioned in the Mahayana literature.

Maitreya

Maitreya is the earliest cult *bodhisattva* mentioned in a Pali *sutra*. He is described as one who in the distant future will arise in the world with thousands of disciples. The Theravada tradition recognises no other *bodhisattva* in the present age but, in practice, Avalokitesvara is popular in some Theravada countries.

Maitreya, unlike the Buddhas before him, is alive, so he can respond to the prayers of worshippers. The Sanskrit root of his name means "benevolent", likewise, he is willing to help those who call to him. Being a high god in this birth, he has the power to grant the requests. His cult therefore offers the advantages of theism and Buddhism combined.

Manjusri

Manjusri shares with Maitreya pre-eminence among the *bodhisattvas* up to about 300 AD. In the *Lotus Sutra* he remembers deeds of former Buddhas that were unknown even to Maitreya. Manjusri means "gentle or sweet glory". He is the crown prince of *Dharma* because, like other tenth-stage *bodhisattvas*, he will next become a king of *Dharma*, a Buddha. Manjusri usually appears to human beings in dreams. Whoever worships him is born time and again into a Buddhist family and is protected by Manjusri's power. Those who meditate on Manjusri's statue and his teaching will eventually reach enlightenment. Manjusri also takes the form of a poor man or an orphan and appears to those who are devoted to him.

Avalokitesvara

Avalokitesvara first appears as a name in the lists at the beginning of the *Vimalakirti* and, later, the *Lotus Sutra*. His first significant role is in the *Sukhavati Sutra* where he is portrayed as one of the two *bodhisattva*s in Sukhavati. The origin of this *bodhisattva* is obscure. His name comes from the roots *avalokita* ("looking down") and *isvara* ("Lord").[17] He is therefore seen as the one who looks down upon the world and responds to people's suffering in compassion. He is also called Lokesvara, "Lord of the World", which is a title of the god Shiva in the Hindu tradition. In the Chinese texts his short name is Kuan-yin ("Sound-regarder") (see figure 8:1).

He adopts many different guises: a *bodhisattva*, a disciple, a god. Avalokitesvara grants many boons to those who worship him. For example, a woman who worships him will give birth to either a son or daughter, depending upon which she wishes. Anyone in distress need only call to him and he or she will be saved from danger.

He has purified his vows for countless ages under millions of Buddhas. He is usually represented in art as a layman wearing a high crown and many jewels. He is especially rich in love and compassion. Like Manjusri, he has played the role of a Buddha but without going on to extinction. In this respect the celestial *bodhisattva*s are superior to the Buddhas.

Mahasthamaprata

Like Avalokitesvara, Mahasthamaprata is mentioned in the lists at the beginning of the *Lotus Sutra* and is placed on a par with him. In Chinese art he is frequently represented standing on the right of Amitabha, with Avalokitesvara standing on the left.

Female deities first appear within the Buddhist pantheon as handmaidens of the great *bodhisattva*s. They are portrayed in a similar way to the small circle of lady companions surrounding Indian princes. Some important female deities are as follows:

Figure 8.1   Bodhisattva Avalokitesvara

Pandaravasini	"White-clad"
Tara	"Saviouress"
Bhrukuti	"Frowning"
Prajnaparamita	"Perfection of Wisdom"
Tathagata-locana	"Buddha Eye"

Tara was very popular because of the assurance of salvation believed to be present in her name. She was quickly regarded as the female counterpart of Avalokitesvara. The goddess Prajnaparamita represents the fundamental wisdom of Mahayana philosophy. These deities become of special importance in Tantra, an expression of Tibetan Buddhism.

Buddhists and the Bible

At the beginning of this chapter it was noted that questions still remain concerning the origins of Mahayana Buddhism. One of the major innovations within the Mahayana tradition is the role of the *bodhisattva* as saviour and source of compassion. In this there are remarkable similarities to the gospel of the Lord Jesus Christ and this has not gone unnoticed.

As Europeans began to study Buddhist texts in the 19th century, many textual similarities resulted in the suggestion that Buddhism had somehow influenced Christianity. This resulted in a heated exchange during the period from 1870 to about 1930. One of the most vocal exponents of the view was Paul Carus who in 1915 published *The Gospel of the Buddha*, which proposes numerous parallels.[18] Some of these now appear far-fetched or even imaginary.

One confusion in the discussion was caused by the belief that all the Buddhist texts in question were older than the gospels. This assumption resulted from the early dating of the Pali texts but, as it has been shown, the Theravada tradition has little in common with Christianity. For example, there is an absence of belief in a supreme God, the soul, and forgiveness of sins. However, by the second century AD, Mahayana was fully operational with many new texts. It is with these texts that similarity can be shown. For example, the role of the *bodhisattva* and the notion of the three bodies of the Buddha were known in China as early as 67 AD. The *Lotus Sutra* has a number of parallels with the gospel narrative, including the famous parable of the prodigal son that occurs in the *Lotus Sutra*, although the elder brother has disappeared from the story.

In 1995 an English edition of Gruber and Kersten's book *The Original Jesus* renewed the debate.[19] This beautifully produced book argues that Buddhism was the source of Christianity; it depicts, in effect, that Jesus was the student of the Buddha. Gruber and Kersten show that communication between India and the Middle East was far easier than formerly supposed. This is especially so for the Gandhara state with its Greek influence.

Derrett helpfully divides those who search for parallels into three classes. First, those he calls "maximalists" such as Carus, Edmunds and, more recently, Gruber and Kersten who consider even the remotest likeness as significant. Second are the "minimalists" such as Pfleiderer who admits the possibility of Buddhist influence on the gospels. Finally, there are "nihilists", such as E. J. Thomas, Lamotte and A. Schweitzer. Derrett in his study concludes:

> Buddhist-Christian contacts were part of a continuum, as we have seen, of Western-Eastern traffic, including the communication of Greek and Jewish themes and stories over many centuries, much of which traffic is still uncharted, unevaluated. It is too early to pretend to strike a balance and find out which gained most, India or the West . . . Missionaries were in the same line of business, the Buddhists were the seniors, their work being on display, established and successful. I am not going to suggest that either party aimed to convert the other . . . Exchange was likely: what is interesting is that our evidence suggests it was modest and superficial. No one, as Beth sarcastically suggested, needed to memorise and stick together broken bits of various Buddhist tales to make a gospel![20]

The debate is still far from over Lindtner, in a review of Derrett's book, states that he holds to the thesis that the New Testament gospels are free translations (imitations) of the Buddhist gospel. "The NT Gospels were not merely influenced by the Buddhist sources. *They were, in all respects, based on them.* The Greek, I hold, was done directly from the Sanskrit, and the first to do so was – not Mark, but Matthew."[21]

The majority of Christians, and many leading Buddhist scholars, have been opposed to any influence of Buddhist ideas in the formation of the gospel. The main reason for this is the continuity of the New Covenant with the Jewish tradition, and Christ being presented as the one spoken of by the Old Testament prophets. Recent evidence has shown that there was greater communication between the Middle East and the kingdom of Gandhara, especially. First century Christian missionaries could easily have travelled east to that area. Although the *Acts of Thomas* is often dismissed as a Christian fiction from the third century, it does suggest this possibility. The story tells of the apostle Thomas ("Doubting Thomas") who in 52 AD preached to King Gundephar of Gandhara.[22] Having converted King Gundephar, Thomas is said to have travelled south into India to the Chola kingdom on the west coast and to the region of present-day Chennai (formerly Madras). Recent archaeological evidence has shown the existence of such a kingdom, suggesting there could be more truth behind the *Acts of Thomas* than was formerly believed. It could be that rather than the Christian missionaries being influenced by the Buddhists, Buddhists may have adopted some Christian ideas that were incorporated into the emerging Mahayana tradition. The debate will undoubtedly continue.

Suggestions for interfaith discussions

What do you think was lacking within the teaching of the *Dharma* that resulted in the emergence of devotion with Buddhism? Is a quest for some transcendent, loving Being an inherent aspect of human nature?

Webwise 8 – The Rise of Mahayana Buddhism

The Lotus Sutra *translated by Burton Watson*

http://www.sgi-usa.org/buddhism/library/Buddhism/LotusSutra/index.html

This is one of the most readable English translations of the *Lotus*

Sutra. Here it is made available by SGI-USA (Soka Gakkai International-USA).

The Heart Sutra *Homepage*

http://members.ozemail.com.au/~mooncharts/heartsutra
This short *sutra* is here presented in a variety of languages plus links to other sites containing commentaries and chanting of the *Heart sutra*.

The Diamond Sutra

http://community.palouse.net/lotus/diamondsutra.htm
This is an English translation of the *Diamond Sutra* by A. F. Price and Wong Mou-Lam.

Temple of Maitreya

http://sangha.net/messengers/maitreya.htm
This site is dedicated to Maitreya, the coming Buddha; it contains photographs of paintings and statues of the *bodhisattva*. It also has links to other sites.

Notes

1. Lamotte, E., *History of Indian Buddhism* (Louvain-le-Neuve: Université Catholique, 1988).
2. Williams, P., *Mahayana Buddhism: The Doctrinal Foundation* (London: Routledge, 1994), p. 24.
3. Conze, E., *A Short History of Buddhism* (Oxford: Oneworld, 1993), p. 41.
4. Conze, *ibid*, p. 41.
5. Gomez, L. O., "Buddhism in India" in Eliade, M. (ed.), *The Encyclopedia of Religion* (London: MacMillan, 1987).
6. Eilert, H. "A brief outline of Pure Land Buddhism in India and in early China" *Japanese Religions* (1985) 14 [1] pp. 1–12.
7. *Rahulabhadra, Prajnaparamitastotra,* v 1.
8. Conze, E., *Buddhist Wisdom Books: The Diamond and the Heart Sutra* (London: Mandala, 1988).
9. Watson, B., *The Lotus Sutra* (New York: Columbia University Press, 1993).

10. Skorupski, T., "The historical spectrum of the bodhisattva ideal", *The Middle Way* 75 (2000), pp. 95–106.
11. Goonewardene, A. "Arhats, Bodhisattvas and Bodhisattvas", *The Middle Way* 74 (2000), pp. 208–210.
12. Akira, H., *A History of Indian Buddhism* (Hawaii: University of Hawaii Press, 1990), p. 300.
13. Hajime, N., "The career of the *Bodhisattva*" in *The Encyclopedia of Religion* (London: MacMillan, 1987).
14. Thomas, E., *The History of Buddhist Thought* (London: Routledge, Kegan & Paul, 1933), p. 209.
15. Dayal, H., *The Bodhisattva Doctrine in Buddhist Sanskrit Literature* (Delhi: Motilal Bararsidass, 1975), p. 294.
16. Dayal, *ibid.*, pp. 295–297.
17. Piyasilo, *Avalokitesvara: Origin, Manifestations and Meaning* (Malaysia: Dharmafarer, 1991).
18. Carus, P., *The Gospel of Buddha* (London: Senate, 1955).
19. Gruber, E. R. and Kersten H., *The Original Jesus: The Buddhist Sayings of Christ* (Dorset: Shaftesbury, 1995).
20. Derrett, J. D., *The Bible and the Buddhists* (Bornato: Sardini Editrice, 2000), pp. 98–99.
21. Lindtner, C., "Review article", *Buddhist Studies Review* 18 (2001), p. 229.
22. Palmer, M., *The Jesus Sutras: Rediscovering the Lost Scrolls of Taoism Christianity* (New York: Ballantine Wellspring, 2001), pp. 109–112.

CHAPTER NINE

THE SILENCE OF THE BUDDHA

What you can learn from this chapter

- the major philosophical schools of Mahayana Buddhism: Madhyamika and Yogacara
- the concept of *sunyata* ("emptiness")
- the argument of the philosopher Nagarjuna
- the Mahayana doctrine of the triple bodies of the Buddha
- the demise of Buddhism in India

A monk named Vacchagotta once asked the Buddha if *atman* existed. To this the Buddha replied with silence. The monk tried again by reversing the thrust of the question: he asked if *atman* does not exist. The reply was the same. After the monk had left, the Buddha explained to Ananda the reason for this silence. If he had said that *atman* existed, it would have meant that he agreed with the same doctrine as held by the monk. If he had answered to the contrary, then it would have meant that he accepted the non-*atman* theory that implied nihilism. Neither an affirmation nor a negation was correct and, facing the limits of language, the Buddha remained silent. The inadequacy of language is an important fact in understanding the problem of the questions unanswered by the Buddha.

> The Buddha's silence indicates a clear philosophical position, although its crystallisation into a philosophy had to await for the genius of Nagarjuna. Indeed, the Buddha's silence was an answer: it was not merely a suspension of judgement or an utter lack of it.[1]

Nagarjuna, some 600 years later, recognised that the highest wisdom of Buddhism was found in the concept of *sunyata* ("emptiness"). From the teaching of Nagarjuna emerged the scholastic tradition of Madhyamika, meaning "middle position". Later, there evolved a second and third school, respectively known as Yogacara and Saramati. It was Madhyamika and Yogacara that dominated Mahayana thought in India and, while the third was short-lived, it did have an important influence on Tibet, as will be mentioned in chapter 13.

The Madhyamika school

It is difficult to fix the dates of Nagarjuna precisely, but all traditions regard him as the founder of this school. Nagarjuna was probably born about 150 AD. His life has become the focus of many legends. He is said to have had a good education as a Brahmin and become a magician able to make himself invisible, a talent that he found useful in seducing women. Legend has it that Nagarjuna was given the *Prajnaparamita Sutra* by the *nagas* (sea serpents) in reward for his wisdom. He read the *sutra* in order to criticise its logic but was unable to do so and became a monk.

Many literary works are attributed to Nagarjuna; two sets of his attributed writings are set some 500 years apart. The first are those of the Madhyamika and the second are Tantric texts. It is more likely that someone of the same, or similar, name wrote the second set, but the Tibetan tradition often claims he lived 600 years. His major work was the *Mula-madhyamika-karika.* According to legend, Nagarjuna is considered to be the discoverer of the *Mahaprajnaparamita Sutra* ("perfection of wisdom"), which became the major text for the school and was commented on frequently by his disciples.

Nagarjuna is believed to have been killed by a Brahmin after an argument over doctrine. His influence on later Buddhist philosophy has been outstanding. Nagarjuna did not aim to establish a fixed dogma but to prove the fallacies of other doctrines. Madhyamika had a devastating effect among Buddhists. If you debunk everything, what is the point of the religious life? In the early part of the fifth century AD, the Madhyamika school subdivided into two schools as a result of a dispute between two great scholars of

Madhyamika. The first was Prasangika, founded by Buddhapalia, and the second Svatanrika, founded by Bhavaviveka.

Empty dharmas

Within early schools of Buddhism, the *atman*, or "soul", did not have an existence and was considered to be the gathering of five attributes, *skandhas*. The Mahayana tradition perceived the nature of reality as reduced to minute entities known as *dharmas*. Care must be taken not to confuse this notion with that of *Dharma*, the wider teaching of the Buddha. Usually in this book the *dharmas* of Mahayana Buddhism are in the plural, while the term for the doctrine is in the singular with an initial capital letter.

Early traditions also considered that all things are unstable, unsubstantial, and impermanent. The Mahayana school went even further than this and maintained that the cosmos is actually unreal. The *dharmas* were believed to have no inherent self-existence, being empty in their very nature. There is no static existence, only continuous flux. The parallel with the modern scientific concept of the atom has not gone unnoticed. Matter has the appearance of solidity and permanence, yet atomic physics has shown that the ultimate components are packets of wave energy. The electron, for example, has the properties of both a particle and an electromagnetic wave. The solid appearance of matter is therefore an illusion brought about by the inherent nature of the components.

Nagarjuna taught that the confusion over the nature of phenomena arises because people do not realise that the Buddha taught according to two levels of truth: "conventional truth" and "profound truth". Conventional truths are those expressed using terms such as "person" and "thing", while profound truth is expressed in terms of *dharmas*. Statements are considered to be true at a conventional level because people agree to use them in certain ways. For example, the statement "ice is cold" is true because "ice" is a word used to describe a particular form of "water" (H_2O) that is experienced as "cold". The language-labels therefore determine how we experience the world through the discrimination made by using a particular name.

Early Buddhism had described three characteristics of all conditioned *dharmas:* suffering, impermanence, and non-self (*anatta*). To these, Nagarjuna added a fourth: emptiness – *sunyata*. *Samsara* is empty, *nirvana* is empty, the Buddhas are empty, as are the beings whom they guide. However, the *Sutra* does not give an explanation of *sunyata*. From the very beginning the concept is presented as something both profound and obscure. It is a concept operating at the limits of language, not understandable in human terms. In seeking to grasp the concept, it is important to understand that the texts were written for practitioners and, more specifically, for people who meditate. Within early Buddhism the emphasis on suffering and impermanence was intended to arouse aversion to worldly life. *Sunyata* summons the hearer to re-evaluate transmigration and achieve release within it, rather than fleeing from it. This is seen in the comparative roles of the *arhat,* who flees, and the *bodhisattva*, who stays. *Sunyata* therefore provides the philosophical basis of the *bodhisattva* path.

Nagarjuna's logic

Nagarjuna believed that *sunyata* was the great discovery of the Lord Buddha. It is an issue that relates to the essential nature of things. In discussing this matter, Nagarjuna used a ruthless negation of opposing pairs. For example:

A. *Dharmas* arise according to the law of dependent origination and so are in a state of flux. *Dharmas* form *dharmas.*
B. Causation does not explain how *dharmas* form *dharmas*, but there can only be four options. A *dharma* is:

1. caused by itself.
2. caused by something else.
3. caused by itself and by something else.
4. caused neither by itself nor something else.

Nagarjuna ruthlessly analysed each possibility, using *reductio ad absurdum.*

Option 1.
If all things are self-existent, there is no need for causation.
If it produced itself it would be both cause and effect.

If it was self-existent before it was produced, then it would not have been caused.

If *dharma* is caused by itself, then there is no inherent causal product.

Option 2.

If it is produced by something else, it suggests that anything can produce anything.

If something is produced from something else, and they are different entities, where is the causal link?

Option 3.

A combination of arguments from options 1 and 2 can be applied.

Option 4.

This implies no causation. The whole cosmos is therefore random.

Whatever option we take we are unable to explain causation, and the ultimate truth must be that there is no causation. *Dharmas* do not truly exist; they are merely designations without a proper nature. As far as a person can imagine them, they are numberless but their definitions are false.

Sunyata

What is *sunyata?* Intellectually, it is the absence of *svabhava* ("own-being"), a term that means having an immutable essence. Emptiness is the claim that nothing can exist of itself. Nothing exists independently of other things; if things cannot exist in this way and they cannot be said to have any inherent nature of their own, then it is difficult to say that they really exist at all. Everything therefore shares *non-nature* as its true nature. *Sunyata* is beyond rational words and cannot be encapsulated by language. As Robinson and Johnson write:

> Because *dharmas* have no own-being, there is nothing bound in *samsara*, nothing freed in *nirvana*, nothing is observed to arise, nothing is observed to cease. There are no beings to save from *samsara*, and yet the *bodhisattva* remains firm in his vow to save all beings. The world is a phantom conjured up by karmic action, the magician, but the phantom maker is itself *maya* (a phantom).[2]

Sunyata is the middle way between affirmations of being and non-being. The extremes of existence and non-existence are avoided by recognising certain causal relations, without predicting a self-existence or immutable essence to either cause or effect. It is therefore necessary to hold to neither the extremes of being nor of non-being; for this reason the system is often called the "school of the middle". The teaching steers a middle path between the extremes of nihilism and eternalism, since the adoption of either of these two is considered to lead to a rejection of the efficaciousness of the Buddhist path.

> When emptiness (*sunyata*) is established,
> The whole world will be established.
> When *sunyata* is not (realised),
> It is absurd that the whole world is (real).[3]

Even from the early period of Mahayana, it was clear that *sunyata* could be misunderstood. On the one hand, there was a danger that it would undermine religious practice and would, in fact provide a licence to infringe the rules of *Vinyana*. On the other hand, it encourages nihilism – nothing exists. For this reason, the *sutras* often give warnings about teaching *sunyata* to those who are not prepared.

Samsara and nirvana

Nagarjuna used the same ruthless logic on the notions of *nirvana* and *samsara*. The very fact that unconditioned *nirvana* is contrasted, at the conventional level, to *samsara* makes it exist only in relationship to it; it is thus empty. The conditioned and the unconditioned cannot be differentiated because both are "emptiness". This led to his famous statement that *samsara* and *nirvana* are the same.

Once this has been established, there are important consequences for the *bodhisattva*. He need not seek to escape *samsara* to attain *nirvana*.

He can tirelessly work to aid suffering beings, sustained by the idea that *nirvana* is something already present in *samsara*. As an advanced *bodhisattva*, he directly experiences this non-duality of *samsara* and *nirvana*, this realisation being fully matured when Buddhahood – *nirvana* in the highest sense – is reached.[4]

All beings are therefore seen to have a nature that is non-differentiated from Buddhahood. The task of beings is not to attain something but to uncover and know that they already possess Buddhahood.

Two truths

The adoption of this approach led to the theory of two kinds of truth, *samvrt-satya* and *paramartha-satya*, mentioned earlier. The first is our everyday, mundane, linguistically constructed truth; the latter is the ultimate, inexpressible truth. However, the two truths depend upon each other, for any distinction between mundane and ultimate is itself empty of reality. In terms of worldly truth, the law of dependent origination asserts that the things of the world come into being through causation. However, in terms of higher truth, all is universal relativity, and hence *sunyata*. Worldly truth is not without its uses, because higher truth can only be reached by going through it.

Generally, Western readers coming to the discussion of *sunyata* ("emptiness") for the first time find it confusing and rather obtuse. In practice, the discussion of "emptiness" only works within a Buddhist frame of reference, hence the difficulty for those from the West trying to understand the concept. Even Buddhists regard *sunyata* as a profound wisdom that is not readily grasped. This was perhaps the reason the concept captured the imagination of many Chinese and Japanese scholars in later centuries.

Yogacara ("Mind Only") school

Approximately 200 years after Nagarjuna, during the period of transition from the Kushan to Gupta dynasty, the Yogacara (or Vijnanavada) school emerged. The founders of the school were the brothers Asanga (c. 310–390) and Vasubandhu (c. 320–400). Asanga, the elder brother, was ordained into the Sarvastivada school. His teacher was said to have been Maitreyanatha, or

Maitreya, who may have been a human teacher or, as some claim, the heavenly *bodhisattva* Maitreya himself. Asanga eventually converted his half-brother to Mahayana, and Vasubandhu became the philosopher who gave the school its characteristic teaching. In contrast, Asanga's writings were deeply rooted in meditative trance. He is often regarded as the author of the *Yogacarabunmi* ("Stages of Yogacara"), one of the earliest Yogacara texts.

This school should not be regarded as in opposition to Nagarjuna, as some scholars have assumed.[5] All regarded Nagarjuna as a great person but Yogacara makes an important affirmation. Yogacara accepts Nagarjuna as correct but assumes that although the cosmos does not exist, the mind does exist. It says that for a starting point, one should take the mind as existent. The central doctrine is *citta-matra* ("mind only", or "nothing but consciousness"). The objects of the world do not exist *per se* but are created from the mind. For this reason the school is often known in the West as the Mind Only school.[6]

The early Buddhists sought to transcend limiting attachments by seeing phenomena as impermanent, unsatisfactory and nonself. The Madhyamikas sought this by seeing phenomena as "empty"; Yogacara sought it by seeing perceived phenomena as mental constructs. The schools should therefore not be considered as separate and opposing trends in Mahayana thought.[7]

Yogacara is therefore concerned about psychological theories which attempt to understand how the mind works to produce the apparent reality. The school proposed the theory of *alaya-vijnana* ("store consciousness"), a kind of collective unconsciousness, the repository of all events in the world. This store consciousness remains imperceptible to us but within it are the "seeds" (*bija*) of all potential phenomena. From this store the seeds continually pour into manifestations and reappear as phenomena, thus explaining the doctrine of *karma*. The mind projects things external to itself. For example, when you sleep you dream, and while you are dreaming it seems so real. When you wake up, you recognise that it was not real. This does not answer the question of why we all perceive it in the same way. The answer the Yogacara school would give is simply that we all have similar consciousness.

The senses, including the mind, work by "grasping" or apprehending objects, so that the six consciousnesses are by that token impure. The aim is therefore to eliminate the impure and so achieve non-duality. When you reach this point, it no longer matters if the mind is real or not. Thus the concept of *sunyata* is totally restored.

The three natures

While the Madhyamikas talk about "two levels of truth", the Yogacaras discuss the "three apparent natures" (*svabhava*). As with the Madhyamikas, the intention is to move from one's ordinary experience to the highest reality. For Yogacara there is an intermediate level of reality, although the Madhyamikas regard this as an impossible mix of reality and unreality.

The first of the three natures is the *parikalpita,* the mentally constructed image, or that which is imagined. This is what is constructed by the subject/object dichotomy. It is the common sense world of self, people and things. The second nature is *paratantra,* the "other-dependent". This is a relative reality which comprehends phenomena as mutually dependent and impermanent. The third and highest nature is *parinispanna,* the "absolutely accomplished". This is the absolutely real level, devoid of the subject/object duality.

A helpful illustration of this teaching relates to the magic shows presented by travelling performers that were popular in India since ancient times. By various devices, the magician produces the illusion that a fierce animal is about to attack the audience. The audience believes for that moment that the wild animal actually exists before them, and they experience fear. The magician also sees the form of the animal but he is not frightened because he knows that the absolute reality is merely a matter of wood and skins. An enlightened person is like the magician who sees the "other-dependent" world free from the fear of the imagination that grips the audience, who are the unenlightened.

The first two natures are the basis of defilements and thus suffering. The aim of Yogacara, therefore, is to understand the dualism constructed so as to undermine the absolute (*parinispanna*). In deep meditation, the mind gradually overcomes the tendency to interpret experiences as indicating external objects.

As this tendency wanes, consciousness is still grasped as a real subject, more real than objects. Finally, there arises the experience of transcending knowledge, which is undifferentiated unity. The path to *nirvana* is a gradual development of virtue, meditative concentration, and insight into the emptiness of "other-dependent" phenomena. The final attainment comes suddenly as a momentous spiritual transition that takes place at the root of the mind.

By adding a third state of "subsequent knowledge", human language and concepts that were negated by Nagarjuna's philosophy could be understood in their own particular terms. They could then be the constituents of the activities of the Buddhas and *bodhisattvas*.

The triple Buddha bodies

The tendency to revere the Buddha as a god had probably existed in his own lifetime. In Indian religion, divinity is not something completely transcendent, as in a monotheistic tradition such as Christianity. In India, godhead manifested itself in many forms, including great sages; religious teachers were looked upon as special manifestations of divinity and, in some sense, a god in human form. How much more divine the Buddha must have appeared, to whom even the great god Brahma did reverence! Yet, according to his teaching, the Buddha had passed completely away from the universe and ceased in any way to be a person.

Ideas concerning the nature of the Buddha gradually developed within the early schools. The Sthaviras spoke about the retribution body that any being acquires as a result of past *karma*. In the case of Sakyamuni he bore the 32 marks of a perfect human being resulting from previous moral lives. The Mahasanghika school raised the possibilities of many worlds and, therefore, many Buddhas. Complex questions emerged as to how these Buddhas relate. These various ideas emerged into the doctrine of the Buddha's three bodies that is so important in the Mahayana teaching. Although the general principles are simple to understand, the repercussions are complex. This concept provides a philosophical foundation for Mahayana Buddhism. About 300 AD, these ideas on the nature of the Buddha were systematised by the Yogacarins into what is known as the *Tri-kaya* ("three bodies") doctrine.

The terms used for these bodies in Sanskrit are based upon the root *kaya* which means "collection" or "body". The three bodies are therefore called: *Dharma-kaya* ("essence"), *Sambhoga-kaya* ("enjoyment body", "bliss"), and *Nirmana-kaya* ("transformation body", "magic"). It was in the latter form only that Sakyamuni Buddha lived on earth.

The first, *Dharma-kaya*, is the *Dharma* body, perfected and all-embracing, in which all the Buddhas participate. It is basically the state of Buddhahood. It is unmanifest; the imagination can only go so far in comprehending its nature. *Dharma-kaya* is the absolute truth. It is like space in the physical cosmos, infinite, all-pervasive, yet beyond human comprehension. In Mahayana it refers to the ultimate nature both of Buddhas and of reality in general, and it has two aspects. The first is the "knowledge body" (*jnana-kaya*), which is the inner nature shared by all the Buddhas. It is the omniscient knowledge, perfect wisdom, and spiritual qualities of the Buddha nature. It is regarded as having a very subtle, shining, limitless material form from which speech can come. In this way, the *Dharma* body has a semi-personalised aspect, making it somewhat like the concept of God in other religions. The second aspect of the *Dharma* body is the "self-existent body" (*svabhavika-kaya*). This is the ultimate nature of reality: the very nature of *dharmas*. It is what is known and realised on attaining Buddhahood – it is *nirvana*!

The manifested bodies are of two forms, one relating to the transcendent and the other to the mundane. The second form, *Sambhoga-kaya* ("enjoyment body") is that which relates to the transcendent manifestation of the Buddha. From a doctrinal point of view, *Sambhoga-kaya* is the body created by the Buddha's merit which is radiated into the world for the "enjoyment" of *bodhisattvas*. It is in this form that he manifests to instruct the advanced *bodhisattvas* in visions, when they hear his voice. However, for the heavenly beings, the Buddha manifests by his direct presence. When I asked a Japanese monk why *bodhisattvas* only hear, and do not see, the Buddha, he replied with the illustration of television. Television channels broadcast in colour but, if

I only have a monochrome set, I will only see the picture in black and white. If I have a colour set, I will see it in its full presentation.

The heavenly Buddha Sakyamuni is of the "enjoyment" type, but there are considered to be many other Buddhas dwelling in various regions of the universe, over which they preside and radiate their merit. The form and powers of the Buddhas and therefore their universes vary slightly according to their past vows and merit. These distinct universes are spoken of as "Buddha lands" (*Buddha-ksetra*) and "pure lands". These are mystical universes created by the Buddha drawing upon the immeasurable store of "merit" and the power of his mind, to realise a universe for the benefit of others. While these pure lands are described in terms of heaven, they are essentially realms where it is easy to hear and practise the *Dharma*. Pure lands are outside the normal system of *karma*, and to be reborn into a pure land requires the transference of some of the huge stock of "merit" from the presiding Buddha. This is usually achieved by devotion and prayer to the particular Buddha. Once a person has been reborn in a pure land, either as a human being or as a god, the person can develop to become a *bodhisattva*.

The third body forms are the various human manifestations such as Sakyamuni – *Nirmana-kaya* ("transformation body"). The argument is presented that if the god Vishnu came to earth, he would take a suitable physical body. Likewise, if the Buddha went to see a god, he would assume a suitable body. If he came to humans, he would take a human body. The "transformation body" refers to earthly Buddhas, seen as teaching devices projected into the world to show people the path to Buddhahood. This notion of a being producing other bodies was not new. In India at this time it was thought that great magicians could produce second bodies. At death, these transformation bodies were drawn back into the heavenly Buddha.

Three spheres of existence may therefore be identified: perfect (absolute), transcendent, and mundane. Buddhists usually do not want to speak about the absolute because it cannot be described with words. A Buddhist monk once said to me: "How do you explain heaven to a person who has never been there? You would struggle to find the words. The Buddha felt the same, and so he did not go beyond the phenomenal."

Disappearance of Buddhism in India

One of the many enigmas that characterise the history of India is the decline and disappearance of Buddhism during the period from the seventh until the thirteenth centuries. The Mahayana philosophers appear to have spent most of their time debating subtle metaphysical logic and even grammatical analysis. Tantra was initially a small minor cult within Buddhism which gradually came to dominate Buddhism in India before this ancient religious tradition finally disappeared. The central axis of Buddhism shifted from India to China and south-east Asia. Before following the development of Mahayana tradition in China and Japan, and considering Tantric Buddhism in Tibet, it is useful first to consider the reasons for the decline of Buddhism in the homeland of the Buddha. Various theories have been suggested; these have been summarised by Mitra in his book *The Decline of Buddhism in India.*[8]

Muslim expansion

An event that clearly had a major effect on Buddhism in India was the Muslim invasions of the twelfth and thirteenth centuries. In their fanatical response to what for them appeared as "idolatry", the Muslims burned the flourishing monasteries and universities of the Sind and killed the monks, who offered no resistance. This passive acceptance was partly due to the vows the monks had taken but also because they believed astrological calculations which predicted that the Muslims would conquer Hindustan.

Even so, that cannot be the whole reason for the extinction of Buddhism in India. First, Hindus and Jains were subject to the same furious attack but have continued to exist. Second, regions of the country untouched by the Muslims, such as Nepal and south India, also saw Buddhism die out, although more slowly. This would suggest that the cause of the decline must be sought as much within Buddhism as from outside.

Withdrawal of royal patronage

An otherworldly religion can only survive if it is able to enlist the support of some wealthy section of society. Indian monarchs were bound by tradition to assist all religions but active support of a particular religion always brought with it increased status and tangible material gain. Buddhism has generally relied on the support of kings; where this has been lacking, the *Sangha* has often had difficulties. The Buddhist laity never formed a distinct social entity but was essentially part of the Brahmanical community, conforming to the caste system and the Brahmanical rituals. The term "Buddhist" itself generally referred only to an individual who had actually left the household and taken the yellow robes of the mendicant.

While there were numerous lay people who supported Buddhism, the *Sangha* was aloof from the laity, as was already noted with the issue of *arhats* as compared to *bodhisattvas*. In contrast, Jain clerics were always closely involved with their lay people and actually produced texts concerning the proper conduct of lay persons.[9] Among these lay persons were wealthy merchants who continued to support the monks. The Jains were far more concerned than the Buddhists to maintain the internal cohesion of their lay community.

Lack of religious creativity

One suggestion for the failure of Buddhism has been "internal corruption and decay".[10] However, lazy monks had been known from early times and it would be wrong to say that this period had a greater proportion. Indian Buddhism was still able to send missionaries to Tibet, which makes it difficult to believe in the degeneracy of Indian Buddhism at this time. What appears to have been missing was religious creativity. During the 1,700 years that Hindus and Buddhists had co-existed in the country, there had been mutual borrowing of many ideas, and the distinctives of Buddhism had become lost.

Mahayana Buddhism, with its doctrine of heavenly *bodhisattvas*, provided a system of heavenly beings that could be interpreted in terms of the Hindu pantheon. Within Buddhist Tantra, the *bodhisattvas* and their consorts became virtually gods who could dispense worldly boons in ways not unlike that of the Hindu deities. The Buddha himself was eventually absorbed in the Hindu pantheon and was sometimes regarded as an avatar of Vishnu. Jains also allowed certain non-human figures to play a part in their rituals but always as lesser spirits. There had been no reformation of Jainism of the type that had produced Mahayana Buddhism. As Edward Conze remarks, "It is a law of history that the co-existence of rival views must lead to some form of eclecticism . . . The same happened to Hinduism and Buddhism. The separate existence of Buddhism no longer served a useful purpose. Its disappearance was no loss to anyone."[11]

Critics of Buddhism have often looked for inherent weaknesses within the philosophy that caused the collapse, and one can identify problems. However, Buddhist scholars had for many centuries spoken of the fall of the *Sangha* 1,500 years after the Sakyamuni's *parinirvana*. Prophecies can be self-fulfilling. When the end came, it was not unexpected.

Suggestions for interfaith discussions

This chapter has dealt with some of the philosophical issues raised within Buddhism, but the underlying issue continues to be the human condition. In order to relate theory to practice, imagine a young Thai woman caught up in prostitution who finally contracts AIDs. What would the Lord Buddha and the Lord Jesus Christ have to say to her?

Ravi Zacharias uses this scenario in his book *The Lotus and the Cross* (Oregon: Multnomah Press, 2001).

Webwise 9 – The Silence of the Buddha

Thinking in Buddhism: Nagarjuna's Middle Way

http://bahai-library.org/personal/jw/other.pubs/nagarjuna
This thesis by Jonah Winter provides a useful introduction to the teaching of Madhyamika.

Studies in Yogacara Buddhism

http://www.uncwil.edu/p&r/yogacara
This website was created to provide a forum for discussion among members of the Studies in Yogacara Buddhism seminar of the American Academy of Religion.

Yogacara Buddhist Research Association

http://www.human.toyogakuen-u.ac.jp/~acmuller/yogacara
Established in January 2000 to serve as an information service of
the Yogacara Buddhism Research Association, this site contains
links to various Yogacara documents and leading contemporary
exponents.

Notes

1. Nagao, G., *Madhyamika and Yogacara* (State University Press: New York, 1991), p. 41.
2. Robinson, R. H. and Johnson, W. L., *The Buddhist Religion: A Historical Introduction* (Belmont, CA: Wadsworth, 1997), p. 87.
3. Nagarjuna, *Mulamadhyamaka*, chapter 24, verse 14.
4. Harvey, P., *An Introduction to Buddhism* (Cambridge: CUP, 1992), p. 104.
5. Harris, I. C., *The Continuity of Mahyanmaka and Yogacara in Indian Mahayana Buddhism* (Leiden: E. J. Brill, 1991).
6. Wood, T. E., *Mind Only: A Philosophical and Doctrinal Analysis of the Vijnanavada* (Honolulu: University of Hawaii Press, 1991).
7. Harris, I. C., *The Continuity of Madhyamika and Yogacara in Indian Mahayana Buddhism* (Leiden: E. J. B. Brill, 1991).
8. Mitra, R.C., *The Decline of Buddhism in India* (Shantinketan: Visva-Bharati, 1954).
9. Jaini, P. S., "The disappearance of Buddhism and the survival of Jainism: a study in contrast" in Narain, *Studies in the History of Buddhism* (Delhi: B. R. Publishing Corporation, 1980), pp. 81–91.
10. Mitra, *op. cit.*
11. Conze, E., *A Short History of Buddhism* (Oxford: Oneworld, 1993), p. 109.

CHAPTER TEN

BUDDHISM IN CHINA

What you can learn from this chapter

- the history of the spread of Buddhism into China
- the formation of a distinctively Chinese expression of Buddhism
- the reasons why the Chinese accepted Buddhism

The introduction of Buddhism into China was one of the great events in Chinese history and provides a remarkable example of cultural borrowing by one civilisation from another. This was all the more remarkable since the Indian civilisation was so different from that of China, and China was so dismissive of all that was foreign. This chapter considers how Buddhism came to be transplanted into China and spread through the whole populace, so that it became one of the three religions of the Chinese. In contrast, Christianity has failed, until recently, to gain a presence in China and has continually been rejected as a "foreign" religion.

Zurcher identifies five stages in the penetration of Buddhist thought into China; this will provide a useful guide.[1]

1. The *embryonic phase* – from the first appearance of Buddhism when it only played a marginal role in the religious and intellectual life of the Chinese (1–300 AD).
2. The *formative phase* (c. 300–589 AD). This marked the penetration of Buddhism into the educated minority, after which it spread to every part of society.

3. The *phase of independent growth* (589–906 AD). This coincided with the second period of imperial unification during the Sui and T'ang dynasties.
4. *Buddhism in pre-modern China* (906–1880 AD). Buddhism gradually lost the support of the social elite and was reduced to a despised popular religion.
5. *Buddhism in modern and contemporary China* (c. 1880–present). The attempt to revive Buddhism remains small and rather elitist.

Conze compares the development of Buddhism to that of the maturation of an individual.[2] The first phase is that of a child who merely copies; in the second phase the wilful child asserts independence; the third stage is that of the true independence of an adult; the fourth is full maturity; the last is that of old age and a waning of powers.

The early period (c. 1–300 AD)

According to legend, Emperor Ming (58–75 AD) had a dream of a "golden image" in the west. When one of his counsellors told him that this was a foreign god called the Buddha, he sent emissaries to north-western India requesting that Buddhist teachers might be sent. The stories of how the monkey god helped bring the scriptures to China along the dangerous path from India have become part of the rich folklore of China. The fanciful story is no longer accepted as an explanation of the coming of Buddhism into China. It was, however, probably about this time that Buddhism entered China with traders who came along the silk route from Central Asia. Envoys travelled back and forth between the growing Han empire and the Kushan empire in north-west India. Migrants and traders could have settled in the towns of China, so Buddhism was initially an urban phenomenon.

The first known Buddhist missionary was Shih-kao, a Parthian prince who, after his arrival in about 148 AD, spent more than 20 years in China. Growth was slow under the Han dynasty. This in part was due to the way in which the emperor was viewed as the "Son of Heaven" and was the focus of the empire in Confucian ideology. Supernatural sanctions held power, position and prestige in correct balance for all members of society.

In addition, there were several major difficulties in communicating Buddhist ideas, and the only way that a translation could be attempted was through Taoist terminology. A word like *tao,* for example, was used to translate *magga,* or "path". This automatically carried with it many Taoist overtones unintended in the original Sanskrit scriptures of India. Buddhism was probably initially regarded in China as a sect of Taoism. As such, there was probably a mixing of Buddhism and Taoism in this early period. Points of similarity included:

a. Many of the assistants of early translations were Taoist scholars.
b. There were similarities in the rituals of Buddhists and Taoists, e.g. no animal sacrifices.
c. Emphasis upon meditation.
d. Abstinence from certain foods.
e. Concern about immortality.

Buddhism was also criticised by Taoists, and in the *T'ai P'ing Ching* text, which is attributed to Yu Chi (fl. 126–144 AD), four criticisms are made:

a. It was unfilial in that young people were encouraged to become monks and leave their parents.
b. It encouraged celibacy and so the neglect of wives and children.
c. It permitted the eating of impurities (use of cow's urine for medicine).
d. It promoted begging.

Buddhism in its teaching was opposed to the indigenous Chinese culture in several fundamental ways. First, the Chinese held the view that life is good and to be enjoyed, and this was counter to the Buddhist teaching that all is suffering and illusion. Second, the Buddhist practice of celibacy conflicted with the Chinese emphasis upon family life and the need for many children.

Third, the mendicant monk was an object of scorn to those who believed that all able-bodied people should be engaged in productive labour. Fourth, the idea of a monastic community possessing its own government and passing its own laws was contrary to Confucian teaching that held to the unity of the empire under one supreme ruler.

During the period of the Han dynasty there was little opportunity for mass response to Buddhist teaching, but it did allow the introduction of the new teaching into society. However, many of the Buddhist texts were translated into Chinese, especially after the fall of the Han dynasty. Most attention seems to have been given to the shorter texts dealing with meditation or trance (*dyana*), probably because of its similarity to the Taoist techniques.

Formative phase (300–589)

The downfall of the Han dynasty in 220 AD brought disunity. By 300 war and chaos had spread over the whole country; in 311 the capital was sacked and the royal court had to flee to the area south of the river Yangtze. The period resulted in a terrible loss in human life and a sharp decline in the population of the north. From this time, China was divided into two halves: northern China ruled by non-Chinese, and southern China governed by a series of short-lived dynasties. It was nearly 300 years before the empire was reunited, during which time Buddhism developed along different routes in the north from that of the south.

Northern China

Throughout Chinese history, northern invaders always struggled to keep their cultural identity amidst the pressure to assimilate into the rich culture of the Chinese. The Huns, like other conquerors, gradually adopted much of Chinese culture but they preferred Buddhism to Confucianism, which was a very powerful force for Sinicisation. At this time, Buddhism was still regarded as a foreign religion by the Chinese. This therefore led to a close connection between the state, with its alien rulers; the *Sangha* in the north in which there was massive government patronage with major building projects. Taoism became something of a rival, competing for the favour of the foreign rulers; and it was through the machinations of the Taoist masters that outbreaks of persecution against the *Sangha* occasionally occurred.

With such imperial patronage, many Buddhist missionaries came to northern China during the fourth and fifth centuries. Buddhist monks became political and diplomatic advisors, gaining great reputations through their healings and magical practices. As a result, the peasants began to adopt Buddhism in large numbers. So rapidly did Buddhism spread in the area that by the early fifth century it has been estimated that nine out of ten families worshipped the Buddha in the northern capital.

The most influential monk of the period was Fo T'u-teng (d. 349 AD), who was the court chaplain of the Hsiung-nu emperors. He established many monasteries in the northern kingdom and created a more complete set of monastic rules. A distinct feature of Buddhism from the start was monastic community and the rules of life codified as the *Vinaya*. The monastic community in China was under the same regulations as the *Sangha* everywhere, but there were some differences in actual practice. The original Indian tradition was mendicant but the Chinese *Sangha* lived in settled communities, usually supported by land-holdings. The economic base of the monastery was the income from lands worked by tenant peasants. This was in part due to a difference in climate. Whereas in India the monks were only unable to wander freely during the rainy season, the winter months can be very cold in China. In part, the change in tradition resulted from the social unacceptability of begging within Chinese society. The monastery became the centre of Buddhist life in China even more than it was in India.

About 400 AD the great translator Kumarajiva (344–413) consolidated Buddhism and gave it even greater prestige. He came from Kucha and was born of an Indian father in about 344. He was carried off as war booty to China in 384 and lived in Leang-chou in Kansu for fifteen years, after which he was taken to the capital of Ch'ang-an where he became the director of religious instruction. He produced a huge number of Chinese versions with the help of a large state-sponsored translation team. The translation of the

Sanskrit texts into Chinese was not an easy task. A statement attributed to Kumarajiva illustrates this most colourfully, "Translating Sanskrit into Chinese is like feeding a man with rice chewed by another; it is not merely tasteless, it is nauseating as well."[3]

Although Kumarajiva was originally a Sarvastivadin monk, he later converted to the doctrines of Nagarjuna, the founder of Madhyamaka teaching, discussed in chapter 9. This school provided an important basis for the teaching of *sunyata,* which became of great interest to Chinese scholars. Perhaps the most influential text was the *Lotus Sutra,* which from that time onwards gripped the Chinese mind through its imaginative style and content.

In 399 AD, another Chinese monk, Fa-Hien, a great scholar, was selected by the emperor to travel to India to obtain accurate information about Buddhism. The imperial authorities wished to obtain copies and correct translations of the sacred books and to establish an official Buddhism that would be both authentic and authoritative. Fa-Hien's fourteen-year journey took him through the Buddhist kingdoms of central Asia into northern India, where he spent ten years copying texts, visiting shrines, and talking to religious leaders. After another two years of study in Ceylon, he returned to China. His account of his travels is one of the major sources of our knowledge of medieval Buddhism and one of the few contemporary accounts of central Asia and Indian Buddhism of this period.[4]

In the north, the most powerful state was the northern Wei dynasty, founded by a people of probable Turkic origins; under their patronage there were massive projects for temple building. Large monasteries were established that became enormously wealthy, with the building of enormous pagodas the size of medieval European cathedrals. Huge cave temples were constructed with ornate sculpture and paintings. The *Sangha* experienced rapid growth in its numbers; in about 520 AD the Wei empire counted 30,000 monasteries and 2 million monks. This encouraged criticism both from Confucian traditionalists and Taoist rivals, and the *Sangha* experienced a number of persecutions. The major ones were in 446 and 574 but in spite of this Buddhism continued to grow.

Southern China

In the south of China, the Chinese dynasty was politically weak, and Confucianism, the official religion, was in decline. This allowed the non-official cults that were always well controlled in periods of stability, to begin to prosper. Taoism became popular among the general population; many people seemed to think that the teachings of Lao-tzu and the Buddha were one and the same. In the third century, Wang Fo wrote a pamphlet in which he represented Buddhism as the result of the conversion of the barbarians by Lao-tzu, and this view was widely accepted. These religions provided alternative ways to deal with the horrors caused by incessant fighting and misery.

Taoism gained many followers among the educated elite who were interested in metaphysical debate. In the same atmosphere, Buddhism was able to gain the attention of the elite, and Buddhist scholars teaching the doctrine of *sunyata* found eager audiences. Although few of the higher classes became monks, they did join the ranks of the laity and accepted the five Buddhist rules of morality, paying frequent visits to monasteries to pray, burn incense and listen to sermons. As such they became great patrons of the *Sangha*, founding monasteries and temples. Buddhism was no longer considered an alien religion favoured by a few foreigners and illiterate members of the population. By the late sixth century, Buddhism had come to be regarded as an acceptable high-class religion in southern China.

Buddhism in the south developed into two different schools: Dhyana and Prajna. Dhyana was a school of meditation, Theravada in nature, which emphasised the control of the mind. The Prajna school followed the Mahayana *sutras* and was concerned with questions about the nature of ultimate reality. For the educated classes, the Mahayana *sutras* brought new ways of dealing with some of the fundamental philosophical problems raised by Taoism. As a result it brought a close relationship between the *Sangha* and the *literati* of Taoism. The *Prajna Sutra* taught that the nature of all phenomena (*dharmas*) was *sunyata*. Nothing conditionally exists of itself; everything is the result of many causes. There is no duality between subject and object, affirmation and negation, *samsara* and *nirvana*; as such this links in well with the concept of the eternal Tao.

During the fourth and fifth centuries, Buddhist masters helped lay the foundation of the Mahayana school of Chinese Buddhism. They were familiar with the teachings of Confucian and Taoist classics, and interpreted the teachings of the great Indian Buddhist thinkers, Ashvaghosha, Nagarjuna, Vasubandhu and Asanga. From this there slowly emerged a distinct Chinese tradition. This eventually came to flower in the Pure Land sects of the T'ang dynasty.

By 400 AD, southern China counted more than 1,700 monasteries and about 80,000 monks and nuns. Buddhist monks gradually increased in influence, and many entered the *Sangha* from impure motives. Monks were exempt from taxation and the usual formalities of reverence due to secular rulers. This sudden expansion caused opposition from anti-Buddhist circles, who urged measures to restrict the growth of Buddhism as "antisocial" and "barbarian". The following two centuries resulted both in the continued progress of Buddhism in China and the gathering storm of opposition.

During the period of political disunity (420–589), Buddhism continued to grow. In the south it gained a strong following in the aristocratic circles connected with the court. Emperor Wu of the Ling dynasty (502–549) was an ardent Buddhist, and built many temples. Imperial patronage was resented by Confucianists and Taoists who were vitriolic in their attacks on Buddhists. Emperor Wu welcomed to the court the famous Indian monk, Paramartha, who arrived in Canton in 546. It was through his translations that the idealistic teachings of Asanga and Vasubandha became influential in China.

Initially, the most popular figures of devotion were Sakyamuni (Chinese: *Shih-chia-mo-ni-fo*) and Maitreya (Chinese: *Mi-lo-fo*). Although Sakyamuni was regarded as the historic Buddha, he was in China spoken of as the glorified heavenly Buddha. Later, this figure was to give way in Chinese devotion to Amitabha (Chinese: *O-mi-t'o-fo*) and Avalokitesvara (Chinese: *Kuan-yin*), as the Pure Land school of Buddhism became increasingly popular.

China had incorporated what is present-day Vietnam as a province of China in 111 BC and it remained under Chinese rule for a thousand years. With the invasion of northern China by the Huns, many Chinese refugees moved to the relatively quieter region of what is now northern Vietnam. This resulted in the gradual spread of the Mahayana tradition into parts of south-east Asia where it came into contact with the Theravada tradition.

During the years of division, Buddhism developed in separate ways in the north and south of China. In both regions it made a strong appeal to the rulers and, at the same time, adapted itself to the needs of the Chinese people by an increasing stress on filial piety, and also by coming to terms with the cult of ancestors by directing that prayers should be chanted for the well-being of the departed. The devotional aspects of Buddhism were increasingly stressed as Buddhism became the religion of the ordinary people. The growth of Buddhism during this period also led to its introduction into Korea in the late fourth century both from the northern and southern states of China. The most important scriptures had been translated into Chinese, and Chinese masters had begun to elaborate their own doctrinal systems that were to become the basis for a particular Chinese character of Buddhism which was to emerge during the next period.

The Chinese Buddhist tradition (589–900)

In 581 the great ruler Yang-chien unified both north and south to form the short-lived Sui dynasty (590–618). He relied on Buddhism to help in the unification and consolidation of the empire. He initiated a series of measures, including establishing monasteries at the foot of each of the five sacred mountains and on the sites of famous battles. This paved the way for the great political, economic and social achievements of the T'ang dynasty (618–906) when Buddhism was patronised on a lavish scale, though not always for religious reasons. The result was a period of creative activity in the whole area of Buddhist thought and practice. The expansion of the empire into central Asia and the opening of trade routes brought many foreigners into China, including pilgrims, the most famous of which was Hsuan-tsang (c. 559–664). Throughout this period, Chinese Buddhism was continually being renewed by contact with

India. Nestorian Christians from the Middle East also entered the region, as later did Muslims.

Eventually, the T'ang rulers saw the need to bring the ever-growing *Sangha* under the control of the state. Throughout the eighth century several measures were introduced to regulate the Buddhist monks but the religion was by then too well established to be seriously affected. The dazzling images, colourful ritual, and beautiful temples impressed the people. Monasteries served as charitable institutions caring for the old and sick. The monks ran dispensaries and hospitals, arranged for the feeding of the poor, and engaged in community projects such as building roads and digging wells. These were all ways in which merit might be accumulated to ensure entrance into Amitabha's heaven.

As long as the T'ang state prospered, it was able to tolerate the immense Buddhist community but later in the dynasty, when it faced political turmoil and economic crises, anti-clericalism became evident. In 845 a census was taken of all Buddhist monastic communities, which revealed that there were some 250,000 monks and nuns, 4,600 temples and over 40,000 lesser shrines. The order was given to destroy all Buddhist buildings, apart from one temple in each prefecture, and four temples in each capital city. The majority of monks and nuns were forced to leave the monastic life and take secular occupations. Although the persecution did not last long it had a disastrous effect, from which Buddhism in China never fully recovered.

Another significant aspect of Buddhism in China was that of martial arts. It is likely that martial arts were practised in China long before the arrival of Buddhism but it is interesting how they have been associated with Buddhism. The myth of the origin of Buddhist martial arts attributes it to an Indian scholar called Bodhidharma, who is said to have travelled to China in the later fifth century. He taught a new style of meditation known as Ch'an and, according to tradition, instructed his followers in breathing and yogic-based martial moves known as the "eighteen hands of the *lohan*". The story associates him with the Shaolin temple in Henan near Loyang. What can be attested is that by the Ming period in the 16th century, martial arts training was associated with the Shaolin temple. It is possible that thirteen Shaolin monks aided the Li family at an incident in 621 AD to establish their control around Loyang.

There are many associations of Buddhism with the martial arts, and sword and warrior imagery abound in Buddhist texts. A particular ethical teaching invoked the concept of "skilful means" to justify violent actions in order to protect the innocent or the *Dharma* and its representatives. Popular ballads, stories and novels have portrayed the exponent as a "Chinese knight errant". As Liu writes:

> In classical Chinese novels and in modern Kung Fu movies the knight errant has long had a place in the fantasy life of the Chinese people. For centuries Chinese martial arts novels have portrayed the young, the physically weak, the elderly, the handicapped, the rebellious, the poor and the alcoholic as knight errants who have used martial arts to defeat awesome adversaries. In both fantasy and reality, powerless, socially marginal Chinese have formed sworn brotherhoods and practised martial arts to enhance their personal and collective strength.[5]

Sworn brotherhoods or martial arts societies and even Triad associations have incorporated the Shaolin legend into the myths of their origin. In China, martial arts have been a non-elitist interest, partly reflecting the Confucian disdain for physical activities.

The pre-modern period (c. 900–c. 1880)

The tenth century was marked by great political, social and economic change during which the agrarian society was transformed into an urbanised bureaucracy with a sophisticated urban elite consisting of rich merchants. Confucian values increasingly dominated society as part of the powerful "neo-Confucian" revival of the eleventh and twelfth centuries.

Throughout this period, Buddhism declined steadily, although it continued to flourish in various forms of popular devotion. After about 1000 AD, two schools of Buddhism ousted all the others: Amidism and Ch'an dominated Buddhist religious thought in China. The decline was mainly intellectual and the interest of the social elite moved from Buddhism to neo-Confucianism. The shift essentially reduced Buddhism to a despised religion of the lower classes, with the exception of Ch'an. Syncretism became the prevailing trend, and the idea of the basic unity of the three teach-ings (Confucianism, Taoism, and Buddhism) gained great popu-larity. Another characteristic of this period was the interest in Tantric Buddhism in its Tibetan form introduced by the Mongol rulers. The influence of Lamaism in China dates from this period and will be discussed further in chapter 14.

During the twelfth century the White Lotus Society devoted to Amitabha emerged, along with many similar groups. The label "White Lotus" came to be used of all heterodox schools of which the government suspected rebellion. In times of unrest it is common for new religious movements to emerge, promising a new glorious age about to dawn. Such movements mushroomed during the Ming dynasty in the 16th century and have continued with varying influence until today.

One fascinating group was the Pure Water sect, which started as a ritualised martial arts brotherhood, under the leadership of Wang Lun. He was a skilful boxer who practised fasting and med-itation to increase his martial skills, as well as powers of healing and exorcism. He acquired a large following and his teaching became increasingly messianic. During the period 1773 to 1774 his rebel army controlled several towns in Shantung, until they were finally defeated by government troops.[6]

Although Europeans such as Marco Polo had made earlier con-tacts with China, it was Matteo Ricci (1552–1610) who first estab-lished himself in the heart of Chinese culture and society. In his coming to China in 1582 he fulfilled the dream of his fellow Jesuit, Francis Xavier. Although the Jesuit method of propagating Christianity in Asia through cultural accommodation was the brainchild of Xavier, it was Ricci who set the pattern of Jesuit work in China. He made the science and technology of Europe known to the Chinese and devised Chinese terminology for Roman Catholic theology and liturgy.

Why did the Chinese accept Buddhism?

It is now possible to return to the question raised at the beginning of the chapter. Why was Indian Buddhism accepted by the Chinese people? Covell lists eight factors.[7]

1. The relative ease of access by land into China by zealous missionaries able to relate well to Chinese life within the general Asian milieu.
2. A Han China open to new ideas and needing revitalisation.
3. An available role as a "sect of Taoism", asserting no exclusive claims.
4. A popular movement among a great number of people such that there was little social dislocation.
5. A philosophy seen by the Chinese as adequate to deal with the incredible human misery and suffering experienced during the period.
6. No external power base that could pose a threat to the Chinese state.
7. A flexible methodology adequate to exploit differing opportunities in northern and southern China.
8. Chinese society was penetrated by Buddhism at all levels of society – linguistically, economically, socially, politically and artistically. Submitting to the state politically was of crucial importance.

As Covell comments, "none of these several advantages were available to the same degree to the emissaries of the Christian faith. Apart from the Nestorians in the seventh century, they came by the sea route: distances were great, communication with the home base was poor, they were not Asians, it was the 'ocean of faith' (*yang jiao*) or 'foreign faith' . . . Christianity was an exclusive faith."[8]

Christianity was not the only religion to fail in China – Islam met the same fate. Several reasons are generally cited for the failure of Islam. First, the Muslims mainly influenced the minority Hui people who were despised by the majority Han people. Second, apart from traders, Islam entered China by invasion and violence. Third, in common with Christians, Muslims refused to blend their faith with Chinese religion and were exclusive in their beliefs. Today, Islam tends to be regarded as more indigenous than Christianity because it took root before the Chinese gained control of the local tribes in central Asia.

1st century AD Han dynasty (25–220 AD)	Stories are told of two Buddhist missionaries who in 68 AD arrive from India at the court of Emperor Ming (58–75). They receive imperial favour and stay on to translate various Buddhist texts including the *Sutra of Forty-two Sections*, which is popular today.
4th century	Translation of Buddhist texts into Chinese by Kumarajiva (344–413) and Hui-yuan (344–416).
5th century	Chinese pilgrim scholar Fa-hsien visits India (399–414). Pure Land school (Ching t'u) emerges in China (402). Persecution of Buddhism under Emperor Wu or Shi-tusu (424–451). Restoration under the new emperor, Wen-ch'eng-ti (454).
6th century T'ang dynasty (618–907)	Bodhidharma arrives in China from India in 520 (or 526) and establishes Ch'an school. This is the golden age of Chinese Buddhism. T'ien-t'ai school established by Chih-i (538–597). Hua-yen school established by Fa-shun (557–640).
7th century	The southern school of Ch'an or new Ch'an begins in earnest with Hui-neng (638–713), the sixth patriarch. The persecution in 845: During the reign of Emperor Wu-tsung (841–847) an order is effected that all Buddhist establishments should be destroyed, causing a decline in Chinese Buddhism. The invention of block printing by Chinese Buddhists. The oldest extant book printed is the Tun-hung book of 868 with excerpts from the *Diamond Sutra*.
10th century Sung dynasty	In 972, the first emperor of the Sung dynasty orders the complete printing of the Chinese *Tipitaka*. This is achieved in 983, known as the *Shu-pen* (Szechuan edition).
12th to 15th century Ming dynasty (1368–1643)	China during Yuan dynasty is under Mongolian rule and the influences of Tibetan *lamas*. The Buddhist–Taoist controversy is brought before Mangu Khan in 1255 and concluded in the Buddhist's favour by an edict of Kublai Khan in 1281. Movement towards unity among the schools develops under the Ming dynasty (1368–1643).

	Master Chu-hung (born 1535) harmonises the different schools (specifically Cha'n and Pure Land) and initiates a lay Buddhist movement.
The modern era	The revolution of 1911 that topples the Manchu dynasty and establishes the Republic of China brings problems for the Buddhist *Sangha*.
	• To combat these trends Tai-hsu (1898–1947), a Buddhist monk, initiates a program of reform that results in the nationwide Chinese Buddhist Society in 1929.
	• A revival of the Idealistic school is initiated by the publication in 1901 of the *Ch'eng-wei-shih-lun* ("Notes on the Completion of the Idealistic Doctrine") of K'uei-chi, long lost in China but brought back from Japan. The leader of this revival is the layman Ou-yang Chien, founder of the Institute of Inner Learning, which he organises in Naking (Nanjing) in 1922.
	• Hsu Yun, Ch'an master (1840–1959), *Dharma* successor of all five Ch'an schools; main reformer in Chinese Buddhism revival (1900–50).
	• Wong Mou-Lam translates *The Platform Sutra* into English and founds the journal *Chinese Buddhism* (1930).
	• The official formation of the Chinese Buddhist Association by the government of the People's Republic of China on 30 May 1953.
	The Cultural Revolution (1965–1975): Buddhist temples and monasteries are sacked and the already weakened *Sangha* further depleted. The excesses of this time have since been regretted, however, and a more liberal policy introduced.

Figure 10.1   Timeline of Buddhism in China

Although a proselytising religion by nature, Islam entered China as the religion of certain ethnic groups, from Persia and other parts of central Asia and beyond. However, Buddhism and Christianity acted differently, arousing much more attention as well as controversy, as each attempted to make its impact upon the larger society.[9]

Lawrence summarises the introduction of Buddhism into China:

The transplantation of Buddhist thought to China is one of the great intercultural movements of history. Among the many lessons we may draw from that movement is that accommodation of a foreign culture is only accomplished as a result of many modifications and reinterpretations that make it comprehensible and even naturalise it. In the case of Buddhism, one must recognise that first there was Indian Buddhism; then there was Indian Buddhism in China; and finally, after many centuries of adjustment, there was Chinese Buddhism.[10]

Suggestions for interfaith discussions

Buddhism was only slowly adopted into Chinese culture and then by a process of adaptation. Which elements of the early teachings of the *Dharma* remained, and which were expressed in Chinese forms? How does this compare with the contextualisation of the Christian gospel into local cultural forms?

Webwise 10 – Buddhism in China

Gateless Passage

http://villa.lakes.com/cdpatton/Dharma/Canon/index.html
This section of the *Gateless Passage* is dedicated to describing the Chinese Buddhist canon as laid out in the Taishoo edition with links to an English translation.

Hsu Yun Buddhist Association

http://home.att.net/~ChuanDao
This website is devoted to presenting the teachings of Grandmaster Hsu Yun ("Empty Cloud") and contains information on Chinese

Buddhism in general. It also offers information on Buddhist practice and other matters.

Silk Road Foundation

http://www.silk-road.com/toc/index.html

The University of Washington uses the "Silk Road" theme to explore cultural interaction across Eurasia from the beginning of the Common Era (AD) to the 16th century. The site contains many excellent historical maps of the region.

Notes

1. Zurcher, E., "Buddhism in China" in Kitagawa, J. M. and Cummings, M. D. (eds.), *Buddhism and Asian History* (London: MacMillan, 1989), pp. 143–144.
2. Conze, E., *A Short History of Buddhism* (Oxford: Oneworld, 1993), pp. 62–63.
3. Goodrich, L. C., *A Short History of the Chinese People* (New York: Harper & Row, 1963), p. 190.
4. Legge, J., *A Record of Buddhist Kingdoms* (New York: Dover, 1965). This is a translation of the recorded travels of Fa-Hien (399–414 AD).
5. Liu, J., *The Chinese Knight Errant* (London: Routledge & Kegan Paul, 1967), pp. 22–23.
6. Nyquil, S., *Shantung Rebellion* (New Haven: Yale, 1981).
7. Covell, R., *Confucius, The Buddha, and Christ* (Maryknoll: Orbis, 1986), p. 147.
8. Covell, *ibid.*, p. 147.
9. Ching, J., *Chinese Religion* (Basingstoke: Macmillan, 1993), p. 121.
10. Thompson, L. G., *Chinese Religion* (Belmont: Wadsworth, 1989), p. 113.

CHAPTER ELEVEN

CHINESE EXPRESSIONS OF BUDDHISM

What you can learn from this chapter

- the Chinese schools of Buddhism
- the nature of "Pure Land" Buddhism
- the figure of Kuan-yin in popular Chinese religion
- the distinctive character of Ch'an and its teaching of immediate enlightenment

The character of the various Chinese schools of Buddhism is best portrayed when they were at their fullest development during the T'ang dynasty of 618–907 AD. As was shown in the previous chapter, their roots go back to earlier times, and some continue much later. By the time Buddhism became firmly established in China, Indian Buddhism had been flourishing for a thousand years and all the great works of the Theravada and Mahayana traditions were already in existence.

The Chinese had a great confidence in the written word and accepted all the Buddhist scriptures in Chinese translations as the literal words of the Buddha. Due to the great volume of Buddhist literature, no scholar could be familiar with all the literature, and the diversity of teaching contained was not often recognised by the Chinese scholars. The voluminous writings of the Indian Mahayanist were eagerly seized upon by the Chinese Buddhist scholars who themselves stimulated new currents of thought.

Distinguished Chinese scholars adopted widely different interpretations of Buddhist truth and claimed their teaching as presenting the perfection of Buddha's *Dharma*. Often a teacher would adopt a particular work as of paramount importance and would consider other writings to be introductory texts leading to the supreme truth. Out of the intense study of the Indian Buddhist scriptures the Chinese scholars formulated new ideas based on their traditional Confucian and Taoist thought.

Most of the Chinese schools were founded during the period of unity under the Sui and T'ang dynasties from the end of the sixth century to the eighth. In any discussion of the schools of Chinese Buddhism it is important to realise that the word translated "school" is the Chinese word *tsung*, which has a variety of meanings, ranging from being a particular doctrine to a philosophical school.

There are eight major schools (see figure 11.1):

1. Pure Land (Ching T'u)   Fourth century
2. Three Treatises, Madhyamika (San Lun)   c. 400 AD
3. Meditation (Ch'an)   c. 520
4. T'ien T'ai, an attempt at harmonisation   c. 550
5. Garland (Hua Yen)   c. 600
6. Wei Shih, or Fa Hsiang based on Yogacara c. 650
7. Discipline, Theravada (Lu)   c. 650
8. Tantric (Chen Yen, or Mi Tsung)   c. 720

San Lun and Wei Shih were too philosophical to exist in their own right for long but their teachings continued to influence the monasteries for some time afterwards. T'ien T'ai and Hua Yen merged into the great Ching T'u (Pure Land) form of Buddhism.

Pure Land Buddhism (Ching T'u)

Pure Land Buddhism emerged as the greatest and most influential of the Mahayana schools in China and dominated the lives of many of the common people. Not only was this one of the earliest schools but it was also the least philosophical. According to the Chinese tradition, the founder is said to be Hui-yuan. He was a

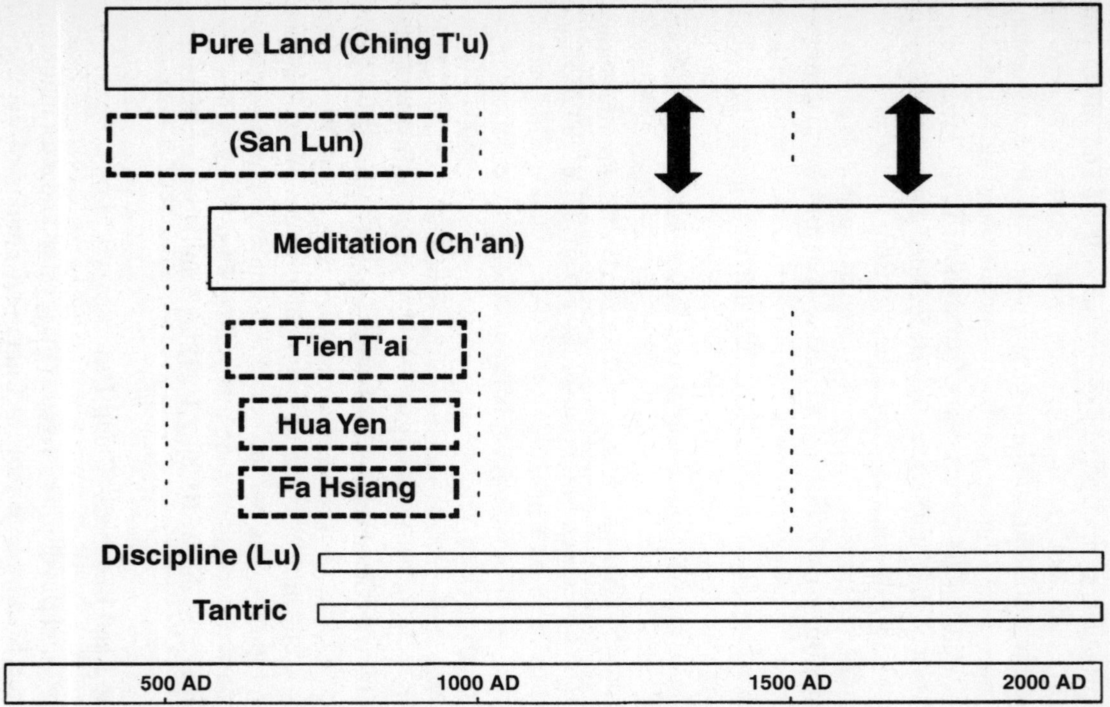

Figure 11.1 Major schools of Chinese Buddhism

zealous Taoist who converted to Buddhism about 380 AD and entered a life-long quest for a real understanding of the Mahayana tradition. In about 400 AD he took as his principal scripture the *Sukhavativyuha Sutra*, a Sanskrit text probably written in the first century AD in India, which in the Chinese translation is known as *Wu-liang-shou Ching*. In the Chinese tradition the Pure Land is attributed to the teaching of Nagarjuna and Vasubandhu but there is little support for this designation. What it does do is provide a respectable ancestry within the Indian school of Madhyamika.

This text taught salvation by faith in Amitabha (*O-mi-to-fo*) and contained vivid descriptions of the heaven over which he was said to rule. Amidism taught that the power inherent in the name of Buddha Amitabha can remove all obstacles to salvation; the mere utterance of his name (*O-mi-to-fo*) can assure rebirth in his kingdom. The legend is based chiefly on the *Sukhavativyuha* and tells the story that aeons ago, the *bodhisattva* Dharmakara made 48 vows, among them the promise that all who call on his name shall be saved. He eventually became the Buddha Amitabha and, ten aeons ago, in accordance with his vows, he established the "pure land" that lies 1 million billion Buddha lands away. The sect honours Amitabha by multiplying copies of his statues as well as the *sutras* that tell of him.

As far as is known, there was little specific devotion to Amitabha before the sixth century; the first dated image of Amitabha is at Lung-men in north China in 519 AD. A dramatic change occurred during the seventh century when many more images of Amitabha were erected. These changes occurred during the collective lifetimes of the three great Chinese patriarchs of Pure Land: T'an-luan, Tao-cho (562–645), and Shan-tao (613–681).

T'an-luan

T'an-luan's major contribution was a commentary on the *Sukhavati Sutra*. In a period of political uncertainty, T'an-luan thought that the golden age of spiritual enlightenment was past and there were no more great sages like the Buddha. In Chinese Buddhism a great gap was opening between the ultimate state of Buddhahood and the conventional realm of *samsara*, and progress from one to the other was almost impossible. How then in this present age could one make spiritual progress? T'an-luan adopted the distinction between the difficult and easy path that had been proposed by Nagarjuna and used this to provide a religion for the majority of people who were unable to make progress through their own actions. Through faith in the power of Amitabha and his great vows, one could be reborn in Sukhavati and there be almost certain to attain enlightenment.

The appeal to the masses lies in its simplicity and ease to follow. It also answers the philosophical and religious problem of how it is possible, through one's own finite deeds, to attain a state of unconditioned enlightenment. T'an-luan adopted five forms of practice mentioned by Vasubandhu but he placed particular emphasis on the virtue of reciting the name of the Buddha Amitabha. Continually repeating the name with a unified mind is said to purify the mind from all its sins and to ensure rebirth in the Pure Land. Through the power of Amitabha, even the worst sinner can attain the Pure Land.

Tao-cho

T'an-luan's disciple was Tao-cho whose main contribution was his response to the critics of Pure Land thought. He experienced the persecution of Buddhism in China and taught that old practices were not suitable for this new age and that people should repent of their sins and call upon Amitabha. He did not condemn the conventional way but pointed out the difficulty of gaining enlightenment in the contemporary, tainted world. It was better therefore to aim at enlightenment in the Pure Land of Sukhavati. This was neither a sensual paradise nor a realm of desire and attachment.

Shan-tao

The third great exponent of Pure Land Buddhism was Shan-tao (613–681) who lived in the Chinese capital of Ch'ang-an. He taught that humans are bound in a vicious circle of sin and error through the three poisons of greed, anger and stupidity. They have little power to save themselves but, through a sincere vow of faith in Amitabha, continually filling the mind with thoughts of him and accepting his mercy and merit, it is guaranteed that all will gain enlightenment. Shan-tao made little impact on the nobility of China but attracted many followers among the ordinary people. Some of these were sufficiently enthusiastic for Sukhavati that they committed suicide in order to hasten their rebirth and subsequent enlightenment. There is even a legend that Shan-tao himself eventually committed suicide.[1]

The teaching of the sect was later condensed into the famous book "Awakening of Faith in the Mahayana" (*Ch'i Hsin Lun*). In this book the reader is directed to the infinite host of Buddhas and *bodhisattvas* who offer assistance to the believer.

> Let those who doubt and desire to give up meditate on this wise. All the Buddhas and *bodhisattvas* of the ten quarters have attained great spiritual and unhindered perception and are able by means of excellent and skilful acts of merit to rescue all distressed beings. Having thus meditated, let them make a great vow that they will with single mind think of conviction. Then at the end of life they will attain entrance into the Buddha's realm and perceiving the Buddhas and *bodhisattvas* with perfect faith they will be everlastingly freed from evil conditions. As a *sutra* says, "If good men and good women would think only on Amitabha in his perfectly blessed world in the western region, and direct all their root of merit towards him, and desire to be born there, then they will assuredly be born there." Faith increases through constant beholding of the Buddhas, and there would never be a relapse.[2]

How shall a person be saved? The answer of the Pure Land masters was through faith in Amitabha. This faith consisted of three features: sincerity, devotion, and desire to be reborn in Sukhavati. These three aspects of faith apply to all beings but if one is missing, then there will be no rebirth in the Pure Land. It is necessary for the devotee to Amitabha to engage in five forms of religious practice. The first is the continual recitation of the name of Amitabha, which is the most important activity. Second, there is chanting the *sutra* of Amitabha. Third, there is meditating on Amitabha. Fourth, there is worshipping him and his images, and the fifth is making offerings.

Shan-tao is said to have told the parable of the white path, which is often used within Pure Land teaching. A man is on a journey to the west when he comes to two rivers. On his left is a river of fire, and on his right waves of water. Between the two rivers runs the white path that is only about the width of a foot, but there are a hundred steps from east to west. As the man stands looking at the situation, a band of thugs comes towards him from one side, while wild animals approach from the other, causing him to be filled with terror. At that very moment, he hears a voice encouraging him to go forward, as to stay would mean death. Then, from the far side of the path comes a voice calling him to walk forward with a fixed purpose and not to fear the fire or the water. As he sets off, the thugs call him to come back but he continues and finally reaches the west bank in safety.

In the parable the shore stands for the world of *samsara*, and the far shore for Sukhavati. The thugs and wild animals are our senses and consciousness. Fire is anger, and water is greed and affection. The white path is the desire for the Pure Land. The voice from this shore is that of Sakyamuni Buddha who points the true way, and that from the far shore is Amitabha and his vow to save. This easily remembered story encapsulates the heart of the teaching of the Pure Land sect.

Kuan-yin

In his saving activity Amitabha was assisted by two great powers, the *bodhisattva* Avalokitesvara (Kuan-yin), known as the Goddess of Mercy, and Mahasthama (Ta-shih-chin) who represented Amitabha's omnipotence and wisdom. Kuan-yin was initially the Indian Avalokitesvara, who was male in India and became female in China sometime after the T'ang dynasty (see figure 8:1).

Chun-Fang Yu, in her important study of Kuan-yin, argues that the feminine Kuan-yin must be studied in the context of new cults of goddesses of that period.[3] These are the cults of the Queen of Heaven and the Goddess of Azure. These may have been in response to the overwhelmingly masculine character of the three religions. Kuan-yin, the Goddess of Mercy, offered new expressions of religiosity that provided the male children necessary for the continuity of the family. Kuan-yin therefore served Confucian family values and was adopted into every home.

Christian parallels

The parallels with this form of parable and the Christian gospel have led some to propose that they actually emerged from a Christian influence. Reichelt, for example, proposed that Nestorian Christianity, which was introduced into China in 635 AD, could have influenced the sect.[4] The Nestorian missionaries were welcomed and favoured by a tolerant Chinese emperor and his successors, with the result that the Nestorian Church prospered. At its height, the Nestorian Church had hundreds of monasteries, 2,000 religious workers, and tens of thousands of adherents. The Nestorian tablets present Christianity in a way that would have appealed to Chinese Buddhists. For example, Jesus is said to have "taken an oar in the vessel of mercy and ascended to the place of lights above", referring probably to the Ascension, and "those who have souls were then completely saved."[5] Here the figure of speech reflects the Buddhist concept of humans lost in a sea of suffering, with the compassionate Saviour filled with mercy providing a vessel for salvation.

The nature, if any, of the interaction is not clear. The Nestorians could have presented Jesus Christ as a *bodhisattva* who descended from God to save humanity, in order to communicate their message. The appeal of Amidism lies in its simplicity and compassion, and this is reflected in the Christian gospel. After the ninth century, Amidism ceased to have a separate existence as a sect and became a general influence pervading all forms of Buddhism in China, even today.

San Lun

The second school to emerge in China was based on the Indian Madhyamika teaching. It was Kumarajiva (344–413) who first translated two of Nagarjuna's writings and one attributed to Aryadeva and Vasubandhu, which came to form the basis of what became known in China as the San Lun.

Taoist thought had for a long time been concerned with the relation of non-being to being, and of non-activity to activity. This was somewhat parallel to the Buddhist relation of *nirvana* to *samsara*. The teachers of the Madhyamika believed that if one was able to describe the nature of ultimate reality, it could no longer be ultimate. Seng-chao (384–414), who was a close associate with Kumarajiva, sought to combine the Madhyamika philosophy with neo-Taoist thought. The central concept of Madhyamika was, as was shown earlier, that *sunyata* (emptiness) is the nature of all *dharmas* and so they are devoid of reality. Thus, all differentiations are only designations and are empty in nature. The only reality is emptiness itself, which is absolute.

It was under the influence of Chi-tsang (549–623) that the San Lun school was systematised. He developed the doctrine of two levels of truth, following Nagarjuna. On the level of ordinary or relative truth things exist as dependent beings, while on the level of absolute truth all *dharmas* are empty. Although everything and every event may be thought of as possessing a temporary reality, in the final resort there is no unity nor diversity, no permanence nor annihilation. Such a philosophy is nihilistic, and proved to be totally unacceptable to the practical Chinese mind. The school rapidly declined during the persecution of 845 AD, but its teachings have been retained to some degree in the Ch'an school.

Ch'an school

Ch'an Buddhism is undoubtedly one of the most original products of Chinese philosophy working upon the basis of Indian thought and developing it through the traditional ideas of Taoism and Confucianism. It was essentially a revolution in Buddhist philosophy and has been thought of as the fourth recreation of the Buddha's thought, the former three being Abidharama, Mahayana and Tantra. Ch'an was almost contemporary with Tantra and they have much in common. The Chinese character *ch'an* is derived from the Sanskrit word for meditation, and so the school was designated the Meditation school.

Later Ch'an traditions claim that it was founded by the Indian monk Bodhidharma (d. 532). He is said to arrived in south China towards the end of the fifth century and then travelled north to the Shaolin monastery, where he spent nine years in "wall-gazing". This story undoubtedly provides Ch'an with a link to the Indian tradition and to the secret teaching of Sakyamuni Buddha. Bodhidharma was reckoned to be the 28th patriarch from Sakyamuni Buddha and the first of the Ch'an school in China. His arrival stimulated a period of rapid growth. A census in 477, in the north, showed that there were 6,500 temples and 80,000 monks. Some 50 years later, another census showed that there were 30,000 temples and 2 million monks, or 5% of the population.

> This undoubtedly included many people who were trying to avoid taxes and conscription or who sought the protection of the Church for other, nonreligious, reasons, but clearly Buddhism was spreading among the common people north of the Yangtze. In the South, it was mainly largely confined to the educated elite until well into the sixth century.[6]

Between Bodhidharma and Hui-neng are four other "patriarchs" who taught a form of Buddhism strongly influenced by Taoism. Hui-neng is credited with the production of the famous *Platform Sutra* of Hui-neng (Liu-tsu-t'an Ching), which became a basic text of Ch'an Buddhism. The key issue of discussion is whether enlightenment is gradual or sudden, and whether learning or practical realisation is more important.

Organisationally, Ch'an only became an independent school during the time of Pochang Hui-hai (720–814). Until this time most Ch'an monks lived in monasteries of the Lu-tsung under the regulations of the *Vinaya*. Pochang made a new set of rules for Ch'an monks, which tried to revive the simplicity of living conditions and combine the teaching of the *Vinaya* with Confucian rules of etiquette. The monks went on their begging round each morning but then they were expected to work. This is a totally new innovation within the life of the *Sangha* but it answered one of the problems that Buddhism had in addressing the Chinese way of life. This resulted in a rapid period of growth during the T'ang dynasty and there was a second period of growth during the Sung period.

The chief tenet of Ch'an is that Buddhahood is achieved through instantaneous enlightenment. The Chinese are a practical people and were not so much interested in theories as practical achievement. Followers of Ch'an worked for enlightenment in this very life and denounced the misuse of piety as an end in itself. In particular, they set themselves against the excessive worship paid to the scriptural tradition and insisted that salvation could not be found by the study of books. This did not mean that they did not study any books. Their writings are full of quotations from the *sutras*, but these were always considered secondary to the practice of meditation and spiritual realisation. In protest against the excesses of devotion, a famous Ch'an master in the eighth century burned a statue of the Buddha when he was cold. Similarly, to correct the contemporary misunderstanding of the role of the Buddha, another Ch'an master coldly stated, "If you meet the Buddha, you ought to kill him if he gets in your way." Ch'an was intent on restoring Buddhism as a spiritual philosophy rather than devotion as within the Pure Land school. For Ch'an, enlightenment was the direct experience of realising the mind-essence in its fullest.

Ch'an claimed that within their ranks numerous people attained "enlightenment" all the time. It is important to note that they did not use the traditional term *p'u-t'i*, which corresponded to the word *bodhi*, but a new word *wu*, meaning "awareness". A new ideal figure then emerged, following the *arhat* in Theravada, *bodhisattvas* in Mahayana, *siddhas* (*lamas*) in Tantrayana. There were now the Ch'an *roshis*.

According to Ch'an, the highest principle is inexpressible, but this school was not content to leave it that way. Ch'an tries to make the insight into a concrete experience by methods of *koan*, "stating it through non-statements". For example:

> In the square pool there is a turtle-nosed serpent.
> Ridiculous indeed, when you come to think of it!
> Who pulled out the serpent's head?

The *koan* is an enigmatic phrase insoluble by the intellect; it is meant to baffle the intellect until it is realised that the intellect is only a matter of thinking *about*. Similarly, the *koan* exhausts the emotions until it is realised that emotion is merely feeling *about*. It is when the disciple is brought to this intellectual and emotional impasse that the experience becomes imminent.

Soon after the death of Hui-neng, the meditation hall came to be used in Ch'an monasteries, and lay persons learned the practice in their own homes. During the T'ang dynasty the Ch'an monasteries attained greater wealth and influence than at any time in the history of Buddhism in China. However, the great monasteries were economically unproductive and this eventually led to the great persecution of 845 when the government confiscated the property of the monasteries and forced the monks and nuns to return to secular work. Ch'an, however, was to have a great influence upon Japan as Zen, which has provided many of the basic elements of the culture of that country.

T'ien T'ai

T'ien T'ai is so called because the founder, Chih-k'ai (538–597) lived and taught in the T'ien T'ai mountains. It is also known as the Lotus school because of its use of the *Lotus Sutra*. It was an attempt to bring order to a mass of contradictory ideas and an attempt at harmonisation. T'ien T'ai has for this reason been regarded as a "watershed" in Chinese philosophy, because all subsequent developments in Buddhism defined their position in its regard.[7]

T'ien T'ai taught that when the Buddha became enlightened he preached the doctrine of the *Hua Yen Sutra* (*Buddhavatamasaka-mahavaipulya sutra*), in which he presented his teaching fully and exactly. However, his disciples were unable to grasp the profound teaching, and so the Buddha preached to them the Theravada scriptures. The disciples then followed these more elementary teachings until they were led to the basic concepts of the Mahayana, and then to the more advanced concepts of *sunyata*. Finally, in old age, the Buddha revealed to a few of his closest followers the doctrines of the *Lotus Sutra*. The result was that an attitude of tolerance pervaded the whole of Chinese Buddhism, because no interpretation of the Buddha's teaching was outside the scheme.

Chih-k'ai also incorporated the ideas of Nagarjuna, as had other Chinese philosophers, using the translation of Kumarajiva. Chih-k'ai taught the mutual identification of the whole and the parts as being identical. Thus, all the Buddhas were present in a grain of sand, and the "absolute mind" embraced the universe in its entirety. The eternal Buddha is represented in innumerable forms working out his purposes, which include the salvation of all suffering beings. T'ien T'ai died out in China after the persecutions of 845, but did spread into Japan.

Hua-yen-tsung

Hua-yen-tsung means literally "wreath" or "garland". This was a link between Yogacara and Tantra, and was one of the most syncretistic expressions of Chinese Buddhism. This sect appealed to the intellect, basing its principal teachings on the *Avatamasaka Sutra* (*Hua Yen*). Tu-shun (557–640) is reputed to be the first master, followed by Chih-yen (602–668) and Fa-tsang (643–712). Like some other schools, it assumes that all beings possess the Buddha nature, and that the universe is present in all beings and all things. Each particle of dust contains all the Buddha lands, and each thought reflects on all that ever was. Unlike Tantra, the school did not seek to use magic to manipulate and control cosmic forces.

Hua-yen-tsung gained popularity among both the uneducated and upper classes. One notable follower was Empress Wu (625–705). Like other schools, it disappeared as a separate school as a result of the persecution of 845.

Wei Shih (Fa Hsiang)

Wei Shih was based on the writings of Asanga and Vasubandhu of the fourth century, who taught Yogacara philosophy. The external world is only a fabrication of human consciousness, the mind consisting of eight consciousnesses – the five senses, the sense centre, a thought centre (*manas*), and a store consciousness (*alaya*). The latter stores and co-ordinates all the ideas reflected in the mind and is the source from which arise all the phenomena of the universe. The *manas* is the connecting link among the six senses of consciousness and is capable of enlightenment. The aim of Buddhist discipline is, therefore, to get *manas* to function so as to feed only good seeds into the storehouse consciousness. This is achieved through the attainment of wisdom, and of truth beyond all duality.

Lu

The Lu, or school of Discipline, was derived mainly from the Theravada tradition, laying great emphasis upon discipline. Its founder was Tao-hsuan (595–667) who used the *Sutra of Brahma's Net* (*Fan Wang Ching*), which contained the rules for the organisation of the life of the *Sangha*. Its high standards for ordination, and the devotion of the monks, provided an example to other schools; it has maintained an influence until the present day.

Mi Tsung

Early in the eighth century, three Buddhist missionaries arrived in China from India, bringing with them the esoteric teachings of Tantric Buddhism. Subhakarasimha (Shan-wu-wei) (637–735) transcribed the scriptures into Chinese. These missionaries taught that although people are sunk in ignorance, they have the Buddha nature within them. The Buddha nature could only be realised, and full salvation attained, by putting into practice certain esoteric teachings that borrowed heavily from Hindu mythology. The cosmos was conceived as a great being, the gods and goddesses being symbols of its function, energy and will. Magic formulae were used to invoke the gods, with the use of *mantras* (mystic sounds), *mundras* (signs), and *mandalas* (diagrams). The mixture of magic and promise of Buddhanature caused it to have great popular appeal. It became known as the school of Mysteries (*Mi Tsung*), as well as the school of the Mantras.

The form of Tantra taught by Amoghavajra was that of the "right hand", derived from the *Mahavaiocana Sutra* (*P'i-lu-chenua Ching*). Ultimate reality was represented as a body divided into two complementary elements, one active and one passive. The parallels with the Taoist concept of *yin* and *yang* were immediately obvious to the Chinese.

Mi Tsung entered China about the same time as Nestorian

Christianity. Reichelt suggested that Amoghavajra introduced masses for the dead into Chinese Buddhism, following the pattern of the Nestorian mass. This became the "Feast of Wandering Spirits", which is one of the most popular Chinese festivals.

*   *   *

The many schools of Chinese Buddhism illustrate the religious creativity that Indian Buddhism caused within China. As was mentioned in the previous chapter, it was the cultural modification and adoption of Indian Buddhism that made it acceptable to the Chinese. During the following centuries, most of the schools disappeared; only Ch'an and Pure Land continued as important elements of Chinese religious life. These two schools were the ones that had been the most radical in their contextualisation of Indian Buddhism, and had made Buddhism uniquely Chinese.

Although these schools have been of significance in the long history of China, it is necessary to realise that much of the actual teaching has been limited to the elite. Most ordinary people have been influenced more by the popular religious movements drawing upon Buddhist ideas and, especially, showing devotion to Amitabha and Maitreya, who will come at the end of the age. These millennial movements have continually arisen in times of difficulty, with leaders proclaiming themselves as the promised Maitreya. Continual oppression of these cults by the Chinese authorities has meant that little written information is available, but recent evidence shows that they have continued until the present day. Estimates state that out of a total population of 1.3 billion in 2000 AD, some 100 million show affiliation to Buddhism.[8]

Suggestions for interfaith discussions

How does the person of Jesus Christ compare with that of Maitreya?

Webwise 11 – Chinese Expressions of Buddhism

Shaolin Monastery

http://www.qigong.ru/Gallery/comments.e/Shaolin.Monastery.html

Hui-neng (638–713 AD), the sixth patriarch of the Chinese Buddhist Ch'an sect, started the tradition of inviting Confucian scholars and Taoists to congregations of Ch'an followers, with the aim of converting them to become Ch'an Buddhists. The monastery is generally acclaimed as a "dominion of Ch'an study and *kung fu* practice". The site contains many photographs of the monastery and local area.

Kuan-yin: goddess of compassion

http://community-2.webtv.net/Ace-Detective/KuanYin

This web page has links to several others relating to Kuan-yin. Notice the number of sites offering images of the goddess.

Notes

1. Weinstein, S., *Buddhism under the T'ang* (Cambridge: CUP, 1987), p. 72.
2. Smith, H., translation of "Awakening of Faith" quoted in *Chinese Religions* (London: Weidenfeld & Nicolson, 1968), p. 127.
3. Yu, C.-F., *Kuan-yin: The Chinese Transformation of Avalokitesvara* (New York: Columbia University Press, 2002).
4. Reichelt, K. L., *Truth and Tradition in Chinese Buddhism* (Shanghai, 1927), p. 132.
5. Covell, R., "Buddhism and the gospel among the peoples of China", *International Journal of Frontier Missions*, Vol. 10, [3] (1993), p. 132.
6. Pine, R., *The Zen Teaching of Bodhidharma* (New York: North Point Press, 1997).
7. Swanson, P. L., *Foundations of T'ien-T'ai Philosophy* (Berkeley: Asian Humanities Press, 1989).
8. McDonald, H., "The Zen of communism", *The Age* (21 September 2002).

CHAPTER TWELVE

BUDDHISM IN JAPAN

What you can learn from this chapter

- the history of the spread of Buddhism from China through Korea to Japan
- The adoption of the Pure Land schools in Japan
- The reformulation of Chinese Ch'an into Zen
- The distinctive role of Nichirenshu in Japanese history
- The various Japanese Buddhist festivals

"The *Dharma* shall be spread to the East." (The Buddha)[1]

As Buddhism was transmitted to Japan by the northern route, Japanese Buddhism is usually classified as a branch of the Mahayana tradition rather than Theravada. Nevertheless, Japanese Buddhism can be regarded as a summary of the whole history of Buddhism from its Indian beginnings to its later manifestations. As Buddhism travelled eastwards from India it went through many modifications before it reached the Japanese archipelago at the extreme east of the Asian continent. Buddhism could travel no further until the sea trade routes with Europe and America were opened centuries later. In its original form it was totally alien to the Japanese culture yet, by various transformations, Buddhism became an integral part of the life of Japan. Not only did this apply to the matters of doctrine but also to the nature of the *Sangha* itself. Today, the great majority of monks marry and pass on their temples to their sons.

Korea

Buddhism came to Japan by way of Korea, which it officially entered in 372 AD; by 525 AD it had penetrated the whole country. Buddhism came to Korea both from the northern and southern Chinese empires, apparently as the result of diplomatic relations. At this time Korea was divided into three independent kingdoms. In the northern kingdom of Koguryo, the king immediately patronised the new religion and made it the official religion. The two southern states of Paekche in the south-west and Silla in the southeast were somewhat slower in their adoption of the new religion.

Buddhism came to Korea not merely as a religious movement but as a channel by which the richness of Chinese civilisation could enter the country. The adoption of Buddhism as the official religion implied a willingness to absorb Chinese culture as a whole. The most important contribution to this process was the introduction of Chinese script, which enabled the Koreans to benefit from the great traditions of Chinese classical literature. Between 550 and 664 AD the Korean monarchs built many magnificent temples, statues and other monuments, which encouraged the rapid adoption of Buddhism. In addition, Mahayana Buddhism was merged with the indigenous Korean snake and dragon cults, and this popularised the new religion. The Mahayana belief in dragons as protectors of the *Dharma* allowed the association of the state with the dragon in the role of protector of Buddhism. The *Sangha* and the state therefore came to a symbiotic relationship in which the monks entreated the Buddhas and *bodhisattvas* to protect the state, and the state provided support for the dissemination of the religion through the country.

The peninsula was finally united under the Silla empire in 668 AD; this introduced a period of unprecedented expansion of Buddhism among the Korean people. All the major schools of Chinese Buddhism were introduced into the country, but a small population could not be expected to retain all the philosophical schools. The general trend in Korea was therefore one of incorporating all elements into an accepted Korean form. One of the most important developments was the introduction of Ch'an teaching, known in Korea as Son, in the seventh century. This remained a separate tradition from that of the scholastic movements for some generations until they were united in the eleventh century. With the advent of the Yi dynasty in 1392 the fortunes of Buddhism in Korea began to wane, but by this time Buddhism had been exported to Japan.

Buddhism enters Japan (552–794)

According to Japan's first official chronicle, the *Nihonshoki* (720), Buddhism was introduced to Japan from Korea in 552 AD. The story tells of how during the reign of Emperor Kinmei-Tenno of Japan, King Syong-Myong of the Korean state of Paekche sent a mission to Japan, hoping to gain an alliance with the Japanese against the two other Korean states. Among the gifts to the emperor were a gold-plated bronze image of the Buddha and several volumes of Buddhist *sutras*. In a letter, the Korean emperor spoke of this most excellent of all doctrines and encouraged the acceptance of this teaching.

The Japanese emperor consulted his advisers as to whether they should adopt this new religion, but they were divided in their opinions. The conservative group opposed it, believing that the adoption of a foreign *kami* (god), as they called the Buddha, would bring the anger of the indigenous *kami*. The emperor decided that it would be good for international relations to accept the new religion and entrusted the image to one of these advisers who immediately turned his home into a shrine for the image. Those who feared the anger of the *kami* appeared to be proved right, for no sooner had the house been turned into a shrine for the Buddha than a plague broke out in the country. As the plague got worse, the emperor had the Buddhist image thrown into a canal, and burned down the house.

In the following year, two logs of camphor wood were found floating in the sea, said to have been accompanied by the miraculous singing of Buddhist chants. The emperor therefore had two Buddha images made out of these logs, and there was a greater openness to Buddhist monks. From the sixth to the 17th century Buddhist teaching was acquired directly from China by official envoys and missionaries; as such it came to Japan in close association with other elements of Chinese culture. Generally, one may consider Chinese civilisation the hub of social development in Asia, to which surrounding people such as the Koreans and Japanese were satellite societies. This was mainly due to China's greater population but also to its growing social and technological skills. China therefore served as the source of new information and cultural skills for the surrounding peoples. When the Japanese first came into contact with imperial China, they were a relatively underdeveloped country in the process of developing a new social order by uniting previously autonomous tribes into a centralised state. Buddhism was therefore welcomed as an element of a highly refined culture.

The Japanese were, however, not always open to outside ideas. Their history is marked by a peculiar pattern of alternating periods when contact with the outside world was eagerly sought, and then shunned. These periods of "outward orientation" and "inward orientation" were of decisive importance with regards to the appropriation of foreign ideas. The periods of insulation enabled the Japanese to be selective in their importation and allowed the indigenisation of alien elements without too much social disruption. For example, the sixth and seventh centuries were periods of "outward orientation", followed by many years of isolation, and then by another period of encounter with the outside world in the 16th century. The next period of openness was in the 19th century when Western technology became the major influence.

It was during the period of openness in the sixth century that Buddhism first entered Japan and found converts among those who were more in contact with Chinese society. These people were primarily members of the imperial family and court officials; for this reason this early stage of Japanese Buddhism has been called "aristocratic". Buddhism did slowly have an influence upon the majority of the population, laying the foundation for a popular movement. However, the acceptance of Buddhism was not without obstructions. For one thing, the position of the emperor was based on the Shinto concept of theocracy which united political and religious functions in the one imperial person. If the emperor therefore embraced a new religion this would threaten the very basis of his political power.

It was Prince Shotoku Taishi (574–622) who provided the way for a deeper understanding of the teaching of Buddhism. He wanted not only to establish a centralised bureaucracy under the emperor but also to enrich the life of the nation by officially endorsing Buddhism. For these reasons he sent officials to the Chinese court in 607 AD to bring back information about Chinese institutions and copies of Buddhist *sutras* and their teaching. This contact allowed some important social changes in Japan that were to have repercussions for Buddhism for many centuries. Shotoku has rightly been called "the father of Japanese Buddhism". After the completion of the first permanent capital of Heijokyo (modern Nara), government support of Buddhism reached a climax. In 741 AD Emperor Shomu built a network of state-subsidised temples in each province. He was the first emperor to confess his personal commitment to Buddhism and elevated it almost to the status of a national religion.

Another important aspect of the Nara period was the developed understanding of Buddhist philosophy and the comprehension of the diverse views within Buddhism. There emerged six schools of Buddhist teaching, each representing the study of a particular text of Indian Buddhism, which flourished in the T'ang capital during the eighth century.

Japanese name	Chinese name	Characteristic text
Ritsu	Lu	Chinese *Vinaya* studies based on the work of Tao-hsuan
Jojitsu		Harivarman's *Satyasiddhi* ("Completion of Truth")
Kusha		Based on Vasubandhu's *Abhidharmakosa* (Japanese: *Kusharon,* "Treasury of Higher Law")
Sanron	San Lun	Based on the *Madhyamika Sutra* and the *Dvadasadvara*, both written by Nagarjuna
Hosso	Fa Hsiang	Yogacara tradition introduced into China by the pilgrim monk Hsuan-tsang
Kegon	Hua Yen	Study of the *Avatamsaka Sutra* (Japanese: *Kegnongyo*, "Flower Garland Sutra")

The first three schools shared a Theravada orientation, while the latter were Mahayana, and covered the range of Buddhist teaching known in China by the eighth century. These distinctions lay only in the academic study of Buddhism and had no influence in the daily life of the people. In fact, many monks received instruction in more than one of these schools. Only three of the schools have survived until today: Ritsu, Hosso and Kegon.

Synthesis of the Heian period (795–1185)

The capital of Japan moved from Nara to Heiankyo (modern Kyoto) in 794 and so initiated the Heian period. The centralised bureaucracy realised in the Nara era slowly began to decline and although power continued to reside with the imperial court, it was the feudal aristocrats who were the effective rulers. Buddhist institutions gained some freedom from the state but had to relate to the local lords. In addition, official contact with China came to an end and the flow of religious ideas halted, resulting in Japanese Buddhism entering a period of indigenisation.

Early in the period, two new schools came into being: Tendai, which followed the teachings of Dengyo Daishi (767–822), and Shingon which followed Kukai (774–835). Although they were very different in many respects, they also had some similarities. For example, both Daishi and Kukai wanted to establish new schools of Japanese Buddhism free from the control of the earlier Nara schools. Both scholars went to China to gain an understanding of the latest forms of Buddhist teaching and practice, and both returned to establish a monastery on sacred mountains outside Kyoto. The Tendai and Shingon schools both illustrate the contextualisation of Buddhist philosophy with Japanese culture.

Tendai

The Tendai school was essentially the Japanese form of Chinese T'ien T'ai, discussed in chapter 11. T'ien T'ai attached particular value to the *Lotus Sutra*, and this was used to develop an elaborate philosophy concerning meditation and the realisation of ultimate truth. Daishi also studied Ch'an and Tantric ritual, which he sought to integrate into a total system. When he returned to Japan he built a major temple north-east of the capital, and for the rest of his life sought to establish the monastery as a distinct school. He was a great favourite with the imperial court, and popular with the ordinary people, who came to regard him as a folk hero.

Shingon

The term *shingon* originates from the Chinese term for *mantra: chen-yen.* A *mantra* is a word that is considered to embody a power that can bring about both spiritual and material results; it was an important aspect of Tantrism, to be discussed in chapter 14. Kukai was converted to Buddhism at the age of 18 and was fortunate to be included as a member of a Japanese mission to China. While in China he devoted himself to the study of Tantric Buddhism, which was then popular in China, and he was considered to have successfully mastered the teaching. When he returned to Japan he established a monastery on Mount Toji near Kyoto to propagate his teaching.

Kukai was a versatile scholar and his most important work on Tantric Buddhism was the "Treatise on the Ten Stages of Spiritual Development" (*Jujushinron*). According to this tradition, ultimate truth is symbolically present in all phenomena, and especially in the three forms of existence: *mantras* (sounds), *mandalas* (diagrams), and *mudras* (ritual gestures). Due to this emphasis upon symbolism, this form of Buddhism has continued to exert a major influence on Japanese art.

Tendai and Shingon primarily addressed themselves to the elite and had little popular appeal. For the general population, Buddhism was considered a religion with magical powers. Monasteries, by their presence on mountains, were considered to preserve the area from earthquakes and plagues. Many monks known as *yama-bushi* ("those who sleep on mountains") lived alone or in little groups in the wild mountains and forests, and were perceived as similar to the traditional shaman.

The process of indigenisation resulted in a syncretism of Buddhism with the traditional religion of Shinto. For example, on the practical level, many shrine-temples for Buddhist rituals were built within the precincts of Shinto temples. On the philosophical level, Shinto *kami* were considered as secondary manifestations in

Japan of certain Buddhas and *bodhisattvas*. This syncretism continued until 1868 when the government decreed against the fusion, and sometimes dealt with it violently. However, even today, many Japanese find it difficult to define themselves as either Buddhists or Shintoists.[2]

Kamakura period (1185–1333)

The establishment of the Kamakura shogunate opened a new period in Japanese history when political power passed from the aristocrats living in the capital to the newly emerged military class. This resulted in a second flowering of Buddhism that took place in the twelfth and thirteenth century when three new schools arose from the Tendai tradition: Pure Land, Zen, and Nichirenshu. Pure Land focused on salvation through faith in Amida Buddha, Zen used the way of meditation, and Nichirenshu followed the path of devotion as taught in the *Lotus Sutra*. In contrast to the comprehensive approach of the Tendai and Shingon schools, all these three were selective and sectarian, and consequently liable to conflicts.

As the year 1000 AD approached, it was widely believed in Anglo-Saxon England that the end of the world was coming, and the beginning of the millennium. Similarly, in Buddhist countries, there was a general sense of apocalypse when it was 1,500 years after the time of the Buddha. This expressed itself in the belief in *mappo,* the notion that Buddhism and society as a whole had entered an era of irreversible decline. This seemed to be confirmed after the country had experienced a series of major crises, including war, famine and epidemics. Most Japanese identified the beginning of the *mappo* with the burning of the temple of Chiokokji in 1052. The new schools reflected this eschatological atmosphere and assumed that none of the normal sources of religious inspiration could be relied upon.

Pure Land schools

The first Amida (Sanskrit: *Amitabha*) sect was known as the Yuzu Nembutsu, founded in 1124 by Ryonin. He taught that salvation could be achieved through the constant recitation of the "nem-butsu", that is, the formula *nama amidu butsu*, up to 60,000 times a day. This school is still in existence but it has never been very popular. It was, however, with Honen (1133–1212), the founder of the Jodo sect, that absolute devotion to Amida became the criterion for sectarian affiliation.[3]

Along with many of his contemporaries, Honen had become disillusioned with his early training in the Nara and Tenai schools and had turned to more charismatic teachers holding to the belief in *mappo*. Honen came to realise the impossibility of attaining salvation through the practice of meditation and knowledge, and concluded that one must seek the path to salvation in the Pure Land through the saving grace of Amida. Honen therefore devoted himself exclusively to the recitation of Amida's name. He said that all that mattered was to "repeat the name of Amida with all your heart – whether walking or standing still, whether sitting or lying, never cease to practise it for even a moment."[4] A simple faith in Amida was all that was needed; it would carry the greatest sinner into Amida's Pure Land. Honen, however, encouraged his followers to avoid sin, to observe the monastic regulations, and to respect the Buddhas. His teaching was immediately successful among the aristocracy, the *samurai*, and the general population.

Although the Jodo school continues today, in the fourteenth century the patriarch Ryoyo Shogei made an important interpretation. He stated that rebirth in the Pure Land does not mean that one is transported into another sphere, or heaven, for the Pure Land is everywhere. To go there means essentially a change of mind and condition, not of place.

Another modification of the Pure Land teaching was made by Shinran in the twelfth century. He was a disciple of Honen; he founded the Shin school, a name coming from an abbreviation of Jodo Shinshu, "The True Jodo Sect". He regarded the constant repetition of the *nembutsu* as unnecessary, and asserted that to call on Amida once only, with faith, was sufficient to obtain rebirth in the Pure Land. Faith in Amida was Amida's own free gift. In practice, he taught that an evil person was more likely to get into Amida's heaven than a good person, because an evil person is less likely to trust in his or her own merit.

Shinran's teachings represent a radical departure from early Buddhism. He reduced the "Three Jewels" (The Buddha, the *Dharma*, and the *Sangha*) to the one "jewel" of Amida's original vow. He rejected the accepted methods of spiritual discipline and meditation, and broke with the monastic traditions. In the religious community that gathered around him there was no distinction between monks and laity; Shinran himself married and had children. Shinran tried to break down the barriers between Buddhism and the common people. This led to a multiplication of images of Amida, and it became popular teaching. Although Shinran never formerly established Jodo Shinshu as an independent sect, his daughter began to organise a "True Pure Land" organisation, and as such it became based upon hereditary leadership. The significance of this development will be explored in the chapter on new religious movements in Japan.

Yet another modification was the Amidist sect founded by Ippen in 1276. It was called Ji, or "The Time", to indicate that this was the necessary religion for the degenerate times in which the people were living. Ippen identified a number of Shinto deities with Amida, and dispensed with the *nembutsu* as unnecessary. One had merely to utter the sound of Amida's name to effect salvation.

Zen Buddhism

During the Nara and Heian periods, *zen* (*Ch'an* in Chinese) was a discipline of meditation practised by all schools of Buddhist sects. It was not until the Kamakura period that Zen emerged as a distinct movement when the Lin-chi (Japanese: Rinzai) and Ts'ao-lung (Japanese: Soto) schools were brought from China.

Rinzai Zen was brought to Japan by Eisai (1141–1215). He had been discouraged by the corruption of Buddhism in the late Heian period and was initially interested in the Tendai tradition. He travelled to China in 1168 hoping to study true Tendai but was introduced to the Lin-chi school of Chinese Ch'an. Although the Ch'an monks refused to pay obeisance to the secular authorities, Eisai was more conciliatory; he believed that one of the major tasks of Buddhism was to protect the nation. Eisai's teaching was therefore favoured by the Kamakura regime and won the following of the

Japanese elite. Although the movement did not become widespread, it did make a significant contribution to the cultural life of Japan.

Dogen (1200–1253) was the founder of the Soto school of Zen and was one of the most influential thinkers in the history of Japanese Buddhism.[5] In his childhood Dogen had two painful experiences that were to be decisive for his spiritual journey. At the age of two his father died, and when he was five his mother died. He was left with an indelible impression of the impermanence of all earthly things. As a member of a noble family he could have had a notable career in politics or the military, but chose, when he was twelve years old, to leave the home of his uncle who had fostered him and become a monk. He entered the Tendai monastery on Mount Hiei and began an intense search for enlightenment. He concentrated upon the study of the various *sutras* but finally concluded that mere knowledge was not enough. His search was for the very heart of truth and he left Mount Hiei to look for other masters. He became a disciple of Eisai who had brought Zen to Japan. It was with Eisai that Dogen realised that only practice and experience would bring him the goals to which he aspired; to achieve this he went to China in 1223, and the Ch'an monastery on Mount Tien-ts'ung.

Eventually, Dogen did achieve enlightenment under the guidance of Ju-ching (1163–1228), and this was to have a major effect on the rest of his life. While meditating in Ju-ching's Zen hall in China, a fellow student sitting next to him started to doze. The master struck the young man with the shout, "Body and mind are cast off!"[6] Upon hearing these words, Dogen is said to have awoken to the great enlightenment; throughout the rest of his life he continued to make use of the phrase "casting-off of body and mind". This enigmatic phrase implied that enlightenment comes through not clinging to bodily and mental functions such as sleep.

Dogen gained enlightenment in 1227 through the practice of *zazen,* a meditative practice that entailed sitting without any thought of effort to achieve enlightenment. Dogen's first written work was in the classical Chinese style and has the title, "The Universal Promotion of the Principles of *Zazen*". In the book he gives clear instructions as to the practice. A person should sit on two cushions, placed one on top of the other, in a quiet room, in the full or half lotus position. The left hand is placed on the right with the thumb tips touching. "Thus sit upright in correct bodily posture, neither inclining to the left or to the right, neither leaning forward or backward . . . Cast aside all involvement and cease all affairs. Do not think good or bad. Do not administer pros and cons. Cease all the movements of the conscious mind, the gauging of all thoughts and views. Have no designs on becoming a Buddha."[7] Dogen's *zazen* was not merely a technique; one must devote oneself to the way with conscious resolve and give up all clinging to the self or the body.

Dogen was convinced of the truth of Buddhism and believed that it was applicable to everyone, regardless of sex, race, intelligence or social status. Dogen also rejected the theory of *mappo* and held that the *Dharma* was true for any time. He believed that everyone could attain enlightenment, even in secular life, and expressed this with the dictum that all beings are the Buddha nature. By this he did not mean that all beings *have* the Buddha nature but that everything *is* the Buddha nature. Dogen wrote: "Grass, trees, and lands are mind; thus they are sentient beings. Because they are sentient beings they are Buddha-nature. Sun, moon, and stars are mind; thus they are sentient beings; thus they are Buddha-nature."[8] For Dogen the Buddha nature is not an essence "hidden" in things; rather, the world of phenomena quite literally is the Buddha nature. Beings are already Buddhas. Dogen's enlightenment is seeing perfectly the present moment as a profound unity with the events at hand, and an openness to its wonders and perfection. As Dogen expressed it, "only Buddhas become Buddhas".[9]

After his death, Dogen's school grew into one of the most politically and socially powerful movements in the later periods. Zen quickly spread throughout Japanese society. The Rinzai form was more popular among the *samurai*, and Soto more with the general population. Among the *samurai*, Zen led to the cult of Bushido, the "Way of the Warrior", one of the most surprising manifestations of Buddhism. There is a Japanese saying, "Rinzai for the *shogun*; Soto for the peasant." D. T. Suzuki gives a very convincing account that the appeal of Zen to the Kamakura warrior elite revolved around the overcoming of cowardice, fear and death.[10]

Nichirenshu

Nichiren (1222–1282) was one of the most charismatic personalities in Japanese history. Although much of his teaching is based on Tendai doctrine, he came to believe that the *Lotus Sutra* contained the ultimate and complete teaching of the Buddha. Rather than assume that the transmission of the *Lotus Sutra* was through ecclesiastic office, he considered that it was through "spiritual succession". Thus, he saw himself as the successor to the transmission that began with Sakyamuni.

Nichiren incorporated many of the practices of Pure Land and advocated the chanting of the title of the *Lotus Sutra*. He even promoted the doctrine of universal salvation that included women and evil persons. The Nichirenshu became the most militant group in Japan and became totally exclusive. In 1260 he presented to the government a manuscript entitled *Rissho Ankoku Ron* ("Establishment of the Legitimate Teaching for the Protection of the Country"). The essay was a dialogue set between the Buddha and his guest, in which the disasters that had befallen Japan were attributed to slanders against the *Lotus Sutra* and worship of Amida Buddha. The government took little notice of the text, but it brought the outrage of Jodo believers. Nichiren was fortunate to escape with his life.[11]

Several modern Japanese movements trace their inspiration to Nichiren, including the Soka Gakka that will be discussed in the final chapter dealing with the Buddhist resurgence.

Muromachi period (1333–1573)

During the fourteenth century, regional government became more autonomous and the warriors more influential. At the same time, the peasants became more productive and there emerged a new class of merchants living in towns. The period was characterised not only by social upheavals but by continual feuding between local warrior groups. The unity of the Japanese finally disintegrated in a confusion of peasant uprisings throughout the period 1467–1573. Many of these rebellions were led by local organisations of the Jodo Shinshu school (the Amida True Sect of the Pure

Land), who fought against the local military rulers and sometimes succeeded in setting up their own autonomous authorities.

By the end of the period, all the schools had become active in seeking converts from the peasant classes. As many as a third of the population were itinerant priests. Although many were unorthodox in their teaching, they helped to spread Buddhism among the whole population. Many intriguing Buddhist figures appeared during this chaotic period.

Ikkyu (1394–1481) was a follower of the Rinzai Zen sect and was said to have been the illegitimate son of the emperor Go-Komatsu. For many years he was an itinerant monk, walking from house to house carrying a skeleton on a pole and warning people, "Be on your guard!" In this way he sought to teach the rejection of thoughts that there is a self. Later in his life, he fell in love with a blind woman and wrote poetry speaking of brothels and explicitly describing sexual desire. In 1474, by order of the emperor, he was appointed chief priest of a temple in Kyoto.

Rennyo (1415–1499) was the eighth patriarch of the Jodo Shinsu (True Sect of the Pure Land) and defended his school against the attacks of the Tendai, who had burned down one of the main temples of Jodo Shinsu. Although Rennyo stressed the unlimited power of the Buddha Amida, he taught the importance of the Confucian virtues of harmony and obedience to authority.

The Rinzai branch of Zen was supported by the military government and it gradually gained great wealth. It developed large estates, gained control of some of the commerce with China, and even engaged in lending money. This wealth led to the creation of what is known as the "culture of the five mountains". The five mountains refer to the five main monasteries of the Rinzai school in Kyoto. This resulted in what is often regarded as the high point of Japanese Zen culture. It contributed to all the arts, such as painting, literature, architecture, printing, gardening, and even medicine. The ideal of conduct became *wabi* or *sabi* ("simple elegance"), which considered that actions must be simple and yet have depth. It was in the 16th century that the tea ceremony was systematised by Zen masters.

It was near the end of this period, when social upheaval was at its height, that Francis Xavier arrived in Japan in 1542. Xavier was a member of the Society of Jesus, which was established in 1540 to propagate the faith wherever the Pope should want its members to go. Xavier's missionary activities relied much on Portuguese trade and colonisation but he soon ran into problems with the Portuguese authorities and "fled" to India. Here he was more tolerant of local customs than other missionaries but in Japan he was challenged by the Buddhist monks. He realised that if Christianity was to succeed in Asia, missionaries would have to learn to speak and read the local language, and to adopt much of the Asian culture.

Xavier sought to debate with the Buddhist monks. To do this he took the role of an aristocrat, wearing expensive clothes and gold chains, and had his attendants wait on him on their knees as he spoke to them. As a result of these debates he became convinced of two main issues. First, future missionaries to Japan would have to be scholars, able to unravel sophisticated arguments and explain the Christian message with relevance. Second, he came to believe that the key to the conversion of the Japanese was the conversion of China. This was because a common criticism of his teaching was how it could be true if the Chinese knew nothing about it. Xavier decided to go to China and preach to the emperor. He held the hope that once the "Son of Heaven" was converted, all the Chinese would follow, and soon all of Asia would be converted to Christianity. He did not succeed in penetrating China's self-imposed isolation, and died in 1552.

Edo period (1573–1867)

After more than 100 years of civil war, which involved not only local rulers but also the large Buddhist schools, Oda Nobunaga (1534–1582) began to establish his authority around the region of Kyoto. He began to challenge and break the military power of the various schools. After a siege of ten years, in 1580 he conquered the Honganji temple that was the military stronghold of the Jodo Shinshu school at Osaka. Nobunaga was assassinated and his position was taken by Toyotomi Hideyoshi (1536–1598), who finally succeeded in reuniting the country. It was his successor, Tokugawa Ieyasu (1542–1616), who took the old title of *Shogun*, and established his government around the castle he had built in Edo (modern Tokyo).

The primary aim of the shogunate was to establish stability in the country, and this was only achieved through the use of drastic measures. For almost 250 years Japan was closed to foreigners. The Buddhist monks were placed under strict control by the government, and it was forbidden to form any new sects. New temples could only be built with permission from the government. The rulers considered that neo-Confucianism was better suited to assure civic obedience than Buddhism, and it became the official ideology. The *Shogun* encouraged the Buddhist monks in scholarly pursuits, hoping to divert them from politics. The result was that the Edo period produced many writings from Japanese scholars.

As Zen no longer enjoyed the privilege of the support of the government during the Edo period, it tried to make its teachings more accessible to the ordinary people. Hakuin (1685–1768) is considered to be the restorer of the Rinzai school in this period. He revived the use of the *koan* to help open the mind to enlightenment. He invented new *koans* himself and adapted old ones to the contemporary situation. One of the most famous is: "The sound produced by the clapping of two hands is easy to perceive, but what is the sound produced by one hand clapping?"

Forms of Buddhism unacceptable to the state had to go underground. This happened to branches of both Amidism and Nichiren Buddhism. Clandestine Daimoku was a branch of the Nichiren tradition which maintained that Japan was a Buddhist country and that its real sovereign was Sakyamuni, not the *Shogun*. As would be imagined, they were one of the most oppressed religious communities of the Edo period, together with the Christians.

Buddhism in modern Japan

The modern period of Japanese history is considered to have begun with the Meiji restoration in 1868, which heralded rapid modernisation. In its attempt to mobilise the nation under the authority of the emperor, the Meiji government gave prominence to Shinto as the state religion. Although this officially brought an end to syncretism between Shintoism and Buddhism, a mixture of the two is still found today. Japanese people continue to pay homage at Shinto shrines while being associated with Buddhist temples. However, during the Meiji period, Buddhism lost its privileged status and faced the challenges of both Shintoism and the new ideas from the Christian West. Buddhist monasteries had served as centres of education and social welfare, but these lost place to the new universities and government institutions. New attempts were therefore made at reinterpreting Buddhist teaching to the modern world order. For example, today, most Japanese monks are married rather than being celibate. In addition, new religious movements began to appear at the fringes of society, such as Reiyukai, Rissho Koseikai and Soka Gakkai. These have grown into national movements, as will be described in chapter 17.

With the end of the Second World War in 1945, the emperor renounced his divine status, and Japanese society went through another period of radical social change. Traditional forms of Buddhism have survived mainly by providing services at funerals and special social occasions. Few Japanese regularly attend a temple or indulge in any religious practice. However, in the census of 1999, the Japanese government reported that almost 96 million people designated themselves as Buddhists, with 311,000 clergy and 75,000 shrines and temples. Most of these people would also reckon themselves as adherents of Shinto.

Some of the major festivals in Japan today are *O bon*, *Higan*, *Hanamatsuri* and New Year. *O bon* occurs on 15 July, and combines Buddhism with traditional Japanese respect for the ancestors. The custom is for people to return to their family village and offer fruit and flowers to the departed. This is also a time for dances and various forms of social activity as the extended family comes together.

The two equinoxes, 21 March and 21 September, were traditionally considered times of danger in the Chinese tradition, when the powers of *yin* and *yang* change prominence. In Buddhism these dates are called *Higan* (meaning "the other shore"), and are a time for festivals with the theme of harmony and peace. During this time, people visit temples and family graves.

The birth of Sakyamuni Buddha is celebrated on 8 April and is called *Hanamatsuri* (meaning "flower festival"). Images of the baby Buddha are bathed with perfumed tea, and many flowers are offered because he is said to have been born in a garden. Once again, this is a time for people to enjoy themselves. The remaining festival is New Year's Eve (31 December) when Buddhist temples ring in the New Year with a peal of 108 bells.

Buddhism has been part of Japanese culture since the beginning of the sixth century. Although its religious significance is not as strong as it once was, it is still an important element of Japanese identity.

Suggestions for interfaith discussions

Is Zen merely a technique for spiritual and physical development, which could be used by Christians? Alternatively, is Zen meditation primarily a means of realising one's inherent Buddha nature, and so not relevant for Christians?

Webwise 12 – Buddhism in Japan

Nichiren schools

The Nichiren schools have made vigorous use of the web and provide many interesting sites.

http://www.nichirenshu.org
This is the site of Nichiren Shu and contains the complete English translation of the *Lotus Sutra* translated by Burton Watson.

http://www.nichiren-shu.org
The Nichiren Shu is a Buddhist order founded by the religious prophet and reformer, Nichiren Shonin (1222–1282), who espoused the doctrine that the *Lotus Sutra* represents the embodiment of the genuine teachings of Sakyamuni Buddha, the founder of Buddhism, the Saviour of this world.

http://www.nichiren.org
Nichiren Buddhist *Sangha*, maintained by the San Francisco Bay *Sangha*, has the expressed aim to foster community, dialogue and trust among all Buddhists. It includes a pictorial life of Nichiren.

Shin Buddhism

http://www.akshin.net/temple.htm
The White Lotus Centre for Shin Buddhism, established in
Anchorage in June 1998, is primarily dedicated to the study,
practice and spreading of the teachings of Shinran Shonin
(1173–1262), founder of the Japanese Pure Land school known as
Jodo Shinshu (True Essence of the Pure Land school). Although
mainly Shin Buddhist in focus, the centre is open to Buddhists of
all denominations and persons interested in Buddhism. The site
illustrates the spread of Japanese Buddhism in the West.

Order of Buddhist Contemplatives

http://www.obcon.org
The Order of Buddhist Contemplatives is dedicated to the practice of the Serene Reflection Meditation tradition, known as
Ts'ao-Tung Ch'an in China and Soto Zen in Japan. The order was
incorporated in 1983 by Reverend Master Jiyu-Kennett.

Vista Buddhist Temple

http://www.vbtemple.org/index.html
The Vista Buddhist Temple is located in north San Diego County,
USA, and seeks to meet the religious aspirations of Jodo Shinshu
Buddhist Japanese families. It is one of 60 Jodo Shinshu Temples
in the Buddhist Churches of America, each independently organised, but joined in the pursuit of the Buddha *Dharma*. The site
contains photographs of recent festivals held by the temple.

Notes

1. Letter from Korea to the emperor of Japan dated 538 AD,
   which concludes with these words, alleged to be those of the
   Buddha.
2. Lewis, D., *The Unseen Face of Japan* (Tunbridge Wells: Monarch,
   1993), p. 59.
3. Blum, M. L., *The Origins and Development of Pure Land
   Buddhism* (Oxford: OUP, 2002).

4. Conze, E., *A Short History of Buddhism* (Oxford: Oneworld, 1993), p. 123.
5. Kodera, T. J., *Dogen's Formative Years in China: An Historical Study and Annotated Translation of the* Hokyo-ki (London: Routledge & Kegan Paul, 1980).
6. Kodera, *ibid.*, pp. 58–63.
7. Quoted in Dumoulin, H., *Zen Enlightenment: Origins and Meaning* (New York: Weatherhill, 1979), p. 91.
8. Dogen, Z., *Shobogenzo,* translated by Nishiyama (1983) IV, p. 134.
9. Cook, F. H., *Hua-yen Buddhism* (Pennsylvania: Pennsylvania University Press, 1977), p. 115.
10. Suzuki, D. T., *Zen and Japanese Culture* (Princeton: Princeton University Press, 1959), pp. 64–79.
11. Yampolsky, P. B., *Selected Writings of Nichiren* (New York: Columbia University Press, 1990), pp. 5–10.

CHAPTER THIRTEEN

HISTORY OF THE TIBETAN TRADITION

What you can learn from this chapter

- the origins of Tantric Buddhism
- the way that Buddhism entered Tibet
- the various schools of Tibetan Buddhism
- the major reform that occurred

Mahayana was not the only innovation to arise within Indian Buddhism. During the period from the third to the seventh century a Tantric tradition was to emerge and constitute a new distinctive phase within Buddhism often known as the "third turning of the wheel". The first turning of the wheel of *Dharma* commenced with the Buddha's sermon in Deer Park when he spoke to the five sages. Here the teaching focused upon the Four Noble Truths, which all schools consider to be a great and unique leap forward, like nothing ever before it or since. The Mahayana tradition is regarded as the second turning of the wheel of *Dharma*, said only to be revealed when people were able to comprehend the deeper teaching of the Buddha. The essence of the Mahayana teaching is the non-substantiality of the elements, their non-arising and non-ceasing, and the great teaching about "emptiness" (*sunyata*).

Traditionally, the explanation given for the origin of Tantra was that it was the esoteric teaching of the Buddha himself.

Linguistically, *tantra* is a kind of scripture in which doctrines described as "Tantric" are set out. The Tantric scriptures provide a third level of literature, of which the first is the *Vinaya*, and the second is the texts of the *Abhidharma*. The texts of the Tantric tradition are called *tantra,* in contrast to the *sutra* for non-Tantric Buddhist texts. Both *tantra* and *sutra* have the implication of a "thread", or a "continuous line". In the case of *tantra*, the "thread" can be understood in various ways but usually it is as the lineage of master to disciple.

As with all other forms of Buddhism, Tantra is concerned with the attainment of Buddhahood. Doctrinally, it is set on Mahayana tradition, but its main contribution is in terms of method. Just as the earlier Mahayana did not replace the teachings of ancient Buddhism, so the new school did not displace the Mahayana. The new school developed within the old and was superimposed upon it. The Tantra movement is known as Mantrayana ("Vehicle of the *Mantra*") after the term *mantra*, meaning a word or sound for meditation and devotion.

Indian Tantra

The uncertainty concerning the dates for the original *tantras* has made scholars hesitant in suggesting any explanations for their origin. It is still a debated issue as to whether Tantric Buddhism emerged from its Hindu counterpart or was a separate development. Within Hinduism there were varieties of Tantric cults based around the great deity Shiva and his consort Shakti. The couple are often depicted in sexual union, and sexual symbolism is an important part of Tantra. Many suggest that Buddhist Tantra may have been a minority religion, essentially being an esoteric cult frowned upon by the Buddhist establishment of the time. It eventually gained momentum and became a significant force of innovation and a vehicle for the expression of dissatisfaction with existing religious organisation. Some asserted that the new path was superior to that of Mahayana, in that it led to spontaneous realisation of Buddhahood in this life. The followers of Tantra criticised the established *Sangha* and asserted that their techniques were superior, as they led to spontaneous realisation of Buddhahood.

Tantrayana was a complex and fragmented teaching that was distinguished into three main types: *Vajrayana, Sahajayana,* and *Kalacakra tantra.* Even though this classification is somewhat artificial, it does provide a useful framework to understand the various expressions.

Vajrayana

Vajrayana derives its name from the central symbol of the *vajra,* which means both "diamond" and "cudgel". It is therefore a metaphor for hardness and destructiveness. At one level it represents the inner state of Buddhahood said to be possessed by all beings, as well as the cutting edge of wisdom. The personification of this condition is a deity known as Vajrasattva.

> By *vajra* is meant emptiness;
> *sattva* means pure cognition.
> The identity of these two is known
> as the essence of *Vajrasattva.*[1]

Vajrasattva stands for the non-dual experience that transcends both emptiness and pure mind. The human person and the essence of *vajra* are said to meet in the human body in this life. The most characteristic aspect of this teaching is the extension of this concept to sexual symbolism. The concept of "thought awakened" (*bodhicitta*) is identified as semen, and dormant wisdom with a woman waiting to be inseminated. Wisdom (*prajna*) is therefore perceived as a female deity, and *upaya* ("skilful means") is visualised as her male consort. The perfect union of these two (*prajnopaya-yuganaddha*) is the union of the non-dual. Behind this Buddhist interpretation one can identify a non-Aryan substratum with the emphasis on fertility and the symbolism of the mother goddess.[2]

Gomez writes, "One may also see radical departure from Buddhist monkish prudery as an attempt to shock the establishment out of its self-righteous complacency."[3] In practice, the higher mysteries of *Vajrasattva* were only for those who had mastered the more elementary Mahayana practices. The practice was established in a system of "five steps" by the Tantric Nagarjuna, and was essentially the esoteric teaching of the school. The followers of this school saw Tantra as the culmination of Mahayana, integrated it with earlier teachings, and followed established monastic discipline. These practitioners lived in the same monastery with the non-Tantric Mahayana, took the *bodhisattva* vows, and received monastic ordination.

Sahajayana

These *tantras* were written first in early Bengali, and although their dates are uncertain, most scholars would suggest a time in the eighth or tenth century. The basic doctrine is very similar to that of *Vajrayana*. *Sahaja* is the innate principle of enlightenment and the *bodhicitta* to be realised in the union of wisdom and skilful means.

The main difference between the two types of Tantra is not their doctrine but the lifestyle of their adepts. The *Vajrayana* became integrated into the curriculum of the universities and was controlled by the *Vinaya* as the monasteries used the methods to cultivate spiritual growth. In contrast, *Sahaja* was a radical lifestyle that saw monastic life as an obstacle, not a help, to true realisation. Many of these practitioners adopted the role of wandering saints called *siddhas* ("possessed of *siddhi*"), and abandoned the rules of the *Sangha*. The ideal of the movement was a homeless madman wandering about with his female consort. In his union with his consort he would seek to actualise that which was only symbolic in *Vajrayana*.

Sahaja rejected the notions of masculinity and celibacy as being higher levels of purity, and regarded women and sexuality as equally sacred. This contrasted with the ascetic paradises of the Mahayana tradition where there were no women or sexual intercourse. It therefore challenged the social as well as the religious life of society, by identifying the bliss of enlightenment with the bliss of sexual union.

Kalacakra

The *Kalacakra tantra* is different from the previous texts in that it had a definite political message, which was to encourage united action to stop the Muslim advance in India. The main argument is that all phenomena, including the rituals of Tantra, are contained within the initiate's body, as are all aspects of time. The concept of time is introduced to explain the means by which the symbolism gives a devotee control over the impermanent world. The absolute and relative, *prajna* and *upaya,* are united, as in the previous two forms of Tantra. The *Kalacakra* also introduces the unusual concept of *Adibuddha,* the primordial Buddha from which everything in the universe arises.

Although Tantra rose as an esoteric, intensely private, visionary and iconoclastic movement, it eventually became an institutionalised literary tradition in India. With this transformation, the magical origins of Tantra were partly disguised by the high Tantra liturgy but remained in the use of secret gestures of the Buddhas, and the charts (*mandalas*). Buddhist Tantra flourished for only a few centuries before Buddhism was extinguished in India. The main line of the Tantric tradition spread into central Asia, as far as Mongolia, Siberia, and finally Tibet, from where we have the most information about the Tantric tradition. A separate line of transmission spread to China and Japan but was only a minor aspect of Buddhism in those countries.

Situated mainly on a vast plateau in central Asia, Tibet has captured the imagination of Western explorers as the mystical Shangri-La (see figure 13.1). The land has fertile valleys watered by great rivers and dominated by majestic mountains of compelling beauty. In this awe-inspiring landscape Buddhism has taken on its particular magical character.

Bon Religion

The original inhabitants of Tibet were a nomadic, warlike people following traditional religions. The most important religious practitioner was the shaman, called the Bon-po, who used the recitation of *mantras* to exorcise spirits of sickness. Bon, with the worship of nature spirits and animal sacrifices, continued to remain as part of popular belief even after the introduction of Buddhism. It is at this point that scholars have had a change of view. In the 1950s Hoffmann proposed that in the eleventh century, when the second transmission of Buddhism had triumphed, a new

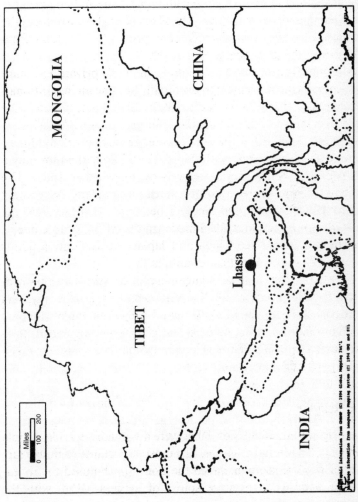

MONGOLIA

CHINA

TIBET

Lhasa

INDIA

Miles
0 100 200

Figure 13.1 Tibet and areas of central Asia influenced by Tibetan Buddhism

expression of Bon emerged to avoid Bon being totally superseded by Buddhism.[4] This new form of Bon copied essential elements of the new religion, such as monastic life, canonical texts, iconography and philosophical speculation. In their hatred of Buddhism they deliberately reversed certain Buddhist customs; for example, the circumambulation of holy objects was performed in a counter-clockwise direction, instead of clockwise.

With the Chinese occupation of Tibet, many monks sought refuge in India and Nepal, bringing with them books that were previously unknown to Western scholars. Snellgrove, in the 1960s, was one of the first Western scholars to seize the opportunity to study these texts of Tibetan Bon-po monks, and advocated a new theory. He claimed that Bon was not a perversion of Buddhism but an eclectic tradition, which accepted some of the traditional beliefs of Bon. Snellgrove's theory can be outlined as follows.

Independently of the official introduction of Buddhism into central Tibet in the eighth century under the patronage of the Tibetan monarchs, Buddhism had penetrated areas in western Tibet which at that time were part of an independent kingdom known as Zhang-zhung. This essentially Tantric form of Buddhism came to be regarded as the native religion of that kingdom, and eventually was known as Bon. Later, Bon was propagated in central Tibet, where it came into conflict with the form of Buddhism that had been imported directly from India. As time progressed, Bon developed a working relationship with the Indian expression, especially the Nyingmapa tradition with which it remains closely connected until the present.[5]

Much work still needs to be done to explain the complex history of Tibet. Even so, the Bon-po do regard themselves as a distinct religion and are considered so by other Tibetan Buddhists. A fundamental difference is the person of the Buddha. Buddhists venerate Sakyamuni Buddha as their primal figure, but in Bon-po the true figure is considered to be Shenrab Miwo who lived long before Sakyamuni. Bon-po also codified its teaching as the "Nine Ways of Bon", which has a goal similar to Buddhist enlightenment. The monks (who are strictly celibate) consider themselves – in the perspective of their own tradition – as "sons of the Buddha".[6]

The First Transmission (c. 640–840)

The introduction of Buddhism into Tibet is usually divided into two distinct stages. The first took place during the era of the so-called "three great religious kings": Songtse Gampo (c. 609–649), Trisong Detsen (704–797), and Ralpachen (805–838). By this time, Buddhism had been flourishing for almost a millennium and had been transmitted throughout south-east Asia and northwards, bypassing Tibet, to China, Korea and Japan. Buddhism in Tibet is called *choas*, meaning "law".

The First Transmission occurred in the seventh century when the diverse clans of the Tibetan highlands were united under a central king and began to harass the western borders of China. When a new young king, Songtse Gampo, came to the throne, the Chinese emperor T'aitsung of the T'ang dynasty was eager to come to gain his favour, so in 641 AD the young king was married to the princess Wench'eng of the Chinese imperial house. Two years previously, Songtse Gampo had married Bhrikuti, a daughter of the king of Nepal. Tradition tells that both these women were ardent Buddhists and influenced the young king, who brought Buddhist teachers, monks and books into Tibet from Nepal and China.

Songtse Gampo became one of the greatest kings of Tibet, introducing literacy and formal education. Legend tells of how he set Buddhism as the state religion of the country, displacing the Bon-po who exerted great influence among the nobility. King Songtse is also credited with sending one of his ministers to India where he developed a system of writing for the Tibetan language. Later, he became regarded as an incarnation of the *bodhisattva* Avalokitesvara ("the Looking-down Lord"); his two consorts known as Tara ("the Saviouress"). The fact that they bore him no children has come to be regarded as evidence of their divine nature. The Chinese princess Wench'eng was deified as the White Tara, while the Nepalese princess was said to be the Green Tara. The significance of these figures will be returned to in the next chapter.

In contrast, Chinese history suggests that King Songtse was for much of his life involved in various wars, doing little to promote

Buddhism beyond building a few temples and translating a few texts into Tibetan. After his death in about 650 AD, Buddhism made little advance against the prevailing Bon beliefs for at least a century. Then, one of his descendants, Tsong Detsen inherited the throne when he was only thirteen years old. Early in his reign, King Tsong Detsen invited an Indian master, Shantarakshita, to Tibet, and he advised him to invite his brother-in-law, Guru Padma-sambhava, a popular leader of the Tantric Yogacara school. The guru promptly responded to the invitation and returned with the messengers in 747 AD. According to legend, on arriving in Tibet he quickly vanquished all the chief devils in the land, sparing them only if they consented to become defenders of Buddhism. In return he guaranteed that they would be duly worshipped and fed, and as a result, some of the pre-Lamaist demons are recognised in the Tibetan pantheon as "*dharma* protectors".[7] In Tibet these deities are generally regarded as "of this world", and able to grant only worldly blessings, as opposed to the great *bodhisattvas* who are "beyond this world".

Under the patronage of King Detsen, Padma-sambhava built the first Tibetan monastery at Samye in 749 AD and instituted the first monastic order, using the Tibetan word *la-ma* meaning "superior one". The term was restricted to the head of the monastery and today applies strictly to the highest monks of the order. The first *lama* is said to be Pal-bans, who succeeded the Indian Shantarakshita. Thereafter, the first Tibetans, traditionally referred to as the "seven elected ones", received ordination as Buddhist monks.

During King Detsen's reign, an important debate took place under the patronage of the king, between the Chinese Mahayana school and the more conservative Indian Mahayana expression. The Chinese monks appear to have been members of the so-called Meditation school, associated with Ch'an (or Zen in Japan). In contrast, the Indian monks advocated the view that final liberation only came about through the continual practice of the *bodhisattva* perfections over countless lives. According to the Tibetan accounts, the debate lasted two years. The verdict finally went in favour of the Indian party, and the Chinese monks were banished from Tibet. From then on, Tibet took its Buddhism exclusively from India, and there was a continual flow of ideas and literature between the Indian and Tibetan Buddhists.

Repression of the *Dharma* (838–c. 1000)

Ralpachen was the last of the pious kings but he was not a strong ruler. He was eventually killed in a court intrigue and his brother Langdarma ascended the throne. Langdarma instigated a vicious repression of the *Dharma* and effectively terminated its first transmission. He did not reign long and was soon killed by a vengeful Buddhist monk who disguised himself as a devil-dancer and shot the king at close quarters.[8]

Centralised power disintegrated and Tibet was once more divided into warring communities. Little is known of this period. The controlling influence of the Buddhists was completely lost and the country went through 150 years of confusion. The *Sangha* did not entirely die out; a few monks continued to exist among isolated communities.

The Second Transmission (c. 1000–1959)

According to tradition, it was in the remote areas of western Tibet that the "Second Transmission of the Doctrine" got under way. Here emerged prosperous, independent kingdoms which received a fresh influx of teachers from India. Among these was Richen Zangpo (958–1055), a great Tibetan translator, and the Indian master Atisha (982–1054) who was persuaded to bring the *Dharma* to the kingdom. Tradition tells of Atisha being heaped with gold by a grateful people. In the east of Tibet, a Nepalese master named Smrt introduced Tantric practices.

New schools of Buddhism developed with their own particular style and teaching. Once again, Tibetan Buddhism was influenced by India but with the Muslim advance into India, Buddhism came to an end in that country – the doorways to Tibet were closed. As Snellgrove writes, "Tibet became a time capsule in which the Mahayana Buddhism of medieval India was reverently preserved by diligent guardians."[9]

Kadam school

Kadam was founded in the eleventh century by the Indian scholar Atisha and his Tibetan disciple Dromton (1005–1064). This school is particularly known for its great emphasis on the practical application of the ideals of a *bodhisattva* within the practitioner's daily life. The word *kadam* means "bound by command", which highlights the laws of abstinence from marriage, intoxicants, travel and possession of money. It accepts "four deities" (Sakyamuni, Avalokitesvara, Tara and Acaia) and "three texts" (the *Tipitaka*).

The Kadam school later evolved into three subdivisions, Lamrimpa, Shungpawa, and Mengapa, each founded by one of the three Kadam brothers, whose names were Potowa, Chekawa, and Phuljungwa. Although there is no existing school of Tibetan Buddhism now explicitly known as Kadam, the teachings in this school are highly respected by all the four major traditions and, in particular, by the Gelug school.

Kagyu ("oral lineage")

The Kagyu tradition also began in the eleventh century; it traces its lineage back to the Indian master Mahasiddha Tilopa (988–1069). He was the teacher of Nalopa (1016–1100), who became the abbot of Nalanda Monastery, the most exalted monastery in India at that time. He was, in turn, the teacher of the first Tibetan exponent of the tradition, Marpa (1012–1097), who had a notable student, Milarepa, (1040–1123) whose biography is one of the best-known pieces of Tibetan literature. The teachings of this school have been transmitted through an unbroken lineage of awakened teachers until the present time.

Although it was particularly known for its great non-monastic teachers, it also developed a monastic tradition beginning with Milarepa's student, Gampopa (1079–1153). The particular feature of the Kagyu lineage is that the teacher, after having mastered the teachings, clears away defects relating to intellectual understanding, meditational experience, and the various levels of realisation. Upon completion of the process, the teacher is able to introduce the text of the *mahamudra* ("great seal") to the disciple.

There are four "great", and eight "lesser", schools in the Kagyu lineage.

Four great Kagyus (directly from Gampopa)

Baram Kagyu	Karma Kagyu	Tsalpa Kagyu	Pagtru Kagyu
founded by Baram Darma Wangchuk	founded by Tusum Khyenpa (1110–1193)	founded by Zhang Yudakpa Tsondu Dakpa (1123–1193)	founded by Phagmo Drupa (1100–1170)

Eight lesser Kagyus (from Phagmodrupa or Pagtru Kagyu)

Drikung Kagyu	Taglung Kagyu	Drukpa (Lingre) Kagyu	Yamsang Kagyu
founded by Jigten Sumgon (1143–1217)	founded by Taglung Thangpa Tashe Pel (1142–1210)	founded by Ling Repa (1128–1189)	founded by Yeshi Senge

Trobu Kagyu	Martsang Kagyu	Yerpa (Yelpa) Kagyu	Shukseb (Shugseb) Kagyu
founded by Rinpoche Gyaltsa	founded by Marpa Rinchen Lodoe	founded by Yelpa Yeshe Tseg	founded by Chokyi Sengey

Today, only the Karma Kagyu, Drikung Kagyu and Taglung Kagyu survive, together with the newer lineage of Shangpa.

Sakya ("grey earth")

Sakya was a third tradition that began in the eleventh century but it was mixed with earlier eighth century teaching. It gained the name "grey earth" because of the colour of the soil on which the monastery was built at Sakya. Khon Lui Wangpo Sungwa became a disciple of Guru Rinpoche in the eighth century. Through the next thirteen generations, the *Dharma* continued to be propagated through the Khon family. In 1073, Sakya Monastery was built by Khon Konchok Gyelpo, who established the Sakya tradition in Tibet. He studied under Drokmi the Translator (992–1072) and became a master of many deep teachings.

Konchok Gyelpo's son, the "Great *Sakyapa*" Gunga Nyingpo (1092–1158), categorised the Sakya teachings. Considered an incarnation of Manjusri, the Buddha of wisdom, he received the teachings directly, some of them when he was still a boy. "Separation from the four attachments" is one of the essential teachings of Buddhism.

Another important Sakya scholar was Gunga Gyeltsen Bel Sangpo (1182–1251). As an infant he would write Sanskrit characters in the dirt and then avoid crawling over them. His contribution to the Sakya school was his ability to understand knowledge of both Buddhist origin and non-Buddhist alike. Widely recognised as a great debater, he answered the challenge to a Vedanta philosopher and succeeded in winning the debate, causing the philosopher to convert to Buddhism.

Tibetan Buddhism has been Tantric from the beginning but the emphasis was made even stronger in the twelfth century, when the masters of Tantric Buddhism fled from India before invading Muslim armies. The Muslims especially attacked the Tantric Buddhists with their many images and icons, and burned down the great centre of Tantric learning at Nalanda. The library was so large that it burned for months. Many refugees took their manuscripts on horseback and fled northward towards Nepal, Bhutan and Tibet. There they established new monastic centres. In the following generations, the Sanskrit manuscripts were translated into Tibetan, Chinese and Nepalese, and the tradition was preserved.

In 1206 AD Tibet was conquered by the great Mongolian emperor Khublai Khan. It is known from the writings of Marco Polo and others that he was a most intelligent man who was wanting to find a religion to weld together the more uncivilised portions of his great empire. Although the Mongols came into contact with Chinese Buddhism as early as the fourth century, it made little impact on them because of the power of their shamans.

Legend tells of how Khublai Khan invited members of several major religions to his court, including Lamaist monks, Muslims, Confucianists and Christians. He is said to have demanded from the Christian missionaries, who had been sent to him by the Pope, the performance of a miracle as a proof to him of the superiority of the Christian religion. If they failed and the *lamas* succeeded in showing him a miracle, then he would adopt Buddhism. In the presence of the missionaries, who were unable to comply with Khublai's demand, the *lamas* caused the emperor's wine cup to rise miraculously to his lips, whereupon the emperor adopted Buddhism; the discomfited missionaries declared that the cup had been lifted by the devil himself, into whose clutches the king had now returned.[10]

Just as Charlemagne recognised the first Christian pope, so Emperor Khublai Khan installed the *lama* of Sakya as head of Lamaist Buddhism, conferring upon him the temporary power as tributary ruler of Tibet. Khublai actively promoted Lamaism and built many monasteries in Mongolia and China. Under the succeeding Mongol emperors, the political supremacy of the Sakya *lamas* was able to suppress rival sects.

The Sakya later divided into two main subsects: Ngorpa and Tsarpa, named after the locations of the monasteries. The Ngorpas are known as scholars, and the Tsarpas for the transmission of the "thirteen golden doctrines". These consist of: cycles of the three dakinis (angels), Naro, Metri and Indra; cycles of three lesser red-coloured deities: Garbhasuvarnasutrasi, Hinudevi and Vasudhara; the three deities, Pranasadhana, Simhanada and Sabalagarudo; and teachings relating to Amaravajradevi, Simhavaktra and white Amitayus. The main text for the Sakyas is the *Lamdre*, which is based on the practice of Hevajra Tantra. The present-day Sakya "throne-holder" lives in Rajpur, India.

The Nyingma (*"old-style ones"*)

The term *nyingma* was probably used of the various individuals and groups who remained devoted to the teaching of the First Transmission once the Second Transmission had begun. As the new schools began to organise themselves, the Nyingma began to regard themselves as a distinct order; they built their own monasteries and ordained monks. They also began to codify their teaching, which they claimed had been hidden during the oppression. Nyingma consider their founder to be Padma-sambhava, who was the leading teacher during the First Transmission. Their teaching distinguishes nine *yana* ("vehicles") to enlightenment, the first three being based on the *sutras* and the remaining six on the *tantras*.

Despite attempts to organise the Nyingma, the *lamas* remained individualistic, following various practices. For example, some of these *lamas* would marry, and many supported themselves by exorcism, rainmaking, divination and shamanistic healing. Those *lamas* who gained a reputation gathered a few disciples around themselves, but they were never a match for the new schools that emerged at the time.

Reform – the Gelug (*dGe-lugs-pa*) school

A further development was brought about by Tsongkhapa (also known as Je Rinpoche (1357–1419) who is today identified as a manifestation of the *bodhisattva* of wisdom, Manjusri. He is said to have come from the region of the great Kokonor lake in north-east Tibet. After travelling and studying widely, he established his first monastery in 1409 in the hills east of Lhasa. He founded two other great monasteries: in Drepung 1416 and in Sera in 1419. Because of their scholarly orientation and their division into colleges, these are often described as Buddhist universities.

Although he is characterised as a self-appointed reformer of Tibetan Buddhism, Tsongkhapa did not consciously set out to found a school of his own. He was strongly scholastic in orientation, and affirmed the monastic virtues and the need to establish a firm basis in the *sutra* teachings before graduating to the *tantras*. He expounded the path to enlightenment in terms of graduated stages, expounded as the *Lam-rim Chenmo* ("stages of enlightenment").

On his death, his body was embalmed and enshrined in a *stupa* at Ganden which was venerated as a holy place. Stories have come out of Tibet that the *stupa* was recently opened by Chinese soldiers, who were shocked to find the body perfectly preserved, with hair and fingernails still growing.[11] Tsongkhapa is also credited with the initiation of the "Great Prayer" festival (*Monlam Chenmo*) that is held in Lhasa after the New Year festival. The annual festival of *Ngacho Chenmo* commemorates Tsongkhapa's death, and is a time when thousands of butter-lamps are lit.

After his death, Tsongkhapa's disciples developed his ideas into a distinctive school separate from the Kadam to which Tsongkhapa had originally belonged. This school is nicknamed "yellow hats", which distinguishes them from the "red hats" of earlier traditions. From these disciples came the line of the *Dalai Lamas*. The word *Dalai* is of Mongolian origin and means "ocean", implying a vast repository of wisdom. The title of the first *Dalai Lama* was bestowed posthumously upon Gendun-drup (1391–1474), the disciple and nephew of Tsongkhapa.

In the 16th century the dGe-Iugs-pa school came to enjoy the favour of a new generation of Mongol Khans. In 1642, Gusri Khana installed Ngawang Lobsang Gyatso (1617–1682), the fifth *Dalai Lama*, as the ruler of Tibet under overall Mongol protection. The fifth *Dalai Lama* proved to be an effective and tolerant ruler. Although other schools were recognised, they were stripped of their wealth and power. Over the ensuing centuries, the regime of the *Dalai Lamas* consolidated its temporal power over the whole country. Despite popular images of the *Dalai Lama* as a "god-king", Tibetan governments were mostly weak and limited. They had little control over the daily lives of the population, most of whom were either peasant cultivators living in isolated and scattered communities, or nomads. Consequently, Buddhism was also decentralised; it survived by catering to local needs. While the ideology of the religion was towards the achievement of enlightenment and the liberation of *samsara,* the everyday activity of the *lamas* and monks was taken up with the performance of rituals for the practical needs of the lay community. There was a large monastic community, a reasonable estimate being about 10–12% of the male population in the main agricultural areas. There were relatively few *lamas* (a word corresponding to the Sanskrit *guru*) who were teachers and leaders of monastic communities. They were often recognised as reincarnations of past *lamas,* sometimes members of *lama* families, and were expected to be competent in the magical rituals. *Lamas* were not necessarily celibate monks or nuns, although in recent centuries most of them were.

Although Tibetan Buddhism is generally thought of as relating only to the country of Tibet, it did have an influence over a much larger area of central Asia. In particular, the Mongolian people of what is now the People's Republic of China, independent Mongolia, and Russia, were Tibetan Buddhists. This includes the present-day Kalmyk and Buryat population of the former Soviet Union, and also the Turkic population of Tua. Tibetan influence in these regions went back to the initial Tibetan–Mongol contact in the thirteenth century and particularly the missionary activities of the dGe-lugs-pa tradition from the 16th century onwards. Tibetan mainly remained the language of instruction and liturgical practice, although much of the canonical literature was translated into the Mongolian language.[12]

Tibetan Buddhism was also important in Nepal, where the Newer people of the Kathmandu valley were in continual contact with Tibet. The northern fringe of Nepal, including the Sherpa region, is culturally Tibetan, and several of the hill peoples to the south have been partially Tibetanised.[13] Connections over these huge areas of difficult terrain were maintained along the trade routes, which allowed students of Buddhism to travel to the central monasteries from the peripheral regions.

Tibetan Buddhism in recent history

By the later 18th century, the Tibetans were growing suspicious of the rise of colonial power as they saw it in India. The country closed its borders to the rest of the world. Its isolation was penetrated by a British military force that briefly occupied Lhasa in 1904, and in 1910 by a Chinese force. With the onset of the First World War the country was left in isolation within the high mountains and shrouded by the clouds. It was this isolation that undoubtedly generated an air of mystery that has gripped the imagination of Western people ever since.

The thirteenth *Dalai Lama* (1878–1933) continued to rule the country as an independent kingdom and made some attempts to introduce modernisation. He did this by selecting what he considered the useful aspects of Western civilisation. The fourteenth *Dalai Lama* was born in 1935 and was only a teenager when the Chinese Communists entered Tibet in 1951. At first, he attempted to compromise with the invaders and combine political Communism with religious freedom. This proved impossible, so in 1959 he fled to India, where he has remained in exile. With him went some 100,000 Tibetans, including many of the leading scholars.

The Chinese made an artificial division between the Tibet Autonomous Region (TAR) and parts of four Chinese provinces. During much of the following period, Tibetan religious and cultural institutions were actively suppressed, and Tibetan activists imprisoned or killed. However, during the 1980s, the Chinese allowed greater freedom in Tibet, and there was a revival of Tibetan religion and culture. The 1.8 million Tibetans in the TAR, and 2.1 million in the Chinese provinces, have little option but to accept the little autonomy they may be granted from the People's Republic of China. The forces for change among the Han Chinese against the strong Communist leadership may eventually cause the fracture of the Chinese state and give some autonomy back to the Tibetans.

The refugees who fled from Chinese domination quickly set about reorganising their religious life along traditional lines. The *Dalai Lama* and the remains of the Lhasa administration eventually settled in the small town of Dharmasala in northern India from where the Indian government gave them considerable scope to organise refugee affairs. They established an autonomous school system within which Tibetan language and aspects of their culture could survive. Within a few years, many of the major Tibetan monasteries had been recreated in India or Nepal. While they were facing new economic challenges, these monasteries were not short of new recruits as the exile had meant that there were many young children without means of support.

There were several traditionally Tibetan Buddhist areas that were not affected by the Chinese occupation. These were the culturally Tibetan regions of northern India (Ladakh, Spiti, Zanskar), Nepal, Bhutan and Sikkim. Although up to the 1950s these areas were backwaters of Tibetan Buddhism, they became places of refuge for the initial wave of refugees, and sources of support for refugee *lamas*.

This meant that Tibetan Buddhism suddenly had many gifted teachers who took their teaching into the Western world. The mystique of Tibet continued in the Western mind, and Tibetan Buddhism came to be regarded by many as the most spiritual of Buddhist schools.

The importance of Tibetan tradition for our time and for the spiritual development of humanity lies in the fact that Tibet is the last living link that connects us with the civilisations of a distant past.[14]

It is perhaps for this reason that the Tibetan tradition is one of the most fascinating for Western Buddhists.

Suggestions for interfaith discussions

Peace has been a distinctive message of the *Dalai Lama*. Compare the attitude of the *Dalai Lama* to the invasion of his country with that which might be held by many Christians in a similar situation. How do Christians and Buddhists respond to the issue of the "just war"?

Webwise 13 – History of the Tibetan Tradition

Tibetan government in exile

http://www.tibet.com/Buddhism/index.html
This is the site of the Tibetan government in exile, giving the "official" teaching of Tibetan Buddhism.

Karmapa

http://www.karmapa.org
This is the site of the 17th *Karmapa*, Trinlay Thaye Dorje, the spiritual head of the Karma Kagyu tradition of Tibetan Buddhism. The *Karmapa* was the first incarnate *lama* (*tulku*) in Tibet. Since the twelfth century, there was a successive line of incarnations of the *Karmapas*. This line of reincarnation is central to the transmission of the Kagyupa lineage. The present 17th *Karmapa* was born in Tibet in 1983.

Nyingma tradition

http://www.nyingma.org
This site provides a history of Buddhism in Tibet from the Nyingma position, and contains many interesting photographs of their central monastery and images. It is currently working on two major projects to retain Tibetan heritage: restoring ancient texts and recreating the ancient art of making ritual wheels.

Drukpa tradition

http://www.drukpa.org
This site contains some of the lectures and teachings of the twelfth *Gyalwang Drukpa* as well as teaching on the particular spiritual practices of this tradition.

His Holiness Sakya Trizin

http://www.aadz12.ukgateway.net
His Holiness Sakya Trizin is the patriarch of the Sakyapa Tibetan tradition.

Website of the fourteenth Dalai Lama

http://www.dalailama.com
This website is dedicated to creating awareness of the life and work of His Holiness Tenzin Gyatso, the fourteenth *Dalai Lama* of Tibet and has been created under the auspices of the Office of Tibet and the Tibetan government in exile.

Notes

1. *Advayavajra Samgraha*, 24.
2. Burnett, D., *Spirit of Hinduism* (Tunbridge Wells: Monarch, 1992).
3. Gomez, L. O., "Buddhism in India" in Kitagawa, J. M. and Cummings, M. D. (eds.), *Buddhism and Asian History* (New York: MacMillan, 1989), p. 90.
4. Hoffmann, H., *Quellen zur Geschichte der tibetischen Bon-Religion* (1950).
5. Kvaeme, P., "The Bon religion of Tibet: a survey of research", *The Buddhist Forum* Vol. III (1991–1993), pp. 131–141.
6. Bechert, H. and Gombrich, R., *The World of Buddhism* (London: Thames & Hudson, 1993), p. 240.
7. Waddell, A., *Buddhism and Lamaism of Tibet* (Kathmundu: Educational Enterprises, 1985), p. 382.
8. Waddell, *ibid.*, p. 34.
9. Snellgrove, D., *The Nine Ways of Bon* (London, OUP, 1980), p. 200.

10. Waddell, *op. cit.*, p. 37
11. Snellgrove, *op. cit.*, p. 207.
12. Jagchid, S., "The rise and fall of Buddhism in Inner Mongolia", in Narain (ed.), *Studies in History of Buddhism* (Delhi, 1980), pp. 93–109.
13. Ortner, S. B., *High Religion: A Cultural and Political History of Sherpa Buddhism* (Princeton: Princeton University Press, 1989).
14. Govinda Lama Angarika, *Foundations of Tibetan Mysticism* (London: Rider & Company, 1969), p. 13.

CHAPTER FOURTEEN

ENTERING THE MANDALA

What you can learn from this chapter

- the spiritual beings associated with Tibetan Buddhism
- the Tibetan teaching on the existence immediately after death
- the "skilful means" of rituals
- the secret rituals of the advanced masters
- why Buddhism took on its distinctive form in Tibet

Tibetans sometimes argue that their tradition includes all three vehicles: Hinayana (Theravada), Mahayana and Mantrayana. Like other Buddhists they believe in the Four Noble Truths, the three marks of life, *karma* and rebirth. Mahayana is seen by Tibetans as the *bodhisattva* path which develops perfection over many lives, as set out in the Mahayana *sutras* that are studied in Tibet. On the other hand, Mantrayana, the "vehicle of the *mantras*", is seen as the direct route, utilising specific practices as a skilful means, enabling Buddhahood to be reached in years rather than many lives. Tantrism refers to an esoteric Buddhism that derives its name from the Sanskrit word *tantra*. It literally means "hidden groundwork", much like the strands underneath a woven tapestry. Tantra designates a religious observance whose purpose is to carry the human mind from the surface of natural existence to the "hidden groundwork", or essence of reality beyond. This is achieved through a variety of ritual practices, especially Tantric yoga, which believes that passion can be exhausted by passion. The craving for food, drink or sex can be overcome by rising above it while it is being satisfied.

Although Mantrayana is regarded as an immediate way, it is also known as a dangerous path reserved for the experienced practitioner at an advanced level. It therefore requires the guidance of a skilled teacher who will lead the practitioner through the initiations and esoteric teaching. So important is this within the northern tradition that the *lama* is often added as the fourth refuge in the Three Jewels of the earlier traditions:

I take refuge in the Buddha
I take refuge in the *Dharma*
I take refuge in the *Sangha*
I take refuge in the *Lama*

The word *bla-ma* is the Tibetan equivalent of the Sanskrit *guru* and refers to a teacher. It is incorrect to apply the term to any Tibetan monk, as is sometimes done, as it applies only to leading teachers of the northern schools. Tibetan monks also object to the name "Lamaism" being used of their religion because it implies that it is not authentic Buddhism.

There are a number of distinguishing features of Tibetan Buddhism: a great variety of spiritual beings, beliefs about the immediate afterlife, elaborate rituals and secret practices.

Yidam

Tibetan Buddhists believe in many colourful spiritual beings, including celestial *bodhisattvas*, demigods and nature spirits. *Yidam* is a term that can apply to any Buddhist deity but it is usually reserved for deities of highest Tantra. Initiation into this level is considered the most dangerous and serious. Initiation includes making some serious vows, such as a commitment to do visualisation every day for the rest of one's life.

Dharma protectors

The notion of "*Dharma* protector" (Sanskrit: *Dharmapala*; Tibetan: *Chos skyong*) is found in most Buddhist traditions and generally is related to any being or object committed to protecting the *Dharma*. In the Tibetan traditions, charms, images and texts are credited with the power of being *Dharma* protectors. These are thought to ward off a host of potential problems. The beings that carry out the function of *Dharma* protectors are divided into two types: worldly and supramundane.[1] Buddhas are supramundane and can sometimes manifest themselves in whatever form is suitable to inspire other beings. Examples of supramundane *Dharma* protectors are Yarmaraja, Vaisravana, Mahakala and Sri Devi. The last is considered to be the special protectoress of the Gelug school and the *Dalai Lama*. In contrast, the mundane protectors are thought of as deities who have not achieved enlightenment but do have the power to help beings in certain circumstances. Examples of mundane *Dharma* protectors are the twelve long-life goddesses and innumerable local Tibetan deities that were bound by the teacher Padmasambhava in the eight and ninth centuries to protect the *Dharma*. Usually, these manifest themselves in a wrathful form to protect the Dharma, and so their images often show them with fearsome expressions, carrying weapons and slaying demons.

One of the most well-known mundane deities is Dorje Shugden, who is disputably an important protective deity of the Gelug school. Legend has it that he is the spirit of a learned and virtuous Gelug monk, Tulku Drakpa Gyaltsen (1619–1655). He had been one of the candidates for selection as the fifth *Dalai Lama*. Another child was chosen for this position in 1642 but there was continuing rivalry between the two. The story says that one day, Tulka Drakpa Gyaltsen defeated the *Dalai Lama* in debate; shortly afterwards, he was found dead, presumably murdered. Soon afterwards, many catastrophes started occurring in the country, and some mysterious force even overturned the dishes of food that were being served to the *Dalai Lama* for his noon meal. Various *lamas* and magicians were called to exorcise the spirit but all failed. The *Dalai Lama* and the leaders of the Gelug school finally asked the spirit to desist from causing harm and become a protector of the Gelug. The spirit agreed and became one of the chief protectors of the sect. One of Shugden's particular functions has been to protect the Gelug from the influence of the Nyingma school.[2]

The worship of Shugden underwent a revival in the early part of the 20th century. The current *Dalai Lama* himself used to include prayers for Shugden in his nightly rituals for many years. Shugden was said to have possessed a man who became the oracle through whom Shugden could give advice to the *Dalai Lama*. After the Chinese invasion of the country, Shugden is said to have given direction as to how the *Dalai Lama* could flee the country and avoid capture by the Chinese soldiers. However, beginning in 1976, the *Dalai Lama* began to discourage the propitiation of Shugden. This caused great upset among the Gelugpa community, and heated debates occurred. In 1996 the *Dalai Lama* renewed his opposition, saying worship of Shugden was a hindrance to Tibetan Buddhism and the cause of Tibetan freedom. One monk who denounced the *Dalai Lama* was Geshe Kelsang Gyatso who founded the New Kadampa Tradition (NKT) in the UK. During visits of the *Dalai Lama* to Britain, members of the NKT have picketed against him, accusing him of intolerance.

Protectors such as Dorje Shugden exert great power over the minds of Tibetan Buddhists, be they high *lamas*, simple Tibetan peasants or even educated Westerners. Although the formal teaching is that taking refuge in the Buddha, the *Dharma* and the *Sangha* is all that is needed, this is invariably supplemented with initiation into a range of protector gods. Stephen Batchelor writes in one of the leading Buddhist magazines:

> If we strip away the exotic veneer of this Tibetan Buddhist dispute, we are confronted with questions that concern the very nature of the Dharma and its practice. In the West we are fond of portraying Buddhism as a tolerant, rational, non-dogmatic and open-minded tradition. But how much is this the result of liberal Western(ized) intellectuals seeking to construct an image of Buddhism that simply confirms their own prejudice and desires?[3]

Heruka Chakrasamvara

The tradition of meditating on this *yidam* is based on the *Chakrasamvara tantra* that is widely studied by all Tibetan schools. The first to discover this path is considered to be the Indian, Saraha. He was a Brahmin who had become a Buddhist

monk but was not satisfied with his learning. In a market place, he
saw a young low-caste woman making arrows. He became deeply
engrossed in watching her working and finally approached her to
ask her about the arrows. She replied, "My dear young man, the
Buddha's meaning can be known through symbols and actions,
not through words and books." Going totally against social con-
vention, Saraha went to live with her, and received her Tantric
teachings. He is especially known for his songs.

This *yidam* has various names but in Tibetan he is called Khorlo
Demchok. The performance of this Tantra is believed to give rise
to supreme bliss. He is often portrayed as standing on a variegated
lotus, in the centre of which is a disc. On the disc are two figures
being trampled under the feet of the *yidam*. Both figures have four
arms, two of which hold a curved knife and a skull cup, while the
other two are raised in devotion to the great figure above them.
They are considered to represent the Hindu god Shiva and
his consort Uma. This illustrates their symbolic defeat by
Chakrasamvara.

Chakrasamvara is dark-skinned with no less than twelve arms.
The central pair embrace his consort Vajravarahi, locked in a sexual
embrace. She is brilliant red with only two arms. Her right arm is
held aloof with a *vajra,* and her left arm embraces her partner's
neck while holding a skull cup. The copulating figures are encircled
by a wall of flames. In Tantric symbolism, Chakrasamvara and his
consort unite all opposites in their sexual embrace.

Tara

Among the fierce deities with their weapons and sexual embraces,
there is the popular cult of Tara. Many ordinary people put their
trust in the goddess. Beyer, in his classic study of the cult, tells one
of the many folk tales about the goddess.

> There was once a man who was fast asleep, when suddenly he was face
> to face with a host of demons, grasping swords and sticks and coming
> towards him. The man was greatly frightened, and so he called out to
> Tara. From beneath his seat there suddenly arose a great wind, which
> blew and scattered the demon army. Again, there was once a woodcut-
> ter carrying a load of firewood on a mountain; he met with a mother

lion, who seized him in her mouth and carried him into her cave. The woodcutter, terrified, loudly cried out to Tara. Suddenly he saw coming a girl, dressed in leaves, who snatched him from the lion's jaws and set him back on the road.[4]

In order to understand the rituals of the Tara cult it is necessary to study the myth of Tara's origin, which is set in the remote past where there was a worldly realm named "Various Lights". In this realm there appeared a Tathagata named "Sound of Drums", and to him the princess of the moon of wisdom showed great faith and devotion. For 1,000 billion years she did reverence to the Buddha and his retinue of *bodhisattvas*. Finally, although she was a woman, she was enlightened. The monks encouraged her to make an earnest wish for her body to become that of a man. She rejected this because the bondage to maleness and femaleness is emptiness, but she took a vow to serve all beings while still in a woman's body. By the power of her meditation she rescues billions of beings each day and has become famed as Tara, the Saviouress ("one who ferries across").[5]

The name of Tara is clearly associated with one of the consorts of King Songtsen who was attributed to be the first Buddhist monarch of Tibet, as discussed in the previous chapter. However, the gentleness and compassion associated with the goddess Tara makes her popular not only among Tibetan people but also among many Western Tibetan Buddhists.[6] The goddess is usually visualised in one of two forms known as Green Tara, considered to be the quick way to wisdom, and White Tara, seen as cheating death.

Immediate state of death (*Bardo*)

The so-called *Tibetan Book of the Dead* has captured the imagination of many Westerners since it was first published in English in 1927.[7] It is more correctly referred to by its actual title, *The Great Liberation upon Hearing in the Intermediate State* (*bar do thos grol chen mo*), and is traditionally regarded as the work of Padmasambhava, the eighth-century founder of the Nyingma-pa Buddhist order. It was used by Tibetan *lamas* as a book of daily recitation and was read or recited on the occasion of death.

Originally, it served as a guide not only for the dying and dead but also for the living.

Tibetan Buddhism, although not believing in a soul in the sense of the Hindu *atman*, has often tried to identify the nature of continuity between one life and the next. Theravada teaching denies any intermediate state and considers that the last act of consciousness in one's life directly conditions the first act of the next. According to Tibetan teaching, the first experience after death is that of a spirit that remains close to the corpse, not realising that it is dead, and trying to communicate to living relatives.

After a while, the earthly scene fades and one experiences clear white light. This is actually one's own consciousness where it is identical with the emptiness of all things and the *Dharmakaya*. If one can recognise this state and submerge oneself in the white light it is possible to achieve enlightenment and Buddhahood without the need for rebirth. Most people are confused by the pure light, and take on the form of a subtle body that is like a ghost.

The *Dalai Lama* described this state in the following way:

> The intermediate being has all five senses, but also clairvoyance, unobstructiveness and an ability to arrive immediately wherever he or she wants. He or she sees other intermediate beings of his or her own type – hell-beings, hungry ghosts, animal, human, demigods or god – and can be seen by clairvoyants.
>
> If a place of birth appropriate to one's predisposition is not found, a small death occurs after seven days, and one is reborn into another intermediate state. This can occur at most six times, with the result that the longest period spent in the intermediate state is forty-nine days. This means that those beings who, even a year after dying, report that they have not found a birthplace are not in the intermediate state but have taken birth as a spirit.[8]

The person is attracted to the future birthplace, even if it is to be hell. For instance, a butcher might see a sheep in the distance, as in a dream; upon his rushing there to kill it, the apparition would fade, causing him to become angry, whereupon the intermediate state would cease and his new life in a hell begin. Fear of the various hells and spirits is therefore an integral part of the lives of ordinary Tibetan people.

Figure 14.1   Tibetan Wheel of Life, illustrating the chain of dependent origination. Mara, the personification of death, holds the whole in his grasp

One of the most striking representations of these ideas is the so-called "Wheel of Life" (see figure 14.1). The outer ring symbolises the twelve links in the chain of dependent origination.[9] The main part of the circle contains the six spheres of existence – going clockwise from the realm of the gods at the top, of the *asuras* or rebel gods, of animals, of hells, of hungry ghosts, and finally of human beings. The half-circles show those who deteriorate spiritually, even in hell, and those who advance towards *nirvana*. In the centre are the three cardinal faults: passion (the cock), hatred (the snake) and delusion (the pig). Mara, the god of death, holds the whole cycle in his clutch.

The scheme of rebirth applies to all but a few at the peak of the cycle of existence, for whom new life begins immediately upon death, so there is the doctrine of the "incarnate lama" or *tulkus*. Originally, the idea was that a past teacher would be reincarnated as a child, or at least be especially connected with a child. The first *Karmapa Lama* (1110–1193 AD) predicted his own immediate rebirth after death. Eventually, the custom of such "lines" of succession was considered to act as the vehicle for the manifestation of the power of a *bodhisattva* or Buddha. The most famous example is the *Dalai Lama* himself, considered to be a focus for Avalokitesvara, the *bodhisattva* of compassion.

The first *Dalai Lama* was Gedun Drub, who founded the monastery at Tashilhunpo in the fifteenth century. The succession of the *Dalai Lama* is determined by special conditions and astrology. Frequently, the *Dalai Lama* himself, before "retiring to the heavenly fields", a euphemism for death, may give indication of the locality. When a male child is found, certain tests are performed, as described by Antoinette Gordon.

> All the male children who were born at the time of the *Dalai Lama's* death and who possess certain physical characteristics are examined, and circumstances at the time of their birth are investigated. The potential applicant is confronted with various personal belongings, among which are articles which belonged to the late *Dalai Lama.* If he selects and recognises those which belong to him, that is another auspicious sign. When the identity of the newly incarnated *Dalai Lama* is finally determined, the child is brought to Lhasa in state. He lives in the palace under tutelage of the Regent until he becomes of age when he assumes full control.[10]

The case of *Lama* Osel, who is said to have been reincarnated as a Spanish boy in 1985, caught the interest of many Western newspapers. His mother Maria was a disciple of the laughing old monk, who had chosen to make his reappearance in her womb. When the child was brought before the *Dalai Lama* in New Delhi, he arrived howling. His mother said, "he hushed immediately as

we entered the room and squirmed out of my arms . . . and went
to a table where there was a white flower among some gifts . . . The
boy waddled over, picked up the flower and tapped the *Dalai
Lama* merrily on the forehead with it."[11]

Tibetan ritual

Tibetan rituals are varied and complex, and involve much symbolism and ritual. They are claimed to be "skilful means" for aiding
people towards liberation and achieving the potential of
Buddhahood.

The prayer wheel (*manichorkor*) is a distinctive feature of
Tibetan Buddhism. It is not strictly a wheel but a barrel that
revolves around on its axis. It contains written prayers and books
of sacred writings and may be turned by hand, water, wind or even
hot air. Tibetans believe that as they spin these cylinders, several
million petitions are released, gaining merit for the wielder.

Prayer flags are a similar religious symbol; these are seen flying
in abundance from houses and hills. Prayers are inscribed on the
cloth and are believed to ascend to heaven as the flags flutter in the
wind. A popular *mantra* is *om mani padme hum*, generally understood to mean "O, the Jewel in the Lotus: Amen." It probably
relates to an invocation to the popular *bodhisattva* Avalokitesvara,
who is depicted holding a jewel and a lotus.[12]

Chorten is the Tibetan for the Sanskrit word *stupa*, mentioned
in chapter 5. In Tibet these structures symbolise the mind of the
Buddha and often represent the five Buddhas of the four directions by means of eyes painted on their walls. Pilgrimages to these
chorten are still very common, with people coming from vast distances. People often practise *kjangchag,* which mainly involves
prostrating themselves for the entire journey. The person falls
prostrate on the ground with hands outstretched. Then the pilgrim
stands upright, placing his (or her) feet where his hands had
reached. These pilgrimages are popular during the fourth month
of the year (equivalent to May), when the Buddha's birth is celebrated.

The most popular places of pilgrimage in Tibet are the cave-
sites of former great teachers. Many of these mountains were

power sites prior to the entry of Buddhism into the country but have gradually become incorporated into the Buddhist tradition.

In Tibetan Buddhism there is no fixed time for going to the temple, and people do not attend as a congregation. Individuals go whenever they wish. They usually take butter, *tsamba* (sweet cakes) and incense. The butter is melted at the monastery and poured into the burners of the lamps in the temple. The *tsamba* is made into small figures shaped like spires, and these are placed on the altar. Then the incense sticks are lit and placed in the incense urns.

Many elaborate festivals punctuated the Tibetan year. A festival that fascinated many travellers was that in which monks chased away the scapegoat representing the evils of humanity. Helen Sawyer, a missionary with the Christian Missionary Alliance in 1949, described the "festival of the scapegoat".

> The Tibetans in Labrang where we lived had a festival similar to the scapegoat of the Old Testament. A man wearing black and white cloths – one side white and the other black; one side of his face painted white, the other black – spent a whole day on the streets and in the market place where the people met him and gave him gifts of money, in order for him to carry away their sins and evil that might befall them in the future year, etc. At dusk the crowds of people chased him from the town – throwing rocks and stones. He crossed the river and fled to the mountains. Usually he received enough money to live comfortably for the coming year.[13]

Secret rituals

There are also secret rituals known only to advanced practitioners of meditation and only partly described in books. Tantra is divided into four main categories:

1. Action Tantra (*Kriyatantra*, "looking")
2. Performance Tantra (*Caryatantra*, "laughing")
3. Yoga Tantra (*Yogatantra*, "holding hands")
4. Supreme Yoga Tantra (*Anuttarayogatantra*, "sexual union")

According to most commentators, these different categories exist because of the differing spiritual abilities of human beings. Each person must find the way appropriate to them. It could be that there is no suitable Tantric path for them at all, and so the person is advised to follow the *sutra* path. The special feature of Supreme Yoga Tantra that distinguishes it from the others is that through practising it, highly qualified persons can attain Buddhahood in one lifetime. It is usually an experienced *lama* who would give advice on which is the most suitable path for a person. It is repeatedly stressed that the Tantric path is dangerous and that improper dabbling may cause psychic damage. Thus, to prevent people rushing into Tantra, many safeguards have been set up.

The first is the secrecy that traditionally surrounds much of Tantra. The Tantra texts are written in an enigmatic language that renders the contents meaningless to the uninitiated. It is the mature *guru* who will instruct and guide the initiate on his or her journey. Snellgrove writes:

> We must now deal with one injunction which can never be transgressed as it is the basis of all tantric practice, namely that of the absolute necessity of total devotion to one's chosen teacher . . . It is noteworthy that it receives in the *tantras,* especially in those of the Supreme Yoga class, where secrecy is also strictly enjoined, a central importance, which it never had in the early history of Buddhism.[14]

When the candidate is ready, they will begin to observe the appropriate practices, and the person will then be given a suitable *mantra.*

The practice of Tantric visualisation (*sadhana*) is an essential part of ritual. The meditator first goes through a gradual process of purification, before visualising the mandala as the illusory universe. The practitioner must thereafter repeat a series of chants and visualisations, make offerings, repeat the relevant *mantra,* and make appropriate gestures (*mudra*) at intervals. Eventually, the visualisation should become joyfully real, only to dissolve again in emptiness. However, even skilled practitioners speak of the complexity of the task.

Visualisation is a complex procedure. It is an art form whose materials are imagination, thought, feeling, and intuition. It takes years of work on one's mind to become truly proficient at it. However, if we have set up the right conditions for practice as described in this chapter, even rudimentary attempts can catalyse a process of inner transformation. Then, with time and sincere practice, the *sadhanas* will become increasingly satisfying. Eventually, it will be possible to produce a true masterpiece: the sublime harmony of all aspects of one's being.[15]

As Buddhism developed, in the Mahayana and Mantrayana especially, increasing emphasis was placed on *Sambhpoga-kaya* (enjoyment body) rather than *Nirmana-kaya* (transformation body). Modern writers say this is due to the fact that one can visualise the Sakyamuni as being in the world of northern India, but the *Sambhpoga-kaya* allows the wider scope of the Buddha archetype. The *Dharma-kaya* would be so great that one would be exhausted with its infinite dimensions.

In visualising the Buddha, two new Buddhas appear that express two great aspects of enlightenment – wisdom and compassion. With time, two further Buddhas appear: those of generosity and action. These four Buddhas take up their posts at the four cardinal points around the central Buddha. It is these five archetypal Buddhas that one often meets in Mantrayana writings and symbolism. Although they are spoken of as five separate Buddhas, there is considered to be only one Buddha; the four surrounding him emphasise different aspects of the one enlightenment experience.

The four surrounding Buddhas in their turn begin to be encircled by other figures. Each Buddha becomes the head of a "family" of figures, each of whom expresses a further aspect of his quality. These figures are the *bodhisattvas* and Tantric deities, who provide a map to help the practitioner move through the complex universe of Tantric meditation.

The map of the five realms of the five Buddhas is arranged in a *mandala* pattern. Buddhists are quick to note that Carl Jung found *mandalas* when working with his patients. He identified the four main functions of the human personality as thinking, feeling, sensation, and intuition. These four would make two pairs, and in each person one of these four would be the most developed. The other of the pair would then be largely unconscious, and these inferior functions would often manifest in dreams or be projected onto other people.

Pictures of Buddhist *mandalas* are two-dimensional but this is only a plan of what is considered three-dimensional. The *mandala* represents the residence of the Buddha or other figures whose *mandala* it is. A *mandala* is like a map of a stately house and the surrounding gardens. The perimeter wall of the garden is usually a great ring of flames that forms a barrier, preventing anything from passing through without being consumed or transformed. Within the flames is another protective barrier: a great wall surrounded by stylised diamond thunderbolts. This is usually the symbol for energy which cannot be stopped and represents the determination needed to get to the centre of the *mandala*.

A common pattern of a Tibetan *mandala* is shown in figure 14.2. It is composed of:

1. Five Buddhas, with Vairocana (Buddha) at the centre.
2. Four Buddha goddesses at the corners: Locana (Buddha Eye), Mamaki (My Very Own), Pandaravasini (Lady with White Garment), Tara (Saviouress).
3. Sixteen *bodhisattvas*, arranged in groups of four, associated with the four Buddhas of the main directions. These are numbered one to 16 in the outer square.
4. Eight goddesses of offerings: Vajralasya (Love-play), Vajramala (Garland), Vajragiti (Song), Vajranritya (Dance), Vajradhupa (Incense), Vajrapusa (Flower), Vajraloka (Lamp), Vajragandha (Scent). These are positioned at the four corners of the two main squares.
5. Four door-guardians: Vajrankusa (Vajra Hook), Vajrapasa (Noose), Vajrasphota (Fetter), Vajraghanta (Bell).

The adept then summons all the Buddhas and *bodhisattvas* from emptiness into the *mandala*. Buddha is envisaged within the *mandala*. The adept then merges with the Buddha, and the transcendence is actualised in the adept's life beyond meditation in the fulfilment of the *bodhisattva* vows. In identifying oneself

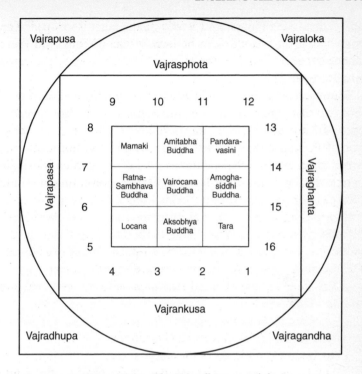

Figure 14.2   The Vajradhatu mandala

with the envisaged Buddha, one may transfer oneself into a Buddha body and leave one's karmic body behind. The continuity of one's own *karma* is therefore cut away. The Tantric way therefore provides a rapid way of release, rather than progress through innumerable lives as in Theravada or Mahayana.

Why Buddhism in Tibet?

In the light of the content of these last two chapters, it is now possible to consider what appear to be two deceptively simple questions, which have been well studied by Geoffrey Samuel in his book *Civilized Shamans*.[16] Why did Buddhism enter into Tibet? Why did it take on this distinctive form? A *lama* would be most likely to answer, "because of the compassionate activity of *Avalokitesvara* (*Chenresig*) and certain other great *bodhisattvas*".

The outstanding thing about Buddhism in Tibet is that it encompasses more of the religious activity of the population than in Thailand or Burma or, for that matter, anywhere else in the Buddhist world.

In the early period of Buddhism in Tibet, there was a process that was also common among many other Asian states from the time of Emperor Asoka onwards. As Samuel writes, "The adoption of Buddhism was at least in part a matter of state policy, and was closely linked to the adoption of other cultural, political, and administrative forms. Buddhist temples and monasteries were part of the panoply of state power."[17] This would have been true of the Tibetan kings of the seventh and eighth centuries. The aim would have been to achieve a fully "clericalised" form of Buddhism, such as largely happened in the Theravada states of south-east Asia. The rulers of the centralised states in all Buddhist countries tended to insist on a well-ordered and celibate *Sangha* for their own protection. They were largely successful in establishing control over the *Sangha* and containing the marginalised shamanistic modes of conduct.

Tibetan rulers and foreign powers tried to do the same, and sought to restrict Tantra and promote the moral teaching of the *Vinaya*. However, the collapse of the Tibetan state in 841 AD demonstrated the fragility of state power within Tibetan society and also the weakness of Buddhism as a branch of state power. Buddhism survived in Tibetan societies and established itself outside the context of state sponsorship, to become part of the life of village communities. There was therefore a lack of centralised state power to enforce the process of clericalisation and reduce the shamanistic aspect of Tibetan Buddhism to the marginal role it had in other societies. Even so, they did aid the growth of the clerical aspect of Buddhism with the formation of monasteries.

The monastic life had its attraction from the point of view of an individual, as it provided an opportunity to withdraw from ordinary life and pursue one's own spiritual path. It also provided the opportunity to acquire an education, and for some to enter a more congenial life than the harsh life of a Tibetan villager or nomad. For his family, the monk could provide valuable connections and reduce pressure on the family's limited resources. Thus, monasteries became an established part of Tibetan life. Samuel writes:

> The folk religion was concerned with power; with defence against the dangerous powers of the physical and social environment, and with the utilisation of the beneficial powers of the Buddhist clergy (primarily the *lamas*) for the good of the community . . . Power here was the power of the personal religious teachers, the *tsawe lama,* and of the Buddhist tantric deities who were accessed through him. Ultimately this power was internalised with the practitioner and became available to help others.[18]

Traditional religion was concerned with the defence against the dangerous powers of the physical and social environment for the good of the community. Within the Buddhist Tantras the power of the Tantric deities became internalised within the practitioner, and was then available to help others. The people therefore respected the celibate Tantric *lamas* who drew together morality, as seen in their celibacy, and power in Tantra. The reincarnate *lama* could be totally selfless, as seen in having no wife or children, and yet he could act with power in the world. He would return in successive rebirths and this implied his inherent selflessness.

Centralised states tend to encourage the clerical form of Buddhism and support it because it legitimises their own existence. There is little reason for people in decentralised societies to adopt such a form, because they are seeking to defend their identity against the domination of state power. Small-scale societies are concerned with local powers, and shamanistic Buddhism is suited to such situations. As Samuel concludes:

> My suggestion is that Tantric Buddhism was adopted by stateless populations throughout the Himalayas and in Tibet in large part because it was believed to provide a superior set of techniques for manipulating these powers.[19]

Although Tibetan Buddhism was based on Indian Buddhist traditions, along with a mixture of Chinese teaching, it became something quite different. The Tibetans achieved a succession of syntheses between Buddhism and local shamanism, each of which provided opportunities to be lived out, and new innovations to be made. Tibetan Buddhism is really a misnomer. It is a complex mixture of ideas and rituals that have been preserved until recently in Tibet, and have manifested themselves in many different ways.

* * *

There is a third context in which Tibetan Buddhism is active today alongside Tibetans under Chinese control and those of the Tibetan diaspora. Many thousands of Westerners have sought the teaching of *lamas,* and by the 1980s there were many temples within the Western world. The effect of this movement upon Western society will be discussed in chapter 16.

Suggestions for interfaith discussions

Earlier, Stephen Batchelor's comment on the dispute between the *Dalai Lama* and the NKT was quoted. "In the West we are fond of portraying Buddhism as a tolerant, rational, non-dogmatic and open-minded tradition. But how much is this the result of liberal Western(ised) intellectuals seeking to construct an image of Buddhism that simply confirms their own prejudice and desires?" Is this a fair comment?

Webwise 14 – Entering the Mandala

Legend of Tara

http://www.holymtn.com/gods/tara.htm
Managed by Holy Mountain Trading Company, this web page gives a brief overview of the story of Tara.

Heruka Chakrasamvara mandala

http://members.tripod.com/~Kalachakra/samvara1.html
This site gives a large picture of the Chakrasamvara mandalas from the *Chakrasamvara Tantra*. This mandala from the Luipa tradition represents a floor plan of the celestial palace of Chakrasamvara. In the centre of the mandala is the figure of Heruka Chakrasamvara with his consort Vajrayogini.

Function of the Dharma *protectors*

http://www.thebuddhistsociety.org.uk/dharma_protectors.htm
This article by Mike Murray on the function of the *Dharma* protectors was published in *The Middle Way* (Volume 76:3, p. 169) in November 2001, and has now been put on the web by publishers.

Position of the Dalai Lama on Dharma *protectors*

http://www.tibet.com/dholgyal/dholgyal3.html
The *Dalai Lama* clarified his position on protectors in the Gelugpa tradition during the Offering to the Spiritual Master at the main temple in Dharamsala to a large gathering of Tibetan and Western disciples in 1986.

Debate concerning Dorja Shugden

http://www.cesnur.org/testi/fr99/gkg.htm
Letter to the editor in response to the article "Cult Mystery" that appeared in *Newsweek International*, 28 April 1997, and in *Newsweek USA*, 5 May 1997. The writer is Geshe Kelsang Gyatso, who is leader of the New Kadampa Tradition.

Transitions to the Otherworld: The Tibetan Book of the Dead

http://www.lib.virginia.edu/speccol/exhibits/dead/otherworld.
html
This site is an exhibition at the University of Virginia library. *The Tibetan Book of the Dead* is traditionally regarded as the work of Padmasambhava, the eighth-century founder of the Nyingma-pa Buddhist order and one of the first to bring Buddhism to Tibet.

Notes

1. Murray, M., "The function of the Dharma protectors", *The Middle Way* 76 (2001) pp. 169–174.
2. Lopez, D. S., "Two sides of the same god", *Tricycle: The Buddhist Review* Spring (1998), pp. 67–69.
3. Batchelor, S., "Letting daylight into magic: the life and time of Dorje Shugden", *Tricycle: The Buddhist Review* Spring (1998), p. 66.

4. Beyer, S., *The Cult of Tara* (Berkeley: University of California, 1978) p. 233.
5. A more detailed account of the story is told by Beyer, *ibid.*, pp. 64–66.
6. Vessantara, *Meeting the Buddhas* (Glasgow: Windhorse, 1993), pp. 171–193.
7. Evens-Wentz, W. Y., *The Tibetan Book of the Dead* (Oxford: OUP, 1960).
8. The fourteenth *Dalai Lama* (1972) quoted in Rinbochay, L. and Hopkins, J., *Death, Intermediate State, and Rebirth* (London: Rider, 1979), p. 10.
9. Goodson, M., "The Wheel of Life" part 3, *The Middle Way* 76 (2002), pp. 225–232.
10. Gordon, A., *Tibetan Religious Art* (New York: Columbia University Press, 1952).
11. McGirk, T., *The Independent,* Saturday 21 January 1989, p. 12.
12. Lopez, D. S., *Prisoners of Shangri-La: Tibetan Buddhism and the West* (Chicago: University of Chicago Press, 1998), pp. 114–134.
13. Quoted by Charis Faith Sy, *A Study of Tibetan Culture and Religion and of Potential Redemptive Analogies which would Heighten the Tibetans' Receptivity to Christianity* (MA Thesis, 1987).
14. Snellgrove, D. *The Nine Ways of Bon* (London: OUP, 1980).
15. Vessantara, *op. cit.*, p. 54.
16. Samuel, G., *Civilized Shamans* (Washington: Smithsonian, 1993).
17. Samuel, *ibid.*, p. 555.
18. Samuel, *ibid.*, p. 556.
19. Samuel, *ibid.*, p. 563.

CHAPTER FIFTEEN

THE CHRISTIAN MISSIONARY IMPACT

What you can learn from this chapter

- The four main waves of Christian mission to the Buddhist world
- The attempts made by Christians to make the gospel relevant to Buddhists
- The problems of translating the gospel into Asian languages

The contact of Christianity with Buddhism has stretched over many centuries and can most simply be considered in four phases. The first was that of the Nestorian Church, the second the Jesuits, the third the Western Protestants, and currently one that can be described as an international mission.

The Nestorians

This Christian church emerged in the Tigris–Euphrates valley in the middle of the second century and gradually founded many bishoprics and great monasteries in the region of modern Persia. The church was not able to win over the local population as it had done in the Roman empire, and its members remained a religious minority. Under the Sassanid rulers ,who in 227 AD succeeded the Parthians, Zoroastrianism was made the state religion; although initially there was no persecution of the Christians, this developed after 300 AD. This pressure from the government produced a small but very committed Christian community, determined to spread its beliefs. The church had an outstanding missionary vision and penetrated Afghanistan, India, Turkestan, Siberia and even as far as China.

In 431 the Christian scholar Nestorius was condemned by the Council of Ephesus on the grounds that he taught a duality in the personhood of Jesus, claiming that he was separately both human and divine. Nestorius and his followers migrated eastward to Persia and infiltrated the existing Christian community; by the end of the fifth century the church was largely Nestorian in its beliefs, hence its name.

The trade routes to the east were open to merchants and missionaries alike, and the first record of Nestorian Christians reaching China was in 578 AD as traders, and as missionaries in 635 AD. Along the trade routes they built cloisters which served as rest centres but which also allowed the copying and distribution of literature, and preaching. Unlike the more wealthy missionaries who were later to come by sea, the Nestorians fitted in well with the local society.

> They travelled on foot wearing sandals, a staff in their hands, and on their backs a basket filled with copies of Scriptures and other religious books. They received gifts – among them some large grants from the rulers of various tribes. They did not keep what they received, except what could be used directly for the extension of their work. They distributed the rest to those who were poorest.[1]

When the Nestorian missionaries arrived in China they were aware that they had arrived in a great civilisation that possessed its own religious tradition. In the seventh century, Buddhism was at its zenith under the T'ang dynasty (589–845), as described in chapter 10.

The Nestorian missionaries headed by Bishop Aloben, were warmly welcomed by the reigning emperor T'ang Tai Zung, who sent his minister of state to the western outposts to meet them. The Chinese empire at this time covered an extensive area, including Manchuria, Mongolia, north Korea, Tibet, and part of central

Asia. This wide area made it easy for visitors to go to China and created within the country a cosmopolitan character to the capital in Ch'an-gan. The emperor was a great patron of learning and welcomed new knowledge, art and literature originating from outside the country. It was this very fact that encouraged the continual flow of Buddhist ideas from India. T'ang Tai Zung encouraged the translation of Nestorian manuscripts in the imperial library. He studied these and gave orders for the propagation of the Nestorian religion, and he himself sponsored the building of a monastery in the capital. This imperial patronage encouraged the spread of Nestorian Christianity and soon, monasteries existed in hundreds of cities. T'ang Tai Zung's son, Gao Zung, was an ardent Buddhist, but he continued to allow the Nestorians to build monasteries and travel widely in the country.

Our knowledge of Nestorian teaching in China is based upon the "Nestorian tablets", and a few manuscripts dating from the eighth century. Emperor T'ang Tai Zung had set, as a first task of the missionaries, the translation of the sacred books they had brought to China. A committee of five translators was responsible for writing the Nestorian tablets, of which one of them appears to have been brought up in China and was known by the Chinese name Jing-Jing. The difficulty of the task facing the translators cannot be overstated. They were new arrivals in the country with little time to adjust to either the language or culture, and were under pressure to produce the translations for the emperor.

The Nestorian tablets show something of how the missionaries sought to relate the Christian message to the Chinese. Martin Palmer, in his recent book, has called these texts *The Jesus Sutras*.[2] They were translated in about 640–660 and sealed in the cave at Dunbuang in about 1005. When the scrolls were rediscovered at the end of the 19th century, they were sold to Japanese and European collectors.

The *Jesus Sutras* illustrate the attempts of the Christian missionaries to answer questions such as the origin of the world.

Every living thing comes from the One Sacred Spirit. Everything originates in the One Sacred Spirit. All that can be seen is created by the One Sacred Spirit. So it is that we know all is created by One Sacred

Spirit. Everything visible and invisible is caused by the One Sacred Spirit. From this we can see that all that exists has its origin quite clearly in the One Sacred Spirit. Because of this Heaven and Earth are stable and nothing changes. Heaven has no need of support to stop it falling down. (*The Sutra of Origins* 1:1–8)[3]

They also seek to tell the basic facts of the life of Christ:

The evil ones brought the Messiah to a place set apart, and after washing his hair led him to the place of execution called Chi-Chu (Golgotha). They hung him high upon a wooden scaffold with two criminals, one on either side of him. He hung there for five hours. That was on the sixth cleansing, vegetation day. Early that morning there was bright sunlight, but as the sun went West, darkness came over the world, the earth quaked, the mountains trembled, the tombs opened and the dead walked. Those who saw this believed that he was who he said he was. How can anyone not believe? Those who take these words to heart are true disciples of the Messiah. As a result . . . [here the text breaks]. (*The Sutra of Jesus Christ*, 5:44–52)[4]

Many phrases are used to describe the work of Jesus, for example, "He laid down the rule of the eight conditions, cleansing from defilement of senses and perfecting truth" and "He rowed the boat of mercy to go up to the palaces of light; those who have souls were then completely saved. His mighty works finished, he ascended at midday to the spiritual spheres."[5] It was Jesus the Messiah who is said to have undone the evil effect of Satan. Jesus is described as "the divided Person of our Three in One". This expression shows the unique doctrine of the Nestorian Church based upon the teachings of Nestorius who said that Jesus was not just one person with two separate natures, but two separate persons.

The Nestorian attempt to communicate the gospel was directed more to the Buddhist way of thought rather than to the Confucian. This was probably because both Buddhism and Christianity were foreign missionary religions, and these religious ideas were most in competition. Buddhism, however, had come onto the scene some 600 years earlier and had met the need lacking in Confucianism, especially in the spiritual dimension. There was therefore no need for a new religion in China in the seventh century.

There has been much discussion concerning the mutual interaction of Nestorian Christianity and Buddhism in China during this period. The Nestorians made strenuous efforts to put the gospel into Chinese thought, but it is questionable whether it reached that stage of syncretism where it lost its distinctiveness from Buddhism. Buddhists fiercely opposed the Christians, and contrasted Buddhism with Christianity as like the Ching and Wei rivers – one of which was very muddy and the other clear. The Nestorians used the same general strategy as did the Buddhists, centring their work about monasteries and supporting themselves by land-holdings.

Not all the subsequent emperors were equally magnanimous. A period of persecution occurred from 695 to 705 under the dowager empress Wu who was a committed Buddhist, but she was forced out and a new emperor restored the T'ang dynasty. Other periods of persecution occurred, but these were interspersed with times of prosperity when the church was able to gain support from the home church in Persia. A common critique of the Nestorians in China was that they depended too much on imperial patronage. When this waned, the church was in a vulnerable position, but the fact that it did continue through times of persecution shows the reality of the commitment of the members. The same can be said of Buddhists, who also suffered during times of persecution.

In 751 Chinese control over most of central Asia was ended with the advance of Arab Muslim armies. Turkic people from the steppes moved into the region. The end of Nestorian Christianity came in 845 with the edict from the emperor that all monks, Buddhist, Taoist and Nestorian, were to "return to the world". By this time the Nestorians had hundreds of monasteries and tens of thousands of followers. Although a small group of believers continued to exist, others seem to have been gradually converted to Islam or become members of a secret society in northern China known as Jin Dan Jiao, the "religion of the golden pill". In 987, Abu'l Faraj, an Arab writer, met a Christian monk in Baghdad and asked him about the state of the Nestorian Church in China. He was told, "Christianity was extinct in China: the native Christians had perished in one way or another; the church which they had used had been destroyed, and there was only one Christian left in the Land."[6]

The Jesuits

Covell graphically describes the dramatic change of approach:

> From long, tattered grey gowns to luxurious dark purple silk robes;
> from clean-shaven faces and close-cropped hair to full beard and long
> hair; from walking to being carried in sedan chairs with several retain-
> ers to bring along their scholarly paraphernalia; from living wherever
> rooms were available in the many temples to having a house of their
> own where visitors would feel welcome to come and admire their many
> volumes of canon law, exquisitely printed and beautifully covered with
> gold ornamentation.[7]

In the early 16th century, a second major approach of
Christianity to Buddhism began. This time it did not come over-
land but by sea around Africa. This symbolised a new era based on
geographical discoveries and economic expansion, and alongside
came new efforts to carry the Christian faith around the world. The
Portuguese were the first Europeans to travel the sea routes to Asia,
spurred on by economic gain.

Ricci and Rugierri were the first Jesuit missionaries who gained
permission to reside in the city of Zhaoqing, a few miles north
of Canton in 1582. The missionaries quickly realised the important role of the scholar within Chinese society and readily adopted
the role for their purposes. They not only adopted the dress of a
scholar but were careful to observe the accepted behaviour when
visiting other scholars. It became evident that they could also con-
tribute European knowledge of science to the benefit of the
Chinese. Ricci taught European scientific theories to interested
Chinese, and the use of simple instruments such as the dial, astro-
labe and quadrant. He was also an excellent cartographer and presented Chinese officials with a map of the world. These were
initially rejected, as he had not portrayed China, the "middle
kingdom", as the centre of the world, nor was it large enough.

In their role of scholars and teachers, the Jesuits were careful to
follow the proper codes of behaviour. They did not refuse to bow
at the proper times, as did many of the later Protestant missionaries of the 19th century. More importantly, they put themselves in

the role of learners, come to study at the source of knowledge, the imperial court. Ricci announced himself in the following terms:

> Li Mao-tou, your Majesty's servant, come from the far west, addresses himself to your Majesty with respect, in order to offer gifts from his country. Your Majesty's servant comes from a far distant land which has never exchanged presents with the middle kingdom. Despite the distance, fame told me of the remarkable teaching and fine instructions with which the imperial court has endowed all its people. I desire to share these advantages and live out my life as one of your Majesty's subjects, hoping in return to be of some small use.[8]

Ricci saw that writing was a better way to penetrate Chinese culture than preaching. As a scholar, he was expected to write, and this he did. He had been asked by the emperor what Europeans thought about friendship, which was regarded by the Chinese as the highest of virtues. Ricci therefore published his first booklet on the subject of friendship, and with it gained both a reputation as a scholar and also gave the Chinese a positive view of European values.

The most important of Ricci's works was *Tianzhu Shiyi* ("The True Idea of God"). This work was prepared as a Christian apologetic for non-Christians, and resulted from nine years of interaction with the Chinese. It was published in 1603 and for the elite of the late Ming period it was the gospel for the contemporary Chinese context. A number of influential scholars did become Christians.

Ricci's approach first made use of the "nature law", which was particularly attractive to Chinese thought. The progression of the argument is as follows. Heaven (or more personally God) is the supreme ruler over the universe, and has given all human beings equally the "law of nature". Therefore in human nature may be found the embryonic virtues of love, justice, propriety and knowledge, which will develop naturally if not hindered by evil external conditions. The norms by which humans seek good and avoid evil are from heaven and are not human inventions. Humans should therefore follow a high moral system because the natural law is part of their very nature. Thus, humans are able to reason from their human nature as to the existence and nature of God, and the kind of moral life that pleases God.

Ricci's second assumption was that contemporary neo-Confucian thought was a perversion of the traditional Confucian legacy that had been accommodated to Buddhism. This was a view that had been proposed by the Confucian scholar Mencius some 400 years earlier. Ricci believed that after the flood in the days of Noah, Jewish missionaries had travelled to China and presented the people with an awareness of a supreme deity. Ricci therefore positioned himself with ancient Confucianism and against Buddhism, Taoism and neo-Confucianism.

Jesuits who followed Ricci could not accept his conclusions about Chinese natural philosophy. For them, the resemblance between Chinese and Christian ideas about the nature of God was purely coincidental. This not only raised the question about the method of mission, but also about the very nature of the gospel. If Ricci was correct, then theological and moral truth could be found in ancient Chinese writings, and the accommodation of the gospel was legitimate. His opponents insisted solely upon the special revelation found in the Christian Bible.

Returning to the *Tianzhu Shiyi,* Ricci, starting from the previous assumption, argues along the following lines. First, human reason, possessed by all persons everywhere, gives the potential for anyone to know God. If this is so, why have so many Chinese not done so? Ricci replies that the fault lies in the way the religions of China have led them astray and have stopped them knowing the true "heavenly Lord". He stresses that the Buddhist doctrine of *sunyata* ("emptiness") is not to be equated with the true God. He argues that just because God does not have a material form, this cannot be used to disprove the existence of God any more than it can be argued that the five moralities do not exist because they have neither form nor sound.

Ricci then goes on to consider the nature of the human soul, which he argues is essentially different from the soul of insects and animals. Like Thomas Aquinas, he describes three classes of soul: the soul of plants that have life and growth; the soul of insects and animals that makes them conscious; and the soul of human beings that allows them also to reason and know truth. He then goes on to give several reasons to show that a person's soul is a spiritual substance, without shape or form, and thus different from the soul of insects and animals. Ricci then continues by presenting several arguments to prove that the human soul will not perish or die. For example, he comments that all persons desire to have a good reputation that will endure after death, and if the soul was to die, then it would not be able to know of the good works left behind.

Ricci also addresses the doctrine of transmigration (*samsara*). He first argues that this did not originate in India with Sakyamuni, but with the ancient Greek philosopher Pythagoras, who speculated that the proper punishment for the wicked was that they would in a future life be changed into a form corresponding to their particular sin. Ricci then gives several arguments against *samsara*. First, in the present life no one remembers a previous existence. Second, it is impossible to interchange the souls of human beings for insects or animals because they are of such markedly different form. Third, what would be the significance of a punishment for the wicked to be changed to animals where in effect they could carry out their wickedness even more easily? Fourth, the implications of the doctrine would make it impossible to carry on necessary human activities such as agriculture, due to the insects and animals that would be killed.

In the next section Ricci is able to ask the question: If the soul is eternal, what happens to it after death? Where is the final resting place? Ricci states that he cannot give a detailed description of either heaven or hell, but that they are everlasting happiness and everlasting misery. The highest good that humans can achieve is to love the heavenly Lord above all else and their neighbours as themselves. Only through trust in God and his gracious provision can help be known for human weakness. Ricci specifically points out that Buddhism and Taoism cannot solve the human problem because of their many errors. In a few short sentences he goes on to explain that God sent Jesus to be the Saviour, and that he was crucified and raised from death. He deliberately does not say too much about this, as these would have been very difficult concepts for the Chinese to have understood, and this was a treatise mainly for non-Christians.

Ricci's text was widely read by Chinese scholars; several

editions were published. The response of the Chinese was, as may be expected, very mixed. Some dismissed the new teaching as false. Others were attracted to the scientific knowledge of the missionaries but felt the religion they taught placed too little emphasis upon traditional Chinese values. There were some who did become Christians, including individuals from the highest sections of Chinese society.

One remarkable mission venture was that of Antonio de Andrada who, after being involved with Jesuit work in India, travelled north into Tibet. After an incredibly difficult journey through the Himalayas he arrived at the capital of the state of Guge in August 1624. The king at that time was surrounded by enemies, particularly his own younger brother and uncle who were influential *lamas*. At first the king thought the visitors were traders, but Andrada explained they had come to tell him about Christianity and to denounce Buddhism. The king was interested and paid for the building of a church. As Tony Lambert points out, Andrada's evangelistic methods were twofold:

1) To win over the ruling-class and preach the faith from the top down. This was a favourite Jesuit strategy, relying on political power to influence the masses.
2) A frontal attack on Tibetan Buddhism to reveal its errors and, by comparison, the truth of Christianity.'[9]

Andrada had amazing success at influencing the king and queen but there were few other converts. During the period 1626–1627 the king decided to reduce the great number of *lamas*, but many of them went underground and began to plot against the king. Soon after Andrada returned to India in 1630, the *lamas* called on the king of the neighbouring kingdom of Ladakh to join them in rebellion against the king. The ailing king was eventually captured and imprisoned. Although some vestiges of Christianity remained for a few more years, the mission to Guge was effectively over.

A major issue that faced the Jesuit missionaries to China was the "rites controversy", which was concerned with the correct name for God in Chinese. In the Chinese classics the terms *tian* and *shangdi* were used, and both can be interpreted in personal or impersonal forms. Most Jesuits recognised the ambiguity but argued that they were terms used by Confucius. In contrast, the Franciscan missionaries, and some Jesuits, were concerned about the danger of compromise with idolatry, and argued for the term *tianzhu* ("heavenly Lord") to signify God. After decades of controversy, it was this term that was finally accepted, following a decision from the Vatican. The argument took on political overtones, with the emperor aligned with the Jesuits against the pope and the Franciscans. Finally, Christians were prohibited in China in 1724, and many priests were deported. The Jesuits were finally disbanded in 1774. Roman Catholics in China may have numbered as many as 300,000, but they had no leadership, and they slowly diminished in number.

The Protestants

As the Jesuit influence was coming to an end, the Protestant era of mission was about to begin. Robert Morrison was the first Protestant missionary to reach China; he settled in Canton in 1807.

Sri Lanka

The British succeeded the Dutch as rulers of the coastal areas of Sri Lanka in 1796, and in 1815 they acquired control of the capital at Kandy and thus political rule of the whole island. It was in this period of advancing colonialism that the Protestant missionaries arrived in Asia. The main missionary organisations to establish themselves in Sri Lanka were the Wesleyans (Methodist Missionary Society) in 1805, and the Anglicans (Church Missionary Society) in 1818. The Protestant strategy was mainly along three lines: by education, preaching and literature. Alongside every mission station there was a school to train teachers and ordinands, which taught English and dedicated the first hour of the day to Christian teaching. Gombrich writes:

> The missionaries were crippled by their inflexibility. They worked hard to learn Sinhala, but then insisted that the Bible be translated into "plain speech", using only one word for "you", the second person

pronoun. The result would be absurd in almost any language but English, and to make matters worse, trying to keep close to the biblical "thou", they chose the pronoun *to*. This was not in ignorance. The chief translator admitted: "To apply *to* to a man of respectable class is an actionable offence . . ."[10]

The Protestant missionaries travelled throughout the country preaching, but they continued to address their audiences using a pronoun which the people regarded as derogatory. They did not take account of the practice of the itinerant Buddhist monks, and often preached at inappropriate times and places. Early missionaries challenged the monks to debate, and were annoyed by the lack of any response.

The great technical innovation of the missionaries was the printing press that was imported by the Methodists in 1815. From the beginning, what was produced was more an attack on Buddhism than an exposition of Christianity. The manager of the Wesleyan Press wrote in 1831, "At present it is by means of the press our main attacks must be made upon this wretched system . . . We must direct our efforts to pull down this stronghold of Satan."[11] In contrast, the Buddhists did not react to the attack and even co-operated with the missionaries. The Methodist missionary Spence Hardy wrote in 1850, "It is almost impossible to move them, even to wrath", but some fifteen years later he was delighted to note that the pernicious vice of tolerance was on the wane.[12]

Some Protestant missionaries did attempt to learn the language and the culture of the people. In 1832 the Methodist missionary Daniel Gogerly started learning Pali, then Sinhala. In 1849 he published *The Evidences and Doctrines of the Christian Religion*. Part 1 of the work compared Buddhism and Christian doctrines, and contained many quotations from the Pali scriptures, appealing to reason rather than just emotions.

The attitude of the Buddhist monks was, however, changing, and in 1862 Guananda (1823–1890), the leading monk in Colombo, founded "The Religious Society for Giving Increase to the Teaching of the Omniscient One".[13] The society took to producing tracts and finally accepted the Christian challenge to public debate. At most of the encounters Guananda took a major part on the Buddhist side. The most important debate in which he took part was held at Panadura, south of Colombo, in 1873. David de Silva, the leader of the Methodist mission of that time, was his principal opponent. The debate lasted two days. On the first day the audience was estimated at 5,000, but on the second day it had increased to 10,000. The Buddhists were fiercely partisan and considered that they had achieved a great victory. The missionaries realised that they had misjudged the situation and issued no further challenge. The whole debate was reported in the national newspaper, and eventually an English edition appeared in book form. It was this book that was to reach Colonel Henry Steel Olcott and was to result in unexpected consequences, as we shall discuss in the next chapter.

The reaction to the Protestant approach was to stimulate many important changes within the *Sangha*. Traditionally, Buddhist monks would preach seated, often holding a fan in front of their faces, in order to render the sermons as impersonal as possible. Guananda, in public debate, adopted the Christian style of preaching. He stood gesticulating, and challenging his evangelical opponents. David de Silva, for example, argued that the Buddhist cosmology of many heavens and hells did not agree with the discoveries of modern science. Guananda responded by asking his opponent to locate the Christian heaven and hell in the universe. This new attitude was not only going to defend traditional Buddhism, but was to revitalise Buddhism in Sri Lanka, as will be discussed in chapter 17.

China

In China the increased openness of the 19th century encouraged a rapid increase in Protestant missionary work. Many new societies entered, but were restricted to the region along the coast. The Protestant missionaries adopted the general patterns of life followed by the rest of the European community living along the coast. It was therefore something of a shock to them when in 1853 a young Englishman called James Hudson Taylor arrived in the country, and after a few years had learned the language and adopted Chinese dress. The Christian historian Stephen Neill writes, "These unconventional proceedings brought them under fierce and almost fanatical opposition of men and women who no less than Taylor were devoted servants of the cause."[14]

In 1860 Hudson Taylor returned to England because of ill health and there began to form an association of like-minded Christians. The China Inland Mission (CIM) was founded in 1865 and was based upon five significant principles. First, the mission was to be interdenominational, and the missionaries would adhere to a simple evangelical statement of doctrine. Second, unlike other missions, the CIM would accept Christians with little formal education. Third, the mission would be directed from China, not England, as were many of the earlier missions. Fourth, the missionaries would wear Chinese dress and, as far as possible, identify themselves with the Chinese people. Finally, the primary aim of the mission was to be widespread evangelism. These principles had far-reaching consequences for the mission and the emerging Chinese Church, in that both would be far more Chinese in character than were the existing missions.

The CIM quickly grew to become the largest mission organisation in China but although they saw many converts their results were not spectacular. Neill comments:

> Numerically, the results of Protestant missions by the end of the nineteenth century were less than impressive. A body of about 1,500 missionaries, including wives, was established in 500 stations, almost all the provinces now having their quota. Around them they had gathered slightly less than half a million adherents, of whom rather more than 80,000 were communicants.

The missionaries were widely regarded as the spearhead of western penetration, and the period 1895–1900 was marked by growing anti-foreign feeling that often resulted in violence. On 24 June 1900 an imperial decree was issued from Peking, ordering the killing of all foreigners. The foreign delegation in the capital was besieged for 55 days, and in many parts of the country foreigners were killed. Many missionaries had to flee to the coast, leaving their converts to the wrath of their countrymen. Many Chinese Christians were killed, or renounced their Christian allegiance.

One interesting attempt to express Protestant Christianity in a Chinese cultural style was that of the Norwegian Lutheran missionary Dr Karl L. Reichelt (1877–1952), who founded the Tao Fong Shan Christian Centre. He used a particular style of Chinese poetry that consists of four lines of four Chinese characters, and expressed Christianity as taking refuge in God the Father, the Son and the Holy Spirit (see figure 15.1).

Reichelt entered into dialogue with the Buddhist monk T'ai-hsu (1890–1949) who had an important impact on the development of Buddhism in 20th century China (see timeline for Buddhism in China, in chapter 10). T'ai-hsu criticised Christian theism and believed that Buddhism could give to Christianity what it desperately needed: a religious spirit that was not in opposition to modern science and that could be a foundation for trust and community. Conversely, China also, according to T'ai-hsu, needed an impulse from Christianity, to the extent that Christianity motivates individuals to bring about harmony and community beyond ethnic boundaries on the basis of the universality of its belief.[15]

T'ai-hsu continually emphasised with great simplicity the differences and similarities between Buddhism and Christianity. He saw these as follows:[16]

Buddhism	Christianity
Similarities	
Ten precepts	Ten commandments
Ten virtues	Eight beatitudes
Ten schools	Ten churches
Mercy	Love
Humans as the children of the Buddha	Rebirth in baptism
Recitation of the Buddha's name	Prayer
Pure Land	Kingdom of God
Bodhisattva vows	The Lord's Prayer
Differences	
Atheism	Theism
Human autonomy	Divine omnipotence
Original enlightenment	Original sin
Causation in mutual dependence	Creation
Analysis of consciousness	Transcendence
Awakening in the Pure Land	The Last Judgement

The main achievement of T'ai-hsu was that he gave many Chinese monks a new confidence in their calling in a rapidly changing world.

至心皈命　Chih hsin kui ming,
無上主宰　Wu shang Chu-tsai
創造諸有　Ch'uang-tsao chu yu,
萬德慈父　Wan te tze Fu!

至心皈命　Chih hsin kui ming,
贖罪基督　Hu tsui Chi-tu
復我性明　Fu wo hsing ming,
圓滿妙道　Yuan man miao Tao!

至心皈命　Chih hsin kui ming,
充滿宇宙　Ch'ung man yu-chou,
隨機應感　Sui chi ying-kan,
清靜聖靈　Ch'ing ching Sheng-ling!

With all my heart I take refuge

In God Most High,

Who created all things,

The merciful Father, source of all goodness!

With all my heart I take refuge

In Christ, the Redeemer of sin,

Who restores my true nature,

The perfect and mysterious Word!

With all my heart I take refuge

In the One who embraces the universe,

Who at all times and in all places

   responds to our needs,

The pure and tranquil Holy Spirit!

Figure 15.1   "The Three Christian Refuges" by Dr Karl Reichelt
(founder of Tao Fong Shan Christian Centre)

Korea

The only Buddhist people that have shown a marked change towards Protestant Christianity are the Koreans. This is probably the result of two unique aspects of Korean history. The first was the influence of the Protestant missionary John L. Nevius, who moved to Korea in 1890 after working in China. He immediately began to implement the same pattern of indigenous principles as employed by the CIM. The missionaries in Korea followed four principles that were known as the "Nevius method".[17] They were as follows:

1. Each Christian should "abide in the calling wherein he was found". The convert would continue to remain in his local community and support himself.
2. The church organisation was to be developed only so far as the Korean Church was able to take responsibility for it.
3. The church was to appoint and support full-time national pastors.
4. The church buildings were to be built in Korean style.

This attempt to establish an indigenous church removed much of the anti-foreign feeling so significant in China.

The second factor important in the growth of the church in Korea was the social trauma the Koreans experienced through Japanese rule, and later, the Communist invasion resulting in the Korean War of 1950. The war left Korea totally destroyed. Through massive US support, South Korea has become one of the economic miracles of Asia. This radical social change has affected every aspect of society, and made all members of society open to the American way of life. As Protestant Christianity is seen as part of that lifestyle, there has been an eager reception of the Protestant Church. Korea now boasts some of the largest congregations in the world, and is now sending many missionaries to other countries.

An international encounter

The 20th century has resulted in immense change within the Buddhist nations of Asia. European colonialism has ended.

Communism has risen to dominate China and many of the southeast Asian countries but now seems to be in decline, following the pattern of the former USSR. Some of these nations have become the "economic tigers" of the new Pacific.

A new class of missionaries has now begun to work among Buddhist peoples. Alongside European, North American and Australian missionaries have come Latin American and African missionaries, but most important have been the Asian missionaries. Korean missionaries are now going to Japan, Thailand and mainland China in increasing numbers. Chinese Christians from Hong Kong and Singapore are working in many parts of Asia and elsewhere in the world. How will they fare in comparison to the previous three attempts to communicate Christianity to Buddhists? For the first time it is Asians who are going to Asians with the Christian message.

This raises the question of the contextualisation of the Christian religion. Can Asian Christians present Christianity in forms that are meaningful to Asian Buddhists? Kosuke Koyama, a former Japanese missionary to Thailand, provides one such attempt in his book significantly entitled *Waterbuffalo Theology*.

> The water buffaloes tell me that I must preach to these farmers in the simplest sentence structure and thought development. They remind me to discard all abstract ideas, and to use exclusively objects that are immediately tangible. "Sticky-rice", "banana", "pepper", "dog", "cat", "bicycle", "rainy season", "leaking house", "fishing", "cockfighting", "lottery", "stomach-ache" – these are meaningful words for them.[18]

Koyama not only seeks to communicate in the everyday symbols of the life of a Thai farmer but engages with some of the major doctrines of Theravada Buddhism.

> The *arhat*-ideal is radically different from the spirituality expressed in the lives of the people of Israel (the Old Testament) and of the church (New Testament). There God is portrayed strongly as an anti-*arhat* God in that he is deeply engaged in history. He rules history. His direction is not *away* from history (detachment – "eyes lowered"), but *towards* history (attachment – "I have seen the affliction of my people

who are in Egypt"). Perhaps this is the basic contrast between Theravada Buddhism and the Judaeo-Christian faith: the two histories, the two eyes.[19]

The Buddhist nations are in a process of rapid change as they drive towards economic development. Will the enticements of wealth through the new industrial revolution draw the people away from any religion, as happened in the West? As a new global culture emerges, it may be here that Christianity finally has a significant impact on the peoples of Asia. The high-tech super-churches of the cities of Asia are all showing rapid growth. However, they could easily become the centres of prosperity teaching, and a pathway to material prosperity rather than spiritual reality.

Suggestions for interfaith discussions

T'ai-hsu sought to make a comparison between Christianity and Buddhism. You may like to make your own table of similarities and differences. What, if anything, is missing from such an exercise in a genuine quest for truth?

Webwise 15 – The Christian Missionary Impact

Exhibition on Jesuits

http://www.nd.edu/~dharley/HistIdeas/Jesuits.html
This site is based on the Vatican library exhibition on Jesuits.

By foot to China

http://www.aina.org/byfoot.htm
This site is still under construction but provides some interesting information on the Nestorian Church and its movement into central Asia.

The Nestorian pages

http://www.oxuscom.com/nestpage.htm
The website of the old Oxus Communications site has been redesigned to give several pages related to central Asia, including the history of the Nestorian Church.

Nestorian tablet and pagoda

http://www.lynnsupdate.com/index.htm

The Good News from China site gives photographs of the Nestorian tablet and the pagoda housed in the Forest of Steles Museum in Xi'an.

Notes

1. Syrdal, R., *To The End of the Earth* (Minneapolis: Augsburg, 1967), p. 74.
2. Palmer, M., *The Jesus Sutras: Rediscovering the Lost Scrolls of Taoism Christianity* (New York: Ballantine Wellspring, 2001).
3. *Ibid.*, p. 147.
4. *Ibid.*, p. 168.
5. Covell, R. R., *Confucius, The Buddha and Christ* (Maryknoll: Orbis, 1986), p. 27.
6. Palmer, *op. cit.*, p. 236.
7. Covell, *op. cit.*, p. 36.
8. Cronin, V., *The Wise Man from the West* (New York: Dutton, 1955), pp. 168–169.
9. Lambert, T., "The Lost Kingdom of Guge", *China Insight*, July/August 2000, p. 4.
10. Gombrich, R., *Theravada Buddhism* (London: Routledge, 1989), p. 178.
11. Quoted in Gombrich, *ibid.*, p. 179.
12. Gombrich, *ibid.*, p. 180.
13. In English it was called the Society for the Propagation of Buddhism in imitation of the Society for the Propagation of the Gospel (SPG).
14. Neill, S., *A History of Christian Mission* (Harmondsworth: Pelican, 1964), p. 333.
15. Lai, W. and von Bruck, M., *Christianity and Buddhism* (New York: Maryknoll, 2001), pp. 84–85.
16. *Ibid.*, p. 85.
17. Nevius, J., *Methods of Mission Work* (London: Morgan & Scott, 1898).

18. Koyama, K., *Waterbuffalo Theology* (London: SCM Press, 1974), pp. vii–viii.
19. Koyama, *ibid.*, p. 153.

CHAPTER SIXTEEN

THE DISCOVERY OF BUDDHISM BY THE WEST

What you can learn from this chapter

- the early contact with Buddhism in the 19th century
- the formation of the first Buddhist societies in Europe and North America
- the formation of Zen and Tibetan organisations in the West during the second half of the 20th century
- the growth of various contemporary movements in the West

> Ah! Blessed Lord! Oh, High Deliverer!
> Forgive this feeble script, which doth thee wrong,
> Measuring with little wit thy lofty Love.
> Ah! Lover! Brother! Guide! Lamp of the Law!
> I take my refuge in thy name and thee!
> I take my refuge in thy Law of Good!
> I take my refuge in thy Order! OM!
> Thy Dew is on the Lotus! – Rise, Great Sun!
> And lift my leaf and mix me with the wave,
> *Om mani padme hum,* the Sunrise comes!
> The Dewdrop slips into the shining Sea!
>   (End of the poem *The Light of Asia* by Edwin Arnold)[1]

Today it seems surprising that only 200 years ago there was almost no knowledge in Europe of the Buddhist tradition. It was only during the 19th century that the Buddha emerged from the realm of myth and stepped onto the stage of Western history. Buddhism was finally distinguished from Hinduism and identified as one of the great religious traditions of Asia.

The discovery of "Buddhism"

European travellers, and especially Jesuit missionaries to Tibet, China and Japan, made record of an obscure cult of the "false god" they wrongly called "Bod".[2] Even in 1802 *The English Encyclopaedia* had the following entry:

> Budun: one of the Ceylonese gods, who is fabled to have arrived at supremacy, after successive transmigrations from the lowest state of an insect, through various species of living animals.

As a result of colonial expansion, information was gradually gathered about the history and customs of the peoples of Asia. Texts were collected and sent back to London and Paris for translation and study; gradually, by the mid-1830s, there emerged an understanding of a religious teaching that was later to be known as "Buddhism".

In 1803 Friedrich Schlegel (1772–1829) coined the term "oriental renaissance" for the discovery of the Asian world with its religions and philosophical traditions. Similarly, Arthur Schopenhauer (1788–1860) began to stir up an interest in Buddhist philosophy and ethics among artists and academics. It was Eugène Burnouf (1801–1852), the Paris philologist, who in 1844 presented an analytical survey of Buddhist material, and in so doing imposed a rational order on the collection of material. Burnouf's *L'Introduction à l'Histoire du Buddhisme Indien* provided the foundation for the European concept of Buddhism, and suddenly there was a boom in the translation and study of Buddhist texts throughout the universities of Europe.[3] Buddhism was not exported to Europe by missionaries but was imported into Europe by Western academics.

So far, the study of Buddhism had been located in the oriental section of university libraries where the discussions revolved around the philosophy of Buddhism. The 1850s saw an increase in the production of cheap literature that was eagerly read by the middle class, and with it came the diffusion of Buddhist ideas into wider society. It was in 1879 that Edwin Arnold, who had been teaching in India, published a poem based upon the life of Sakyamuni Buddha called *The Light of Asia*. This was to become one of the most popular long Victorian poems; it went through at least 100 editions in Britain and America. Not only did the poem bring fame to Edwin Arnold but it spread the Buddha's name among English-speaking people around the world. It did so in the context of the mystery of India that spun a web of romance around the Enlightened One.

The Christian Church was quick to criticise the content, if not the structure, of the blank verse. The rejection was powerfully expressed by missionaries such as Reverend Richard Collins who had been a missionary in India and Ceylon from 1854 to 1878. He claimed that "the Buddha of *The Light of Asia* is no more a picture of the genuine and real Buddha than Alfred Tennyson's King Arthur is a picture of the actual King Arthur."[4] The polarisation of attitude to Arnold's poem illustrated the divergent reactions within Western society towards the non-Western world in general. On one side, non-Western people were perceived as savages who needed to be converted and civilised, while on the other, the Romantic tradition saw them as "noble savages" who had retained their identity with nature.

Theravada tradition

In 1824 the first Pali grammar was published in Colombo by the Wesleyan missionary Benjamin Clough, but this had little influence for some years, as Burnouf had used the Sanskrit texts. There was much discussion as to which texts were earlier, the Pali or the Sanskrit; it was not until the 1870s that the Pali versions were regarded as the earliest. T. W. Rhys Davids, who had been with the civil service in Ceylon (Sri Lanka), became interested in Buddhism and formed the Pali Text Society in 1881. The Society collected, translated and published many of the Theravada texts. Initially, the interest in these texts was among academic scholars who admired the philosophy and ethics of Buddhism, and sought to study the historical development of the philosophical concepts.

Gordon Douglas, who was ordained as Asoka at the Jayase-kerarama, Colombo in 1899, was one of the first Europeans to be ordained a Buddhist monk, but he had little impact as he died in 1905. Alan Bennett McGregor (1872–1923), a former member of the Hermetic Order of the Golden Dawn, an occultist association, entered a Burmese monastery in 1901 and took the name Ananda Metteyya.[5] He returned to Britain in 1908 and formed a small Buddhist society that was supported by members of the Theosophical Society, including the influential Christmas Humphreys. A year later, a small group of Buddhist missionaries came from Sri Lanka and settled in Britain. In 1924 Humphreys, with others, formed the Buddhist Lodge of the Theosophical Society. Angarika Dharmapala visited London and founded the Maha Bodhi Society. In 1926 the first issue of *Buddhism in England* was produced. The first *Vihara* was opened in Hampstead in 1929 but closed after a few years.

The Society struggled to survive in its early years. "More than once, Mr and Mrs Humphreys stood on the doorstep of the house to welcome people but no one came to the meetings. So they went inside and read the Scriptures together, and waited for the next meeting."[6] In 1943 the name was changed to the Buddhist Society of Great Britain, and the journal to *The Middle Way*. After the war, the Society was greatly helped by substantial donations from Burma.

During the period 1880–1920, the adoption of Buddhism was dominated by ethical and intellectual interest in the Theravada tradition. These early Buddhists stressed particular advantages in Buddhism that they considered were the disadvantages of the Christianity that they had previously rejected. For example, they argued that Buddhism was a religion of reason, and rested on insight and knowledge alone. Apart from intellectual motives, there appear to have been two other motives for these early Western Buddhists to take up this religion. The first of these was an interest in the esoteric; most of these early converts came into contact with Buddhism by way of the Theosophical Society, or through occultism or spiritism. The second influence was that of the Romantic movement, mentioned earlier, which glorified ancient wisdom and culture. Buddhism was presented as the oldest and wisest religion that would enable European culture to step out of the gloom into a new and glorious century. In practice, most of these early Buddhists approached the subject as little more than a hobby, which left other aspects of their lives unchanged.

The Theravada form of meditation also gained popularity in Britain through the Thai master Ajahn Chah (1918–1992). He founded the Chithurst Forest Monastery in West Sussex in 1978, which was the first successful Theravada *Sangha* comprising Western members. Under its British abbot, Ajahn Sumedho (formerly Robert Jackman), other centres were established in Britain, Germany, Italy and Switzerland. Meditation practice gave Buddhism a hitherto unknown popularity and widened the social groups to which the religion appealed. In the early period, it was the better-educated elite who were attracted to Buddhism. Meditation opened the tradition to a wider class of the university-educated, who were at this same time increasing in number.

The history of Buddhism in the USA differs in several respects from what happened in Europe. The earliest phase of American Buddhism resulted through Asian immigrants arriving during the latter half of the 19th century. The early Chinese population reached its peak in the 1880s when it numbered slightly over 100,000. The Chinese brought with them ancestor veneration and meditational devotion upon O-mi-t o fo (Amitabha Buddha) and Kuan-yin (Avalokitesvara).[7] The Chinese settled along the west coast of America and generally had little influence upon those of European descent.

In 1889 a young Japanese priest entered Hawaii and established a branch of the Jodo Shinshu (True Pure Land school). Soryu Kagahi set up a small temple in Hawaii and then returned to Japan, leaving the lay people to run the temple.[8] This branch was soon to grow into the largest denomination of Buddhism in Hawaii, attracting mostly Americans of Japanese decent. In 1900 missions of Jodoshu (Pure Land school) and the Soto branch of Zen Buddhism also became active among the ethnic Japanese living on the island. All the schools succeeded in establishing several temples. Until the commencement of the Second World War, the establishments were under the influence of their Japanese parent organisation but in 1944 this was changed and the Buddhist Churches of America was formed. The Japanese-Americans had great difficulty passing on their cultural heritage to their younger generation. To arrest the decline, they formed so-called "*Dharma* schools", based on Christian Sunday schools.

The World Parliament of Religions that was held at the Chicago World Fair of 1893 had a greater influence upon American opinion of Buddhism than any other single event. Some Americans had been influenced by ideas of the Theosophical Society and were familiar with the Theravada tradition. At the Parliament two Buddhists spoke: Anagarika Dharmapala from Sri Lanka, and Soen Shaku, a master of the Rinzai school of Zen. (The importance of Dharmapala in Sri Lanka will be discussed in the following chapter.) Paul Carns, the owner of the Open Court Publishing House, was so impressed by what he learned about Buddhism that he invited a disciple of Soen Shaku to work with his publishing house. The person sent was Daisetzu Teitaro Suzuki (1870–1966), who wrote many books on Zen and Mahayana which have been translated into many languages. It was Suzuki who did more than any other person to bring knowledge of Zen to the West, especially the USA. Zen has played an important part in American Buddhism from that time.

Zen Buddhism

The Second World War marked an end to all Buddhist activities within Europe, but in the new post-war period there was a re-organisation of the former Theravada-based associations. Christmas Humphreys started writing many books on Buddhism tailored to a Western readership, and these sold in large numbers.

The first book in English on Japanese Zen Buddhism was that written by D. T. Suzuki in 1927 but it was not until after the Second World War that it gained popularity in Europe. Zen caught the imagination of many young people in the USA during the 1950s, in the so-called "beatnik" generation that spread around the Western world. Zen became part of the mixture of ideas common among the young people of the 1960s; books such as *Zen and the Art of Motor Cycle Maintenance* became of cult status. More serious practitioners of Buddhism criticised the superficial presentation of the religious tradition to the wider public, but it brought to Buddhism a "with-it" image.

The main emphasis during the 1960s was the interest in meditation and experience. In Western Europe it was through the Zen teachers Testu Nagaya Kiichi Rochi (1895–1993, Rinzai school) and Taisen Deshimam Roshi (1914–1982, Soto school) that a continuing interest was maintained. In addition to Zen masters, European and American Zen disciples have increasingly started to conduct meditation courses in the West. The Jesuit missionary Hugo Makibi Enomiya-Lassalle (1898–1990) incorporated Zen meditation practice into Catholic worship and proposed "Zen for Christians".

Martial arts first occurred in Britain with the founding of the Budokwai club in London in 1918. This school taught *ju-jutsu*, from which *judo* and *kenjutsu* (sword fighting) developed. Initially, the patrons were middle-class gentlemen interested in oriental culture, and the teachers were Japanese long-term residents in the UK. By the 1950s the ethos of the club had shifted to that of a serious *judo* school in which the core group of black belts had trained in Japan. They had a serious interest in Zen practice, but by the 1960s this interest had almost vanished due possibly to the admission of *judo* as an Olympic sport in the 1964 Tokyo Olympics. As *judo* became more popularised, those interested in the Zen philosophy gravitated towards *aikido*. *Aikido* was developed in the 1930s by Ueshiba Morihei; like *judo*, it is based on the fighting methods of the *samurai*. During the 1960s *karate* became of interest, mainly as a result of the exposure to it of US military personnel on Okinawa and the Japanese mainland after the Second World War.

The 1970s saw the *kung fu* explosion, and a much higher profile for Chinese martial arts. Much of this was due to the films of Bruce Lee, a Chinese American who was trained in *wing chun*, a southern Shaolin boxing style. He developed his own eclectic approach, which incorporated elements of mystical Taoism, Zen and Krishnamurti.[9] His grace and power were demonstrated in the many films he made, before his death from a brain embolism in 1973. As a result of his brief career, interest in Chinese martial arts soared in the West. The blend of dazzling martial skills and esoteric mystical teaching was irresistible to popular culture; it continues to find an eager market, with "Ninja Turtles" and films like *Crouching Tiger Hidden Dragon*.[10]

Associated with this is the move to employ methods and

concepts derived from Buddhism but not articulated in traditional Buddhist terms. These have variously been called "inner warrior" or "lifestyle warrior". A notable exponent is Paul Shane, an American martial artist and former executive. He employs martial arts-based fitness and *ki* exercises, combined with a programme of self-reflection and analysis through creative meditation and visualisation to produce the "inner warrior".[11] This Zen-orientated method is claimed to provide a way of facing the battle of ordinary life and business.

The 1950s and 1960s saw the rise of what was to become known as the "New Age" movement. It was greatly influenced by both Hindu and Buddhist traditions with the result that many Christians tend to think of Buddhism as part of what they perceive as "New Age". While there are direct influences from Buddhism there are some marked differences, such that today most Western Buddhists would be adamant that they are not New Age, even though they may have experimented with New Age practices on previous occasions. A brief outline of the similarities and differences would be as follows:

Similarities between Buddhism and New Age teaching
Holistic view generally based upon monistic philosophy
Reincarnation (rebirth) a common assumption
The greatest human problem is "ignorance" rather than sin
The quest therefore is for "enlightenment"

Differences between Buddhism and New Age philosophy
Buddhism is not "new", but draws upon the ancient teaching of the Buddha
The monastic discipline of Buddhism has no counterpart in "New Age"
"New Age" often draws upon ideas and practices from traditions other than Buddhism
"New Age" primarily concerned with coping with the present life while Buddhism seeks ultimate liberation

Tibetan tradition

After the popularisation of Zen during the late 1960s and 1970s, a third wave of interest came to the West with the flight of the

Dalai Lama from Tibet in 1959. With the *Dalai Lama* journeyed many leading teachers, some of whom came to the West. They did not come as missionaries but as political refugees or as students, university teachers and researchers. The administration of the *Dalai Lama* in Dharamsala in north India was initially preoccupied with the settlement and housing of refugees. They were therefore surprised by the influx of young Westerners wanting to study Buddhism in the later 1960s and early 1970s. Slowly they began to provide classes, which were formally established in 1971 under the direction of Geshe Ngawang Dhargyay (1921–1995).

In other parts of India and Nepal, other Westerners were forming links with individual refugee *lamas*. A significant centre was established in the small town of Kopan, near Kathmundu, where two *lamas* first met Western travellers in 1965. The *lamas* were Thubten Yeshe (1935–1984) and his student, a young dGe-lugs-pa incarnate *lama* from Nepal, Thubten Zopa Rinpoche (b. 1946).

In 1975 *Lama* Yeshe named his fledgling network of centres the Foundation for the Preservation of the Mahayana Tradition (FPMT). Now, more than 130 centres and other activities in 26 countries make up the FPMT, and it grows yearly.[12]

The FPMT was eventually given approval by the Dharamsala administration even though the two *lamas* had no followers from the Tibetan community. It is probably the loose administrative structure of the Tibetan system that has allowed the rapid expansion of this form of Buddhism into the Western world. The *lamas* had traditionally been entrepreneurial and were therefore able to take advantage of new opportunities and draw from the breadth of ritual and teaching that was of particular interest to their new Western students.

Two Tibetan spiritual leaders have shown themselves to be charismatic personalities, and have attracted many Americans and Europeans through their writings. The first was Chogyam Trungpa who escaped from Tibet in 1959 and later proceeded to England to study at Oxford. He began to teach in the late 1960s in England, where he established the Samye-ling Meditation Centre. He was involved in a serious car accident in 1969, after which he gave up the monk's robe and moved to Vermont, USA, where some of his disciples had set up the Karme Choling Meditation Centre. He soon founded other centres in the USA and wrote many books interpreting the *Dharma* by means of dynamic translation into English.

The other charismatic personality was Tarthang Tulku, who also fled from Tibet in 1959, and was selected by the *Dalai Lama* as a teacher of the *rNying-ma-pa* tradition at the University of Tibetan Studies in Varanasi. He also gave up the monk's robe before going to America. There he founded the Nyingma Meditation Centre in Berkeley. This form of Buddhism is presented and practised in such a way that it allows Americans to combine its study and practice together with a professional life.

In 1970 John Blofeld's book *The Way of Power* caught the imagination of many students.[13] In one short section he wrote about the visualisation of the Buddha Vajrasattva, in which the symbolism of Tibet is brought together with the philosophy of Buddhism. Vessantra is another convert to Tibetan Buddhism and wrote of this mixing: "Here was all the richness and symbol, and even magic, that I had ever been looking for, harmoniously married to the clear reason of the Buddha, and devoted to the highest goal that a human being is capable of attaining."[14] Vessantra is typical of many leading European Buddhists. Born in 1950 in a middle-class family, he was interested in Buddhism from his teenage years. He gained an MA at Cambridge and was ordained into the Western Buddhist Order (WBO) in 1974. In 1975 he gave up a career in social work to become chair of the Brighton Buddhist Centre. Since then he has divided his time between meditating, studying Buddhism and aiding the development of Buddhist centres in Europe.

The dGe-lugs-pa tradition, headed by the fourteenth *Dalai Lama,* has established study and practice centres in Switzerland and Germany; by 1990 it had more than 50 centres. Following his first visit to the West in 1973, the *Dalai Lama* has made many visits and has inspired his Western followers. The Kagyu tradition has also been very successful. The Kagyu head, the 16th *Gyalwa Karapa* (1923–1981) made his first visit to Europe and North America in 1975; it is claimed that he has founded more than 50 centres throughout Europe.

What was the attraction of Buddhism among the students of the West? Martin Baumann concisely sums up the observations of many writers:

> Evidently, Buddhism in the West serves both romantics and rationalists by providing a religious home. Rationalists stress the cognitive, scientific and anti-ritualistic aspects of Buddhism. Romantics, especially the adherents of Tibetan traditions, emphasise the devotional, spiritual and mystical elements of Buddhism.[15]

The main appeal was the colourful art and rituals of Tibetan Buddhism, but many followers modified the teaching to the emerging drug culture of the period. Within this broad movement some serious practitioners emerged. Some Westerners became monks and nuns, but although some have taken three-year retreats, very few have remained in the monastic *Sangha*.

Some Westerners have travelled to Tibetan monasteries in Nepal and India to receive the highest levels of initiation. This experience has not always proved to be all that they expected. I know of a case where the seeker was welcomed into the monastery for the initiation, but was shocked to find that this included a sexual act with one of the nuns. On refusing the ritual, the young man was sent out from the monastery with the beating of drums to chase away the "bad influence" that he was considered to have brought to the monastery.

New movements

Although Zen and Tibetan Buddhism are still popular in the West, more recently there has been a growing response to some new schools of Buddhism.

In 1967, Venerable Sangharakshita, an Englishman, founded the Western Buddhist Order (WBO) in Britain.[16] This is the first Buddhist tradition to be founded in Britain and although basically Mahayana in outlook, the movement stresses the basic unity of all forms of Buddhism rather than the collection of oriental customs that have grown up around it. The WBO itself is a new way of taking Buddhist practice seriously, providing ordination that does not necessarily involve adopting the traditional lifestyle of a monk or nun. It sees itself as a practical form of Buddhism suited to the Western world.

The 1970s and 1980s have seen the introduction and growth in popularity of Nichiren Buddhism in Britain and America. The origin and development of this movement will be discussed more fully in the following chapter. Nichiren Shoshu in America was established in 1960; the original members were nearly all Japanese brides of American GIs. By the mid-1970s, when the association claimed more than 200,000 adherents, 90% were occidental. Nichiren Shoshu did not become established in Britain until 1974 when Richard Causton (1920–1995), an English businessman who had started to practise while working in Japan, returned to the UK. Under his leadership, Soka Gakkai International-UK (SGI-UK) now claims a membership of about 6,000,[17] but possibly only 4,000 may be counted as active.[18]

According to Barker, in Britain only a handful of SGI-UK members are employed by the movement; the majority are middle-class people living ordinary lives.[19] No special lifestyle or dress is adopted. The members have two centres, the larger being at Taplow Hall near Maidenhead. The movement is not so aggressive in its propagation as in other countries and has therefore not been subject to the same sort of criticism as experienced in Japan, for example. SGI-UK not only promotes lectures but also well-produced artistic events.

Because of the various forms of Buddhism currently practised in the West it is difficult to give accurate figures. The Buddhist Directory gives the most complete listing of Buddhist groups and centres in the UK.[20] Martin Baumann has made a brave attempt to estimate the number of Buddhists in various nations.[21] He would be the first to acknowledge the limitations of his study, but he has assembled some of the most accurate data.

These figures only give an estimate of the number of Buddhists living in each country. The definition of what constitutes membership varies considerably. Although the numbers are small as a percentage of the population, the influence of Buddhist ideas and thought is far more significant. Meditation has become a common practice among many people, primarily as a means of reducing

Country	Buddhists (sum)	Euro/ American Buddhists	Centres	National Population	Percentage Buddhists
USA	3–4 million	800,000	500–800	261 million	1.6
Australia	140,000	14,000	150	18 million	0.8
South Africa	5,000	2,500	40	42 million	0.01
UK	180,000	50,000	300	58 million	0.01
France	650,000	150,000	130	58 million	1.15
Germany	150,000	40,000	400	81 million	0.2
Italy	75,000	50,000	30	57 million	0.1
Switzerland	20–25,000	?	80	7 million	0.3
Netherlands	20,000	5,000	40	15 million	0.1
Denmark	8,000	5,000	32	5 million	0.16
Austria	13,000	5,000	25	8 million	0.16
Hungary	6,500	6,000	12	10 million	0.07
Czech Republic	2,100	2,000	15	10 million	0.02
Poland	4,500	4,000	15	38 million	0.01
Russia	1 million	40,000	100	149 million	0.7

Figure 16.1   Buddhists and Buddhist groups in mid-1990s

stress in the frantic pace of technological society. Many management development courses make use of Buddhist teaching, although it has been packaged to make it appropriate to modern businesses. Talking to one businessman about why his company made use of such methods, he answered that competition was so great, the competitive advantage lay with developing the full potential of one's managers by any means available.

The discussion has so far related to people of European descent but there are now an increasing number of Asian Buddhists in Europe. The majority of Hindus, Muslims and Sikhs in Britain are immigrants from different parts of the British Commonwealth. There have been few immigrants who have been Buddhist. Some of the largest communities have been Vietnamese refugees – the "boat people". They have established numerous local groups and built some large pagodas in Paris and Hanover.

In general, Asian Buddhists have only a few contacts with European Buddhists, and have little interest in propagating Buddhism. Thus, as in the USA, two distinct lines of Buddhism have developed. In order to improve communications between

Buddhists in Europe, the European Buddhist Union (EBU) was formed in 1975. Its last congress in Berlin had the title "Unity in diversity – Buddhism in Europe".

In summary, Buddhism has within a period of 200 years moved from being a misunderstood religion to become a significant, if not numerous, religious tradition in the West. Although Western converts have been few, their numbers have been increasing. A more important trend has been the attitude of the general public to the religion. Although most Europeans and Americans have only a superficial knowledge of Buddhism, it is seen in a positive way, and is not regarded as a threat, as some other religions. Various elements of Buddhist teaching and practice have been adopted by exponents of the New Age movement, and have had a surprising influence in the media as seen in films like *The Matrix*.

Why are Western people accepting Buddhism? This is *not* the result of Asian missionaries but a demand by Western people for a new and radically different philosophy of life. There was a growing dissatisfaction with the secular materialist worldview during the 20th century, and the sharp distinction between observer and observed was challenged. Geoffrey Samuel comments, "Westerners are, by necessity, beginning to accept what the Buddhists have always asserted: that the world cannot be separated from the human beings who observe it and interact with it."[22] The social sciences have begun to respond to this situation, but there have been few comments from Christian scholars.

A second reason which is commonly stated by converts to Buddhism is that it claims to offer peace in a stress-filled life. Terry Muck in his research comments, "The idea seemed to be that American culture is so hectic and busy and stressful, and the various kinds of Buddhist meditation techniques (are) an antidote they hadn't found in . . . the Christianity that they had grown up with."[23]

A third reason is that people are looking for answers to the question of suffering. In the midst of material prosperity, they still feel a lack of satisfaction, and this is the very starting point of the Four Noble Truths. Western converts are therefore seeking to discover for themselves whether the Middle Way provides them with a satisfactory answer. Today, Asian monks are finding a ready number of disciples who are willing to support them and help establish new Buddhist centres. I was once in discussion with one of these monks, who had recently arrived from Thailand. We were having an amicable discussion on the subjects we had been studying together in the Buddhist Studies class we had just left. We had been talking about the Noble Truth of *dukkha*, when suddenly he asked me, "What do Christians do with the sadness inside?" Out of mutual friendship, a Christian and a Buddhist had come to realise their common humanity.

It remains to be seen to what extent Buddhism can adapt itself to Western culture. The novelty and elegance of the *Dharma* gradually permeated the great civilisations of China and Japan, even though this was only after being greatly modified over hundreds of years. If the *Dharma* can be adapted to such radically different societies as India and China, it seems likely that the *Dharma* can, in time, take on a particularly Western expression. Films such as *The Little Buddha* with Keanu Reeves have certainly presented Buddhism in a way relevant to a Western audience.

Suggestions for interfaith discussions

Why have Western people converted to Buddhism? This question can provide an opportunity for individuals to share accounts of their own religious quest. It is always important to listen to the other person and not just be eager to speak.

Webwise 16 – The Discovery of Buddhism by the West

The Light of Asia

http://www.theosophy-nw.org/theosnw/books/lightasi/asia-hp.htm

Theosophical University Press has published this online edition of *The Light of Asia*, or *The Great Renunciation* (*Mahabhinishkramana*) by Edwin Arnold.

Pali Text Society

http://www.palitext.demon.co.uk

The Society was founded in 1881 by T.W. Rhys Davids "to foster and promote the study of Pali texts". It publishes Pali texts in roman characters, translations in English and ancillary works including dictionaries, concordances, books for students of Pali, and a journal.

The Buddhist Society UK

http://www.thebuddhistsociety.org.uk
This is the official site of the Buddhist Society UK, founded in 1924. The site contains a variety of material including an online catalogue of books in the library in Eccleston Square, London.

Forest Sangha *newsletter*

http://www.abm.ndirect.co.uk/fsn/index.html
The Forest *Sangha* is a worldwide Buddhist community in the Thai Forest tradition of Ajahn Chah. This site is for the magazine and contains many interesting articles and other information.

Parliament of religions

http://www.cpwr.org
The first Parliament of Religions was held in Chicago in 1893. In 1993 the Parliament of the World's Religions was again convened in Chicago, with 8,000 people from all over the world coming together to celebrate diversity and harmony and to explore religious and spiritual responses to the critical issues which confront us all.

Friends of the Western Buddhist Order (*FWBO*)

http://www.fwbo.org
This is a big site containing everything from cartoons to teaching on Buddhism. It gives extensive information on the FWBO and the addresses of their meetings.

Foundation for the Preservation of the Mahayana Tradition

http://www.fpmt.org/organization/history.asp
The FPMT was founded in 1975 by *Lama* Yeshe and advocated the teaching of the *Dalai Lama*. The site contains links to other useful sites.

Notes

1. Arnold, E., *The Light of Asia* (New York: Cowell, 1884).
2. Wessels, C., *Early Jesuit Travellers in Central Asia 1603–1721* (New Delhi: Motilal Banarsidass, 1992).
3. Burnouf, E., *L'Introduction à l'Histoire du Buddhisme Indien* (Paris: Imprimerie Royale, 1844).
4. Quoted in Almond, P. C., *The British Discovery of Buddhism* (Cambridge: CUP, 1988), p. 2.
5. Harris, E. J., *Ananda Metteyya: The First British Emissary of Buddhism* (Kandy: Buddhist Publication Society, 1998).
6. *The Buddhist Society Prospectus* 1994–1995 (London: The Buddhist Society 1995), p. 4.
7. Chandler, S., "Chinese Buddhism in America: identity and practice" in Prebish, C. S. and Tanaka, K. K. (eds.), *The Faces of Buddhism in America* (Berkeley: University of California Press, 1998), pp. 14–30.
8. Bloom A., "Shin Buddhism in America: a social perspective", in Prebish, C. S. and Tanaka, K. K. (eds.), *The Faces of Buddhism in America* (Berkeley: University of California Press, 1998), pp. 32–47.
9. Lee, B., *Tao of Jeet Kune Do* (Ohara: Burbank, 1975).
10. *Crouching Tiger Hidden Dragon* (United China Vision Incorporated, 2000).
11. Shane, P., *The Warrior Within* (Colorado: Delta, 1983).
12. http://www.fpmt.org/organization/history.asp (December 2002)
13. Blofeld, J., *The Way of Power* (London: Allen & Unwin, 1970).
14. Vessantra, *Meeting the Buddhas* (Glasgow: Windhorse, 1993), p. 1.
15. Baumann, M., "Creating a European path to nirvana: historical and contemporary developments of Buddhism in Europe", *Journal of Contemporary Religion* (1995) vol. 10 [1], p. 62.
16. Subhuti, *Bringing Buddhism to the West: A Life of Sangharakshita* (Birmingham: Windhorse, 1995).
17. *Daily Telegraph*, 25 January 1995.
18. Wilson, B., "The British movement and its members" in

Machacek, D. and Wilson, B. (eds.), *Global Citizens: The Soka Gakkai Buddhist Movement in the World* (Oxford: OUP, 2000), p. 373.

19. Barker, E., *New Religious Movements* (London: HMSO, 1989), pp. 193–195.

20. *Buddhist Directory 2000* (London: The Buddhist Society, 2000).

21. Baumann, M., "The Dharma has come west: a survey of recent studies and sources" *Journal of Contemporary Religion* 10 (1995).

22. Samuel, G., *Civilized Shamans* (Washington: Smithsonian, 1993), p. 565.

23. Muck, T., *Those Other Religions in Your Neighbourhood* (Wheaton: Victor Books, 1990).

CHAPTER SEVENTEEN

THE BUDDHIST RESURGENCE

What you can learn from this chapter

- the ways that European colonialism helped inspire various Buddhist movements
- information about some of the contemporary Buddhist movements
- the various movements seeking to unite Buddhism into a worldwide religion
- the diverse nature of newer Buddhist movements

In spite of the intensity of various Christian missions, converts from Buddhism to Christianity have remained the exception rather than the rule. Towards the end of the 19th century the assimilation of Western culture was arrested and a new feeling of cultural identity began to emerge. The Buddhist revival began among the educated middle class in association with the movement towards national independence. Wars and Communist rule affected Asia throughout the 20th century but in many areas Buddhism underwent a resurgence that had a worldwide influence. Once again, Buddhism achieved this by expressing itself in ways that were relevant to contemporary society. In this final chapter a few of the major modern Buddhist movements will be considered. They provide examples of how old traditional philosophies and practices have been reworked for the modern world and a global community. One notable feature of these movements is the important role played by the Buddhist laity.

"Protestant Buddhism" in Sri Lanka

In their book *Buddhism Transformed*, Gombrich and Obeyesekere described some recent developments in Buddhism in Sri Lanka as "Protestant Buddhism". The basis of the thesis is that the Buddhist revival was largely an externally driven one brought about by what they consider to be the "Protestant" ideas of Colonel Olcott and others. Although the term "Protestant Buddhism" has been questioned, it does reveal a notable revival movement in Buddhism in Sri Lanka.[1]

Don David Hevavitarana (1864–1933) who became known as Anagarika Dharmapala, was born into a Buddhist family in Colombo which belonged to the new social elite of colonial rule.[2] They had not accepted the Christian religion of their new rulers but instead had become ardent lay supporters of Buddhism. Hevavitarana was educated at a Roman Catholic primary school and an Anglican secondary school, primarily because there were no Buddhist schools in Colombo at that time. The experience left him with an impression of Christianity as fanatical and intolerant of other religions. His biographer tells the account:

> One Sunday he was quietly reading a pamphlet on the Four Noble Truths, when the boarding master of the school came up to him and, true to missionary tradition, demanded the offending work from him and had it flung out of the room . . . The climax of his criticism was reached when he drew a picture of a monkey and wrote underneath it "Jesus Christ", for which piece of juvenile imprudence he was threatened with expulsion from the school.[3]

As a schoolboy aged ten, Hevavitarana was present at the famous debate at Panadura, and the enthusiasm that it generated moved the boy towards the emerging Buddhist revival. In 1880 he first met Colonel Olcott during his visit to Colombo. In 1884 he was initiated as a member of the newly formed Buddhist order of the Theosophical Society, and became a favourite of Olcott and Madame Blavatsky. Later in the same year, despite his father's opposition, he visited India with Blavatsky. It was while in India that she is said to have told him that "he should not devote himself to the occultism with which he had become fascinated but should work for the good of Humanity and that he should take up the study of Pali."[4] In the following year he assumed the name Dharmapala meaning "Protector of the *Dharma*" or "Defender of the Faith". The title Anagarika was an innovation based upon a Pali word meaning "homeless" and was traditionally used of a monk, although not as a title.

In 1891 Dharmapala visited the Boddhigaya, the place where Sakyamuni Buddha gained enlightenment. He was shocked at the deplorable state of this most sacred of Buddhist sites, which was crumbling under Hindu control. He decided to work for its restoration, and initiated the Budh-Gaya-Mohabodhi Society in Colombo. This was the first international Buddhist organisation. In 1892 the society moved its headquarters to Calcutta where the reconversion of Indians to Buddhism became one of its main concerns. One of the reasons that the organisation moved was that it was involved with militant Buddhist nationalism and this was causing difficulties with the colonial authorities in Colombo.

In 1893 Dharmapala, under the patronage of the Theosophical Society, was invited to represent Buddhism at the World Parliament of Religions in Chicago. He made less of an impact than Vivekananda, who was representing Hinduism, but it did make him a world-renowned figure.[5] Dharmapala and Vivekananda occupied comparable positions in their respective religious traditions and shared many common aspirations. However, the two never co-operated, and appear to have had a disagreement in 1897.

Dharmapala linked Buddhism and nationalism, and sought to revive the traditional myth of the *Mahavamsa* ("The Great Chronicle of Ceylon"). According to the *Mahavamsa*, the Sinhala race was to be the guardian of the *Dhamma,* so modern Sinhalese must identify themselves with King Dutugamunu, who rescued Buddhism. In 1906 Dharmapala founded a nationalist newspaper called the *Simhala Bauddhaya* ("The Sinhalese Buddhist"). The literary style employed owes much to his Christian education, but his sharp sarcasm was used to full effect to attack British influence. He wrote: "The sweet gentle Aryan children of an ancient historic race are sacrificed at the altar of the whiskey-drinking, beef-eating belly-god of heathenism. How long, oh! how long will unrighteousness last in Ceylon?"[6]

Dharmapala also gave the lay person a new place in Buddhism that went much further than organisational leadership. Traditionally, lay Theravada Buddhists did not meditate; those who wished to do so became monks. In 1890 Dharmapala found in an old Buddhist temple a text on meditation, which he began to read and practise. As far as is known he was the first Buddhist to learn meditation from a book and not from a master, as was the practice. He developed the practice and it became popular among the elite of Colombo and Rangoon.

The title Anagarika actually encapsulated a new status invented by Dharmapala that was halfway between monk and lay person. Instead of the monk's saffron robe, he wore a white robe and did not shave his head. He did, however, formally undertake a life of chastity and took the eight precepts (see chapter 3). Traditionally, lay persons may take these vows on Buddhist holy days for a period of 24 hours, and some old people may take them permanently. Dharmapala, however, took them for life while he was still a young man, and made a public pronouncement about the fact. The Anagarika became a popular symbol but few actually adopted the role. The primary reason was that the actual roles of monk and lay began to converge: monks became more socially active, and the lay became more devout. The two roles have in fact become more like those of a Protestant minister and a Protestant lay person, with monks acting as prison chaplains, and the laity active even in doctrinal debate.

Dharmapala accepted the Western Protestant view of religion as one and the same for everybody. It would never have occurred even to his anti-Christian friends, the Theosophists, with their own Protestant backgrounds, to question this assumption. So Dharmapala saw Buddhist soteriological doctrine and activity as equally applicable to everyone. Lay people should meditate. "Gods and priests", the stuff of communal religion, could have no place in the lives of good Buddhists. The communal religion which in fact the Sinhalese were practising must therefore be due to pernicious Hindu influence.[7]

Another important force in the Buddhist resurgence was the Young Men's Buddhist Association (YMBA) modelled upon the Young Men's Christian Association (YMCA). Their YMBA was founded in 1898 in Colombo by C. S. Dissanayake, who had previously converted from Roman Catholicism. Many branch associations were opened during the following few years in Sri Lanka and elsewhere in Asia.

Reintroduction of Buddhism into India

At the partition of India in 1947 few Buddhists lived in the country where Buddhism had first begun. The reintroduction of Buddhism into India was primarily the work of Dr Bhimrao Ramhi Ambedkar (1891–1956) who was born in Maharashtra state. His family belonged to the Mahars, who are considered one of the untouchable castes (now called *dalits*); they traditionally work as street cleaners. Through a number of fortunate circumstances, Ambedkar was able to receive a high school and college education and was granted a scholarship to study at Columbia University in New York, where he received his doctoral degree in 1916. After further studies in England he returned to India to practise law.

By 1930 many untouchables considered Ambedkar their political and spiritual leader. He disagreed with Gandhi's view that the caste system was beneficial to India and only needed to be reformed to remove abuses of untouchability. For Ambedkar, the caste system actually was the cause of untouchability. In 1936 he formed the Independent Labour Party and was appointed Minister of Law in the new government in 1947. His attempt to bring about major reforms in the law met with much opposition and in 1951 he withdrew from the government.

In 1935 Ambedkar had publicly declared that he would not die as a Hindu. Twice he nearly converted to Christianity; for eight years he engaged in dialogue with Bishop Pickett and others in Bombay.[8] It was not until 1950 that he made known his allegiance to Buddhism. He argued that Buddhism was preferable to all other religions because it is based on wisdom and understanding, not upon belief in the supernatural. Its message of love and equality deny the inequality of the caste system, and it has an Indian cultural heritage. Ambedkar called upon all untouchables to accept Buddhism. On 14 October 1956 Ambedkar and his followers took part in a great ceremony at Nagpur. With this event India's "new Buddhism" emerged. About 3.5 million untouchables followed him, which was about 5% of all *dalits* or 0.7% of the entire population of India at the time. Unfortunately, Ambedkar died soon after the event, and without its charismatic leader the movement faltered.

An interesting aspect of this particular movement was that an English Buddhist, Sangharakshita (Dennis Lingwood, b. 1925), was active among these neo-Buddhists.[9] When he returned to Britain he established the Friends of the Western Buddhist Order (FWBO), mentioned in the previous chapter. Since 1979 the FWBO has been actively involved with the movement in building schools, producing literature, and generally giving teaching to the people on Buddhism.

Recently, there have been further mass conversions among the *dalits*, who currently make up some 16% of the population of India. The most widely publicised occurred in 2001 when claims of a possible 1 million possible converts caused a hostile reaction from the Hindu BJP political party. Finally, some 3–4,000 *dalits* publicly converted to Buddhism on 4 November 2001 in the Indian capital. This movement was clearly a reaction against the oppression of the caste system which, although legally abolished in India, continues in practice in thousands of villages.[10]

Some Christians spoke to leading members of the *dalit* movement, trying to persuade them of the advantages of converting to Christianity, but with little success. This was due to a number of factors. First, the movement was essentially a reaction against caste oppression and its Hindu foundation. Second, Buddhism is seen as an Indian religion and not one that is foreign. Third, conversion to Christianity would probably have caused even greater outrage among the Hindus than conversion to Buddhism. Religious conversion continues to be a very contentious issue in India.

Soka Gakkai in Japan

During the latter part of the 20th century many religious movements emerged in Japan. Although the Aum Shinrikyo is the most well-known because of the sarin gas attack in 1995, this is a small movement compared to others. Most of the Buddhist-affiliated religious movements have been generally limited to the Japanese people. However, there is one movement that has not only grown to have great influence in Japan but has won converts around the world. Soka Gakkai (Value Creation Society) is a lay Buddhist movement following the teaching of Nichiren Shoshu that claims 12 million members in 183 countries and territories worldwide.[11]

Nichiren was a thirteenth-century Japanese Buddhist scholar, discussed in chapter 12. Nichiren's teaching was focused upon the *Lotus Sutra*, which was regarded as the highest work of Sakyamuni Buddha. Nichiren's teaching was that the *Lotus Sutra* aimed to draw people away from dependence on Buddha's mercy and make them reliant upon the wisdom latent within themselves. The doctrine therefore challenged the popular Pure Land school with its emphasis upon the mercy of Amida. It was, however, regarded as teaching which was especially valuable for the last days.

According to the Nichiren tradition, the *Lotus Sutra* reveals that Sakyamuni attained Buddhahood for the first time, not in India in Guatama's lifetime but in the remote past. The text does not reveal the law by which he acquired that enlightenment; this is left to a later reincarnation identified as Jogyo – the supreme leader of the *bodhisattvas* of the earth. As Nichiren claimed to make this revelation, he in practice was also claiming to identify himself as Jogyo. The "mystic law" is the phrase *nam-myoho-renge-kyo*, which invokes the *Lotus Sutra*. The "true law" is applied to a scroll inscribed with many Chinese and two Sanskrit characters, and known as the *gohonzon*. The basic practice of Nichiren Shoshu consists of chanting the *nam-myoho-renge-kyo* to the *gohonzon*. This practice is the law by which people may gain enlightenment in the latter days.

Nichiren promoted his teaching strongly and condemned other Japanese schools of Mahayana. The resulting persecutions were considered merely to confirm the predictions of the *sutra* of the latter days and to legitimise his status as the eternal Buddha. The Nichiren Shoshu sect was one of some 31 divisions of Nichiren's teaching that emerged after his death. The sect was one of the smaller, and at times was faced with merger with others. The sect actually took the name Nichiren Shoshu in 1912.

The major change that occurred to the group was the conversion, in the 1920s, of the Japanese educationalist, Tsunesaburo Makiguchi (1871–1944). He had already pronounced some radical educational policies and had thought much about philosophy, stressing three cardinal virtues: benefit, beauty, and goodness. These ideas were to become significant in the lay people's educational association that he formed within the Nichiren Shoshu. Makiguchi's association was established in 1937 and was called Soka Kyoiku Gakkai. Initially, it had only 60 members and slowly increased to 300–400 in 1940. In the following year the movement produced a magazine, *Kachi Sozo* ("The Creation of Value"), showing a commitment to the ideas of Nichiren Shoshu and including testimonies of healing. Japan was in the midst of war and the people were living through much suffering. The publication thus addressed important areas of need among the Japanese people.

Friction between the Nichiren Shoshu priesthood and the Soka Gakkai occurred almost from the beginning of the movement. In 1943 the Japanese wartime government ordered Makiguchi to enshrine a Shinto talisman of the sun goddess Tensho Daijin, but he refused seeing this as being against his Buddhist faith. He and his disciple Josei Toda (1900–1958) were imprisoned, and there Makiguchi died in 1944. In contrast, the priests accepted the Shinto amulets in order to appease the authorities.

When the war ended, Toda took over as the leader of the reconstituted lay organisation of the Nichiren Shoshu now known as the Soka Gakkai (Value Creation Society). During his presidency, the movement was vigorous, growing from 500 families in 1951 to a goal of 750,000 before his death in 1958. The growth of the movement was largely the result of a particular theory of conversion that Toda endorsed known as *shakubuku* ("break and subdue"). *Shakubuku* was not an innovation of Soka Gakkai but was the second of two principal historical methods of propagating Buddhism. The first was *shoju,* the more moderate approach through dialogue and example, which was considered suitable for non-Buddhist countries. The second was *shakubuku,* an uncompromising method of recruitment which Nichiren said would be necessary in Buddhist countries in the latter days. Nichiren was dogmatic that his interpretation of Buddhism and the *Lotus Sutra* was the only true faith and that all other forms of Buddhism were corrupt and evil. Toda adopted this view and frequently advocated the use of *shakubuku*.

After the death of Toda, Daisaku Ikeda (b. 1928) became the third president, and the Soka Gakkai has continued to grow. Ikeda promoted the extension of a wide variety of cultural projects, such as the creation of art museums, scholarships for musicians, founding of schools and a thriving university in Tokyo. He also established an autonomous political party Komeito ("Clean Government Party") in 1964, which has become the third largest party in the Japanese parliament.

As the Soka Gakkai gained increasing political influence, opposition grew in proportion. The movement had previously been regarded as an off-beat religious sect, but now it began to cause alarm in Japan. Most Japanese were nominal Buddhists belonging to many different schools and head temples, but one thing they agreed upon was that Nichiren Shoshu was heretical and not even "Buddhist". A socialist writer, Hirotatsu Fujiwara, brought the issue to public attention in his book *I Denounce Sokagakkai,* in which he accused Ikeda of being a "fascist".[12] Soka Gakkai faced such criticism that Ikeda was finally required to apologise and agreed to withdraw his influence from the political party.

Ikeda was also required to withdraw on two other controversial issues. The first was the policy of *shakubuku,* which had been much criticised, and which he said would be no longer used. The second related to the construction of a head temple of Nichiren Shoshu, which was originally to have been funded by the government but would instead be built with its own funds.

The head temple of Nichiren Soshu, Taiseki-ji, was founded by Nikko in 1270 after he left Mount Minobu. In 1298 he had established a new temple two miles away at Hommon-ji. The two temples have disputed the title of "head temple" ever since; they also disagreed about theology. Taiseki-ji was not a great centre for pilgrimage, unlike Hommon-ji where the tomb of Nichiren was housed. However, what Taiseki-ji did have was the *dai-gohonzon*, the original *mandala* of the *gohonzon*. According to Toda, "The cardinal point of faith lies first and foremost in pilgrimage (to Taiseki-ji). No one can develop true faith unless and until he faces and worships the *dai-gohonzon* directly."[13] Both Toda and Ikeda have embellished the temple at Taiseki-ji and made it a major pilgrimage site which attracts millions of pilgrims each year. The movement regards this centre as the third "great secret law", in addition to that of the chant and the *gohonzon*.

As the lay movement grew, the friction with the priests continued to emerge. In 1977–1979 the priests objected to certain speeches made by Ikeda in 1977, in which he advocated that Soka Gakkai is an organisation that carries out the function of both priests and the lay people. He went on to assert that inner heart and attitude, not the shaven head and the robe, determined who was to be regarded as the true priest. He concluded for Soka Gakkai, "We are the true *shukke,* or clergy of today. Lay believers and clergy members are in fact absolutely equal in rank . . ."[14] The tensions between the priests and Ikeda finally led to his resignation in 1979, but he was soon appointed as president of Soka Gakkai International (SGI).

The complex ongoing argument between the two parties is beyond the scope of this current text, but it is necessary to comment on the schism of 1990–1991. In 1990 the general administrator of the Nichiren Shoshu head temple accused Ikeda of making heretical remarks and showing bad temper in meetings between the two groups. The specific charges were quickly overtaken by escalating recriminations, and in the spring of 1991 Nichiren Shoshu withdrew its recognition of President Ikeda as leader of SGI. The head temple sent missionary priests abroad to establish the so-called Danto ("believers") movement, and some British and other European members defected.

The underlying problem is that Soka Gakkai is a mass movement, lay in membership, dedicated to making Nichiren's teachings known throughout the world and relevant to modern life. In contrast, the Nichiren priesthood is an ancient ritualistic, monastic system, concerned with the preservation of its authority and its monopoly of sacred teaching. The priesthood holds to many aspects of traditional Japanese culture, such as ancestor veneration and the importance of funeral and memorial ceremonies. Litigation and dispute between the two parties has continued in the 21st century.

For Western members of Soka Gakkai International, the priesthood was never a vital part of their experience; the full practices of the funeral rites have not been imported to the West. The major problem that this has caused for members in the West has been the authentication of the *gohonzon* for new members. Previously, copies were printed by a wood-block process under the authority of the high priest, but this is no longer available to members of the SGI. While chanting is in itself efficacious, the *gohonzon* has always been the vital element of complete religious performance by which the individual realises his or her own Buddhahood.

In earlier times the SGI raised the funds to build an impressive building known as the Sho Hondo ("main temple") in the grounds of the priest headquarters at Taisek-ji. This was considered the high sanctuary of Buddhism that housed the *gohonzon* from which the truths were to be promulgated to protect humanity in the disastrous age of *mappo*. In 1998, the chief priest had this building demolished, despite international protests. Bryan Wilson, a sociologist and leading authority on SGI, believes that the split may have even benefited the lay movement. Even the SGI are equating the division to the Christian Reformation.[15]

What attracts Westerners to Soka Gakkai? Wilson and Dobbelaere have made a study of Soka Gakkai Buddhists in Britain and have examined the question.[16] More than a third of the respondents said that they were attracted by the friendliness, sincerity and general integrity of the members. They were made to feel welcome, and this was attributed to the quality of the philosophy that lay behind the movement. Some were attracted by the practical benefits which they understood they would obtain from regular chanting and from the *gohonzon*. In particular, they wanted wealth, health and various other material benefits. Others were attracted by the simplicity of the rituals, and the aesthetic appeal of the chanting. Yet others were attracted by the moral freedom of the association. Nichiren Buddhism taught that moral rules were set aside as individuals took responsibility for themselves; this gives the movement great tolerance. For some respondents such as self-confessed homosexuals, the absence of a moral code was a particular attraction.

Buddhism among the Chinese

It is difficult to determine the condition of Buddhism in China at the present time. Neither the numbers of monks, nuns and laity, nor the schools of allegiance are known. In the 1930s there were about half a million monks and 250,000 nuns in China, inhabiting over 200,000 monastic buildings.[17] In 1947 the Chinese Buddhist Association (CBA) claimed 4,620,000 members, all of whom were theoretically supposed to have taken the Three Refuges. This was equivalent to about 1% of the total population.[18] The monasteries were important landowners; during the early 1950s they lost most of their property and income. Many of the monks returned to lay life, and the monasteries closed. By the time of the Cultural Revolution in 1965–1975 there were only a few surviving monasteries. During this period public displays of worship were suppressed, and many monks and nuns were imprisoned and forced to work in labour camps. Many temples and Buddhist libraries were destroyed or turned into community projects. The temple complex at Zhaojue, for example, was turned into a zoo during this period.

Chinese Buddhist Association

From the early 1980s the situation eased somewhat, and the government-sponsored Chinese Buddhist Association encouraged the training of monks and nuns. Observers estimate that there were only about 25,000 monks surviving by this time, and most of them had been in labour camps or working as peasants for many years previously. The majority of these monks were over 60 years old because there had been no ordinations since 1949. The CBA urgently began to establish new Buddhist academies, the first of which was the Buddhist Institute, for monks, which opened in Beijing in 1981. A similar institute for nuns was later opened in Sichuan. The training lasts from two to four years depending on previous education; more recently some members have been sponsored to continue their training at Buddhist faculties of British and American universities. It is estimated that the total enrolment of students at the Buddhist Institutes in China is only about 1,500. One study suggests that the total of new ordinations during the period 1980–1990 might only be in the region of 10,000.[19] A fifteen-day ordination ceremony took place in Guangdong province in 1988 in which 800 monks and nuns took part.

Temples are expected to be self-supporting. Those on the tourist routes tend to prosper and often obtain foreign donations, but most have to rely on weaving and farming to cover their costs. Donations from the local people are low, because the government has decreed that "all monks shall take part in productive labour". Most of those who attend the temples are old people, but they are now bringing along their grandchildren. Parents are busy at work, so it is the grandparents who, while looking after the children, are passing on their traditions to the younger generation.

Tien Tao

As was mentioned in an earlier chapter, popular forms of Buddhism had often expressed themselves as religious movements regarded as heterodox by the Chinese government. These movements were not destroyed by the Cultural Revolution and began to re-emerge during the greater religious freedom in the 1980s. Most of the sects are small, and little information is available about the extent of these movements. One of the largest is the I-kuan Tao, which has combined Christian-style studies of scriptures and personal evangelism with esoteric elements such as spirit-writing. In Taiwan the I-kuan Tao has rapidly grown to have a membership in excess of 1 million by 1991 (5% of the population).[20] It has spread through the Chinese communities around the world, and in Britain there is a growing group which prefers the name Tien Tao.

Falun Gong

Another religious movement that, in part, owes its origins to Buddhism is Falun Gong. It is a branch of Qigong, which is the generic name for a complex of techniques for physical and spiritual well-being that originated in China several thousand years ago. It is sometimes referred to as Chinese *yoga* and consists of a blend of mind and body to harness energy called *qi*. This notion of a life force or vital energy is believed to circulate both within the body and throughout the world. The practice of *tai chi* and martial arts is based upon this teaching. The *falun* is considered to be located at the lower abdomen and can absorb energy from the universe and relieve the body of bad elements.

The founder, Li Hongzi, claims to have been born on 13 May 1951. However, the Chinese authorities say he was born on 7 July and fraudulently altered his recorded date of birth to 13 May which in that year was the birthday of Gautama Buddha according to the lunar calendar. It was during the 1980s that Li began to develop his ideas of Qigong, and in May 1992 Li made public his teaching. His first published book was *China Falun Gong* which described his discoveries. A second book, *Zhuan Falun*, was published illegally in January 1994. Between 1992 and 1994 Li went on a national speaking tour. He seems to have started by making his ideas accessible and affordable to the poor; he began by teaching in the public parks. Reports say that the China Qigong Research Society charged fees, but Li would say that they were not for himself. Quickly a disagreement began between Li and the Qigong Society, which was soon to result in a political dispute. His teaching immediately became popular in China with a greater following than the Chinese Communist Party itself. The Party began to refuse to approve any Falun Gong conventions, and finally Li Hongzi left the country for the USA in 1996. Li moved first to Dallas and then to New York City, from where he oversees the expansion of Falun Gong internationally. Small groups now exist in the main metropolitan areas of the US and Canada, and also in some 30 other countries.

The world media paid little attention to the movement until 25 April 1999. On that day some 10,000–15,000 Falun Gong practitioners quietly surrounded Zhongnanhai, the government headquarters in the heart of Beijing, not far from Tiananmen Square. They lined the streets quietly without placards and simply stood or sat quietly for twelve hours. Some meditated and others read books. This was meant as an appeal against what they considered inaccurate and even slanderous attacks on Falun Gong made by He Zouxiu, a physicist and member of the Chinese Academy of

Sciences. This right of appeal was within the constitution, but it came as a shock to China's rulers to see that Falun Gong could mobilise so many thousands of people to quietly stand around their residence. Massimo Introvigne comments: "The regime was particularly scared by the failure of its intelligence services to prevent the demonstration, and by membership in Falun Gong by some medium-level political and military leaders."[21] Unofficial sources think that so many civil servants were practitioners of Falun Gong that they could have closed down the workings of government.

Between May and June 1999, in the aftermath of the protest, the Communist Party leadership was divided in how to respond. It is said that Premier Zhu Rongji came out and spoke to the protesters and was sympathetic to their cause. President Jiang, however, feared that there could be a loss of party authority. Eventually the hard-liners prevailed. The NATO bombing of the Chinese embassy in Belgrade gave them an opportunity to encourage nationwide protest and deep-seated nationalism. This became the opportunity to crack down on Falun Gong, especially as its leader was then resident in the USA. Newspaper articles, comics and booklets were written presenting Falun Gong as a dangerous cult.[22] An arrest order was then issued for Li Hongzhi. Interpol refused to serve the warrant because there was no criminal wrongdoing, and considered it blatantly political.

The Chinese Communist Party (CCP) focuses upon four main criticisms of the movement. First, that it has fabricated heretical ideas, and practises mind control. Li Hongzhi is accused of inventing a series of fallacies, such as the "doomsday of the world", in order to frighten his disciples into following his instructions without question. This is the same argument used by many in the West in the 1970s and 1980s who claimed that "cults" brainwashed their members. In much of their literature the CCP place Falun Gong alongside Aum Shinrikyo in Japan (1986), Branch Dravidians in the USA (1993), Solar Temple in Canada and Switzerland (1994), and Movement for the Restoration of the Ten Commandments of God in Uganda (2000).

Second, Falun Gong is accused of collecting money by illegal means. The sale of books and videos on their teaching is especially noted. "They purchased villas and cars, obtained visas for entry to foreign countries and bought green cards, frequented gambling dens and other places of ill repute abroad and spent money like water."[23]

Third, Falun Gong is accused of disturbing public order. "Since 1996, the 'Falun Gong' organisation illegally besieged schools, media and publishing establishments and government organs or held sit-ins with more than 300 'Falun Gong' practitioners participating on each of 78 occasions. In April 1999 more than 10,000 people besieged Zhongnanhai, the seat of the Central Government, which seriously undermined the normal public order and gravely disrupted the normal life of citizens."[24] The accompanying photographs show people three or four deep sitting quietly at the side of the pavement.

Fourth, a more dramatic accusation is that over 1,500 people have died from practising Falun Gong. Many Falun Gong practitioners are said to have refused to take medicine after becoming ill, and have then died as a result of delayed treatment. Others are said to have suffered from mental disorders, and some have committed suicide. Horrific pictures of those who hanged themselves, burned themselves, and committed murder accompany these accusations. On 23 January 2001, on the Spring Festival Eve, seven Falun Gong practitioners entered Tiananmen Square and set fire to themselves. Of the seven, two were stopped before they could harm themselves, but the other five suffered horrific burns, and one died on the spot.

Although the persecution has scared many followers and driven them underground, millions remain in China and several thousand abroad. Exactly how many "members" Falun Gong has is a matter of dispute (the government uses a figure of 2 million; Li claims 100 million); "membership" may not be an entirely applicable concept. Although the movement recommends a nine-day introduction course and frequent contacts with local centres, it also states that anybody can simply start practising Falun Gong by following the instructions from one of the many books, cassettes and websites quickly available in a variety of languages. The possibility of such a self-initiation, without a master and a lengthy discipline, is at the core of the criticism by other Qigong groups against Li and his movement.

A remarkable feature of Falun Gong is the way that it has made use of the Internet. The Falun Gong makes their material available to anyone free on the Internet. A banner on the home page reinforces the point: "All Falun Gong activities are free of charge." E-books are available free, as are the viewing of videos showing how to do the exercises on their official site.[25] This site is maintained by Falun Gong itself, with mirror sites elsewhere. The web pages present a message of non-aggression, health, human rights, and openness. If people want to attend a group they can e-mail to find the nearest group. Before they join they are often asked to read the basic text called *Zhuan Falun*.

Buddhism has been an integral part of Chinese life and culture for many generations, and it is unlikely that it will disappear even after the atrocities of the Cultural Revolution. Some estimates say that in 2002, 100 million of the country's 1.3 billion people show some affiliation with Buddhism.[26] Greater religious freedom in China has not only allowed the rapid growth of Christianity but also of the new Buddhist movements referred to previously.

International Buddhist associations

The aim of bringing together Buddhists from all countries and all denominations for the renewal of their Buddhism has been present from the beginning of the revival movements in about 1890. The first international Buddhist organisation was the Maha Bodhi Society founded by Dharmapala in 1891, mentioned earlier. Wars and political changes interrupted the progress towards international Buddhist co-operation, and it was only in 1950 that Buddhists succeeded in forming the World Fellowship of Buddhism (WFB). Apart from being a common platform for the promotion of Buddhism, the WFB understood its mission to be that of contributing towards a solution of the problems of the world. The compilation of the *Encyclopaedia of Buddhism* began in 1956 as an international venture.

The World Buddhist Sangha Council was established in Colombo in 1966 as an international association of Buddhist monks and nuns. It has defined its aims as to "unite all Buddhist monks in the world today, both Theravada and Mahayana, as one solid organisation in spite of superficial minor differences and in order to develop their ethical, intellectual and spiritual standards and adapt themselves to changing social and economic conditions in the modern world."[27]

Buddhists are not only concerned with the promotion of Buddhism but see themselves as making a contribution towards the solution of world problems. At the 1978 conference of WFB held in Tokyo, Professor Hajime Nakamura said in his keynote address,

> There is no doubt that, from now on, all the nations on earth will inter-act and influence one another more intensely. Precisely because of this state of affairs, mankind is now confronted with the crisis as to whether it will survive or perish. The teaching of Buddhism which has been transmitted through various countries should reveal the path which mankind is obliged to follow. We Buddhists are obliged to reflect upon ourselves from the point of view of this task and put it into practice so that we are able to expect a brighter future.[28]

In recent years many books have been produced with Buddhist approaches to ecology, the role of women, race, and various social issues. Buddhism has moved out of Asia and has come to perceive itself as a world religion addressing world problems. This universalist orientation is bringing about a new, integrative self-understanding. In Asia, the many different traditions had little contact with each other, but now an improving co-operation of Buddhist schools is observable in the West and increasingly so in Asia. This points to a radical new development in the history of Buddhism, and the emergence of a "global Buddhism".

Conclusion

Buddhism has fascinated many during the 2,500 years since the time of Sakaymuni Buddha. During the 20th century it faced the pressures of Communist rule in most of the traditional Buddhist nations, while in other countries it felt the dynamics of a capitalist economy. Now Buddhist monks travel around the world bringing their particular teaching to the Christianised peoples of Europe and America. It is here that it has found a growing response among those who are asking questions about the meaning of life. The revolutionary ideas of the Buddha now find a new audience among those who have rejected Western secular culture and are seeking a spiritual experience.

A few Christians have tried to incorporate Buddhist practices, such as meditation, in order to add a new spiritual dimension to Christianity. Others see the revival of Buddhism in East and West as a challenge to the spread of the Christian faith, which should be a spur to renewed missionary effort. Buddhism and Christianity are both missionary faiths that have established great civilisations, but they are based on totally different assumptions and soteriologies. In our growing global society, the only thing that is certain is that during the 21st century the debate between these two great religions will grow ever more fervent.

Suggestions for interfaith discussions

Can Buddhism adapt to the scientific culture of the emerging global society and provide new answers to the meaning of life? Can Western Christianity free itself from secularism and find a new spirituality and hope for the world?

Webwise 17 – The Buddhist Resurgence

Dalitstan Journal

http://www.dalitstan.org/journal/buddhism/bud001/idxbud001.html

This site presents news from a *dalit* perspective and shows something of the difficulty *dalits* face in converting to another religion.

Dr Ambedkar and his people

http://www.ambedkar.org

This extensive site contains sound and video clips as well as text containing much information about the state of *dalits* in India and their conversion to Buddhism.

Dharmapala

http://www.vipassana.com/resources/dharmapala/index.php

This site is in honour of Dharmapala and his teaching. It contains various articles written by him, including "What is Buddhism?", "What Buddhism is not", and "Our duties to the people of the West".

The Official Soka Gakkai International

http://www.sgi.org
This high quality site presents the official image of the SGI. It contains links to sites in various countries including www.sgi-uk.org. It shows the SGI's concern for refugees, the environment, and nuclear arms. More interesting information is found in some of the "unofficial" sites.

World Fellowship of Buddhists

http://www.wfb-hq.org/main.htm
The World Fellowship of Buddhists (WFB) was founded on 25 May 1950 in Colombo, Sri Lanka, where representatives from 27 countries in Asia, Europe and North America (including Hawaii) met for this purpose. The current president is Phan Wannamethee (1999 –)

World Buddhist Sangha Council

http://www.wbsc886.org/oldpage/eindex.htm
A lively site presenting material from the World Buddhist *Sangha*.

Buddhalife

http://www.buddhalife.org
This is a site created and managed by members of the SGI-UK, and contains many downloadable articles.

Falun Gong (*Falun Dafa*)

http://falundafa.org
This site not only contains the writings of Master Li, the founder of Falun Gong, but many by ordinary practitioners of the movement. It contains an online version of the key books on the teaching in various languages.

Notes

1. Goonatilake, S., *Anthropologizing Sri Lanka* (Bloomington: Indian University Press, 2001).
2. Bond, G. D., *The Buddhist Revival in Sri Lanka* (Columbia: University of South Carolina Press, 1988).
3. Gombrich, R., *Theravada Buddhism* (London: Routledge, 1988), pp. 188–189.
4. Bond, *op. cit.*, p. 53.
5. Burnett, D., *Spirit of Hinduism* (Tunbridge Wells: Monarch, 1991), pp. 225–227.
6. Quoted by Gombrich, *op. cit.*, p. 191.
7. Gombrich, *op. cit.*, p. 194.
8. Pradkar, B. A. M., "The religious quest of Ambedkar" in Wilkinsons, T. S. and Thomas M. M. (eds.), *Ambedkar and the Neo-Buddhist Movement* (Madras: CLS, 1972).
9. Subhuti, *Bringing Buddhism to the West: A Life of Sangharakshita* (Birmingham: Windhorse, 1995), pp. 71–74.
10. *Dalitstan Journal* provides many news clippings (see Webwise 17).
11. SGI official website, 2002 (see Webwise 17).
12. Fujiwara, H., *I Denounce Sokagakkai* (Tokyo: Nisshin Hodo, 1970).
13. Quoted in Montgomery, D. B., *Fire in the Lotus* (London: Mandala, 1991), p. 198.
14. Ikeda, D., *A History of Buddhism* (Tokyo: Soka Gakkai, 1977), pp. 14–15.
15. Machacek, D. and Wilson, B. (eds.), *Global Citizens: The Soka Gakkai Buddhist Movement in the World* (Oxford: OUP, 2000).
16. Wilson, B. and Dobbelaere, A., *A Time to Chant* (Oxford: OUP, 1994).
17. Welch, H., *The Practice of Chinese Buddhism* (Cambridge: Harvard University Press, 1967), p. 4.
18. Welch, *ibid.*, p. 393.
19. Hahn, T., "New developments concerning Buddhist and Taoist monasteries", in Pas, J. F. (ed.), *The Turning of the Tide* (Hong Kong: OUP, 1989), p. 93.

20. Jordon, D. K. and Overmeyer, D. L., *The Flying Phoenix: Aspects of Chinese Sectarianism in Taiwan* (Princetown: University Press, 1986).
21. Introvigne, Massimo, "Falun Gong" http://www.cesnur.org/testi/falung101.htm (14 April 2001).
22. *"Falun Gong" is a Cult* (Beijing: New Star Publishers, 1999).
23. *"Falun Gong" is a Cult* (New Star Publishers, 2000), pamphlet.
24. *Ibid.*
25. http://www.falundafa.org
26. McDonald, H., *The Age* (21 September 2002)
27. Quoted in Bechert and Gombrich, *The World of Buddhism* (London: Thames & Hudson, 1993), p. 285.
28. Quoted in Bechert and Gombrich, *ibid.*, p. 285.

GLOSSARY

Buddhism uses terms from many languages. The normal one used in the text is Sanskrit (S), but where the language is different the following abbreviations will be used: Chinese (C), Japanese (J), Pali (P), Tibetan (T). A word or phrase in inverted commas represents a literal translation of the term.

Abhidharma	Buddhist systematic philosophy
Adhidharma-pitaka	The third corpus ("basket") of the Pali canon (*Tripitaka*)
Ahimsa	Non-violence
Ananda	Cousin of the Buddha and favourite disciple
Anagarika	Homeless
Anatman (P: *anatta*)	Non-self
Anicca	Impermanence
Arhat (P: *arahat*)	An enlightened person
Atman	"I", self
Avalokitesvara (C: *Kuan-yin*)	A *Bodhisattva*
Avidya	Ignorance
Bhavana	Meditation
Bhiksu (P: *Bhikkhu*)	Buddhist monk
Bhiksuni (P: *Bhikkhuni*)	Buddhist nun
Bhukti	Worldly goods
Bla-ma (T)	Religious teacher (see *Lama*)
Bodhi	Enlightenment, illumination
Bodhisattva (P: *bodhisatta*)	One who has taken a vow to become a Buddha

Bon-po (T)	Priest of the pre-Buddhist religion of Tibet
Buddha (S and P)	Enlightened; especially a title for Gautama
Butsudo (J)	"The way of the Buddha", Buddhism
Byung-po	A demon or malevolent spirit
Cakra	"Wheel"; a common symbol for the Buddha's teaching
Ch'an (C)	Chinese school teaching sudden enlightenment (see Zen)
Chos (T)	*Dharma*, the Buddha's teaching
Citta	Thought
Citta-matra	"Thought only"
Culavamsa	A Sri Lankan chronicle
Dalai Lama (T)	"Ocean (of wisdom) *Lama*"
Dana	Giving
Deva	A god
dGe-lups-pa	Tibetan school of Buddhism acknowledging the authority of the *Dalai Lama*
Dharma (P: *Dhamma*)	The Buddha's teaching
dharma(*s*)	Basic elements
Dharma-kaya	Body of *Dharma*
Dharma-raja	"Righteous ruler"
Dhyana	Meditation exercise to concentrate the mind
Digha-nikaya	The first collection of *sutras* in the *Tripitaka*
Dipavamsa	A Sri Lankan chronicle
Duhkha (P: *Dukkha*)	Suffering, of unsatisfactory nature
Hua Yen (C)	"Garland"; school of Chinese Buddhism

Jataka	Stories of the previous lives of the Buddha
Jhana	Stages of meditation
Jiva	Life principle
Jodo (J)	"Pure land"; the western paradise of Amida Buddha
Jodo-shu (J)	Pure Land school
Kalacakra	A school of Tantric Buddhism
Kama	Sensuous enjoyment
Kanakamuni	A former Buddha
Karmi (J)	An indigenous (Shinto) deity, a nature god
Kaya	Body
Koan (C)	Ch'an technique to achieve enlightenment
Ksanti	Patience
Lama (T)	Religious teacher
Madhyamika (C: *San Lun*)	A major school of Mahayana philosophy
Magga	"Path"
Mahavamsa	A Sri Lankan chronicle
Mahayana (S and P)	"The great vehicle"; a movement that began in the first century AD and dominates northern Asia
Maitreya (C: *Milofo*)	A *bodhisattva* popular in China
Mandala	A religious diagram, "circle"
Manichorkor (T)	Prayer wheel
Mantra	A ritual sound normally confined to Tantra
Mantrayana	Tantric Buddhism
Mara	God of death
Marana	Death
Maya	The power of illusion
Moksha	Spiritual liberation
Muni	Sage, religious ascetic

Naga	Serpent deity
Nana	Knowledge
Nat	A god, spirit, "lord"
Nirvana (P: *nibbana*)	"Blowing out" of greed and delusions, which is equivalent to enlightenment
rNying-ma-pa (T)	Followers of the old Tantras
Pacittiya	Offence requiring confession
Pali	"Text"; now used of the original language of the canon
Parinayika	Insight
Parinirvana	Death of an enlightened being
Pitaka	"Basket" of scriptures
Prajna	Wisdom
Pratimoksa (P: *Patimokkha*)	The code of monastic discipline
Preta	Ghost, spirit
Rahula	The son of Sakyamuni
Raja	Ruler, king
Roshi (J)	Advanced Zen master
Rupa	Form, material shape
Saddha	Faith
Saddharma	True (or good) *Dharma*
Sadhana	Tantric visualisation
Sahajayana	School of Tantric Buddhism
Sakya	Tribe into which Gautama Buddha was born
Sakyamuni	Sage of the Sakyas; title of the Buddha
Samadhi	Mental concentration
Samana	Recluse, ascetic
Samjna	Cognition
Samkhya	One of the six schools of Hindu philosophy
Samsara	Sequence of repeated rebirths
Sangha	The assembly of monks

Shinto (J)	The systematised form of *kami* worship
Shomoyo (J)	Buddhist chanting
Shu (J)	A school of Japanese Buddhism
Siddha	Tantric *yogi* who has acquired magical powers
Sila	The precepts, ethical principles
Skandha	The five groups of phenomena: body, feelings, perceptions, volitions, and consciousness
Stupa	Monument commemorating death of the Buddha
Sunyata	Emptiness
Sutra	Buddhist scripture
Sutta-Pitaka	The second "basket" of the Pali canon
Svabharva	"Own-being", immutable essence
Tanha	Craving
Tantra (C: *Chen Yen*)	A form of Buddhism making use of magic and ritual to achieve enlightenment
Tathagata	A title for the Buddha, "Thus-gone"
Tathata	"Such-ness"
Tendai (J)	A school of Japanese Buddhism
Theravada (P)	"The doctrine of elders", the form of Buddhism based upon the Pali canon; sometimes called *Hinaya*
Tripitaka (P: *Tipitaka*)	The "three baskets" of the Pali canon
Tsung (C)	A Chinese school of Buddhism
Tulkus	Incarnate *lama*
Upaya (C)	"Skilful means"

Vajra	"Diamond"; symbol of emptiness.
Vajrayana	"Unsplittable"; a school of Tibetan Buddhism
Vinaya	Monastic discipline; the first section of the Pali canon
Vipassana	Insight meditation
Virya	Effort
Visaya	Object of sensory cognition
Yana (T)	"Vehicle"; a path for spiritual development
Yidam (T)	A high deity in Tantra
Yogacara	A Mahayana school of philosophy
Zen (J)	Japanese school advocating immediate enlightenment

BIBLIOGRAPHY

A Buddhist scriptures

The following are some of the more accessible translations.

Conze, E., *Buddhist Wisdom Books: The Diamond and the Heart Sutra* (Vintage Books, 2002).
Conze, E., *Buddhist Texts through the Ages* (Oxford: Oneworld, 1995).
Carter, J., *Dhammapada* (Oxford: Oneworld, 2000).
Cowell, E. B., *Buddhist Mahayana Texts: Sacred Books of the East* (Dover, 1989).
Smith, E. G., *Among Tibetan Texts* (Wisdom Books, 2001).
Watson, B., *The Lotus Sutra* (New York: Columbia University Press, 1993).

B General bibliography

Akira, H., *A History of Indian Buddhism* (Hawaii: University of Hawaii Press, 1990).
Almond, P. C., *The British Discovery of Buddhism* (Cambridge: CUP, 1988).
Armstrong, K., *Buddha* (London: Phoenix, 2000).
Arnold, E., *The Light of Asia* (New York: Cowell, 1884).
Barker, E., *New Religious Movements* (London: HMSO, 1989).
Basham, A. L., *The Wonder that was India* (London: Sidwick & Jackson, 1988).
Batchelor, S., "Letting daylight into magic: the life and time of Dorje Shugden", *Tricycle: The Buddhist Review* Spring (1998).

Baumann, M., "Creating a European path to Nirvana: historical and contemporary developments of Buddhism in Europe", *Journal of Contemporary Religion* 10 (1995), pp. 55–72.

Baumann, M., "The Dharma has come west: a survey of recent studies and sources" *Journal of Contemporary Religion* 10 (1995), pp. 55–70.

Bechert, H. and Gombrich, R., *The World of Buddhism* (London: Thames & Hudson, 1993).

Beyer, S., *The Cult of Tara* (Berkeley: University of California, 1978).

Blofeld, J., *The Way of Power* (London: Allen & Unwin, 1970).

Bloom, A., "Shin Buddhism in America: a social perspective", in Prebish, C. S. and Tanaka, K. K. (eds.), *The Faces of Buddhism in America* (Berkeley: University of California Press, 1998), pp. 32–47.

Blum, M. L., *The Origins and Development of Pure Land Buddhism* (Oxford: OUP, 2002).

Bond, G. D., *The Buddhist Revival in Sri Lanka* (Columbia: University of South Carolina Press, 1988).

Buddhaghosa, B., *The Path of Purification* (Singapore: Singapore Buddhist Meditation Centre, 1956).

Buddhist Directory 2000 (London: The Buddhist Society, 2000).

Burnett, D., *The Spirit of Hinduism* (Tunbridge Wells: Monarch, 1992).

Burnouf, E., *L'Introduction a l'Histoire du Buddhisme Indien* (Paris: Imprimerie Royale, 1844).

Carrithers, M., *The Buddha* (Oxford: OUP, 1983), pp. 83–84.

Carus, P., *The Gospel of Buddha* (London: Senate, 1955).

Chandler, S., "Chinese Buddhism in America: identity and practice" in Prebish, C. S. and Tanaka, K. K. (eds.), *The Faces of Buddhism in America* (Berkeley: University of California Press, 1998), pp. 14–30.

Ching, J., *Chinese Religion* (Basingstoke: Macmillan, 1993).

Conze, E., *A Short History of Buddhism* (Oxford: Oneworld, 1993).

Cook, F. H., *Hua-yen Buddhism* (Pennsylvania: Pennsylvania University Press, 1977).

Covell, R., "Buddhism and the Gospel among the peoples of

China", *International Journal of Frontier Missions* 10, [3] (1993), pp. 131–142.

Covell, R. R., *Confucius, The Buddha and Christ* (Maryknoll: Orbis, 1986).

Cronin, V., *The Wise Man from the West* (New York: Dutton, 1955).

Crouching Tiger Hidden Dragon (United China Vision Incorporated, 2000).

Daily Telegraph, 25 January 1995.

Dalitstan Journal (provides many news clippings, see Webwise 17).

Dayal, H., *The Bodhisattva Doctrine in Buddhist Sanskrit Literature* (Delhi: Motilal Bararsidass, 1975).

De Silva, L. A., *Buddhism: Beliefs and Practices* (Colombo: Wesley Press, 1974).

Derrett, J. D., *The Bible and the Buddhists* (Bornato: Sardini Editrice, 2000).

Dhamma, Ven. Dr R., "Buddhism in Myanmar", *The Middle Way* 74 (1999), pp. 114–117.

Dogen, Z., *Shobogenzo,* translated by Nishiyama (1983) IV.

Dumoulin, H. *Zen Enlightenment: Origins and Meaning* (Weatherhill: New York, 1979).

Dutt, S., *Buddhist Monks and Monasteries of India* (London: George Allen & Unwin, 1962).

Eilert, H., "A brief outline of Pure Land Buddhism in India and in early China" *Japanese Religions*, 14, [1] (1985), pp. 1–12.

Eliade, M., *A History of Religious Ideas* (Chicago: University of Chicago, 1982), Vol. 2.

Evens-Wentz, W. Y., *The Tibetan Book of the Dead* (Oxford: OUP, 1960).

Falun Gong is a Cult (Beijing: New Star Publishers, 1999)

Foster, R., *Celebration of Discipline: The Path to Spiritual Growth* (London: Hodder & Stoughton, 1983).

Fujiwara, H., *I Denounce Sokagakkai* (Tokyo, Nisshin Hodo, 1970).

Gombrich, R., *Theravada Buddhism* (London: Routledge, 1994).

Gomez, L. O., "Buddhism in India" in Eds. Kitagawa, J. M. and Cummings M. D. (eds.), *Buddhism and Asian History* (New York: MacMillan, 1989) pp. 51–104.

Goodrich, L. C., *A Short History of the Chinese People* (New York: Harper & Row, 1963).

Goodson, M., "The Wheel of Life", part 3, *The Middle Way* 76 (2002).

Goonatilake, S., *Anthropologizing Sri Lanka* (Bloomington: Indian University Press, 2001).

Goonewardene, A., "Arhats, Bodhisattvas and Bodhisattvas", *The Middle Way* 74 (2000), pp. 208–210.

Gordon, A., *Tibetan Religious Art* (New York: Columbia University Press, 1952).

Govinda, Lama A., *Foundations of Tibetan Mysticism* (London: Rider, 1969).

Gruber, E. R. and Kersten H., *The Original Jesus: The Buddhist Sayings of Christ* (Dorset: Shaftesbury, 1995).

Hahn, T., "New developments concerning Buddhist and Taoist monasteries", in Pas J. F. (ed.), *The Turning of the Tide* (Hong Kong: OUP, 1989).

Hajime, N. "The career of the *Bodhisattva*" in *The Encyclopedia of Religion* (London: MacMillan, 1987).

Harris, E. J., *Ananda Metteyya: The First British Emissary of Buddhism* (Kandy: Buddhist Publication Society, 1998).

Harris, E. J., *What Buddhists Believe* (Oxford: Oneworld, 1998).

Harris, I.C., *The Continuity of Madhyamika and Yogacara in Indian Mahayana Buddhism* (Leiden: E. J. Brill, 1991).

Harvey, P., *An Introduction to Buddhism* (Cambridge: CUP, 1992).

Hinnells, J. R., *A Handbook of Living Religions* (Harmondsworth: Penguin, 1991).

Hoffmann, H., *Quellen zur Geschichte der Tibetischen Bon-Religion* (1950).

Hopkins, J., *Death, Intermediate State, and Rebirth* (London: Rider, 1979).

Horner, I. B., *The Book of the Discipline* (London: Luzac, 1936–66), vol. 1, xii.

Horner, I. B., *The Early Buddhist Theory of Man Perfected* (London: Routledge, 1936).

Ikeda, D., *A History of Buddhism* (Tokyo: Soka Gakkai, 1977).

Introvigne, M., "Falun Gong" http://www.cesnur.org/testi/ falung 101.htm (14 April 2001).

Jagchid, S., "The rise and fall of Buddhism in Inner Mongolia", in Narain (ed.), *Studies in the History of Buddhism* (Delhi, 1980).

Jaini, P. S., "The disappearance of Buddhism and the survival of Jainism: a study in contrast" in Narain (ed.), *Studies in the History of Buddhism* (Delhi, 1980), pp. 81–91.

Jordon, D. K. and Overmeyer, D. L., *The Flying Phoenix: Aspects of Chinese Sectarianism* in *Taiwan* (Princetown: University Press, 1986).

King, W., "Buddhist meditation" in Kitagawa, J. and Cummings, M. (eds.), *Buddhism and Asian History* (New York: MacMillan, 1987), p. 331–339.

Kodera, T. J., *Dogen's Formative Years in China: An Historical Study and Annotated Translation of the Hokyo-ki* (London: Routledge & Kegan Paul, 1980).

Koyama, K., *Waterbuffalo Theology* (London: SCM Press, 1974).

Kvaeme, P., "The Bon religion of Tibet: a survey of research", *The Buddhist Forum* 3 (1991–1993), pp. 131–141.

Lai, W. and von Bruck, M., *Christianity and Buddhism* (New York: Maryknoll, 2001).

Lamb, C., "Rites of Passage" in Harvey, P. (ed.), *Buddhism* (London: Continuum, 2001), pp. 151–180.

Lambert, T., "The lost kingdom of Guge", *China Insight*, July/August, 2000.

Lamotte, E., *History of Indian Buddhism* (Louvain-le-Neuve: Université Catholique, 1988).

Lamotte, E., *The Spirit of Ancient Buddhism* (Venice: San Giorgio Maggiore, 1988).

Lee, Bruce., *Tao of Jeet Kune Do* (Burbank: O'hara, 1975).

Legge, J., *A Record of Buddhist Kingdoms* (New York: Dover Publications, 1965).

Leggett, T., "The Buddha's teaching and ministry", *The Middle Way* 75 (2001), pp. 231–233.

Lewis, D., *The Unseen Face of Japan* (Tunbridge Wells: Monarch, 1993).

Lindtner, C., "Review Article", *Buddhist Studies Review* 18 (2001), pp. 229–242.

Liu, J., *The Chinese Knight Errant* (London: Routledge & Kegan Paul, 1967).

Lopez, D. S., *Prisoners of Shangri-La: Tibetan Buddhism and the West* (Chicago: University of Chicago Press, 1998).

Lopez, D. S., "Two sides of the same god", *Tricycle: The Buddhist Review* Spring (1998), pp. 67–69.

Machacek, D. and Wilson, B., (eds.), *Global Citizens: The Soka Gakkai Buddhist Movement in the World* (Oxford: OUP, 2000).

McDonald, H., *The Age*, September 21, 2002.

McGirk, T., *The Independent,* Saturday 21 January, 1989, p. 12.

Mitra, R. C., *The Decline of Buddhism in India* (Shantinketan, 1954).

Montgomery, D. B., *Fire in the Lotus* (London: Mandala, 1991).

Muck, T., *Those Other Religions in Your Neighbourhood* (Wheaton: Victor Books, 1990).

Murray, M., "The function of the Dharma protectors", *The Middle Way* 76 (2001) pp. 169–174.

Nagao, G., *Madhyamika and Yogacara* (New York: State University Press, 1991).

Narada M. T., *The Manual of the Abidhamma* (Colombo: Vajirarama, 1956).

Neill, S., *A History of Christian Mission* (Harmondsworth: Pelican, 1964).

Nevius, J., *Methods of Mission Work* (London: Morgan & Scott, 1898).

Noraratrajmanit, C., *Towards Buddha-Dhamma* (Bangkok: Thai Buddhist Temple, undated).

Nyquil, S., *Shantung Rebellion* (New Haven: Yale, 1981).

Obeysekera, G., "The great tradition and the little in the perspective of Singhalese Buddhism", *Journal of Asian Studies,* 22 (1963), pp. 138–153.

Oechanet, J-M., *Christian Yoga* (Tunbridge Wells: Search Press, 1984).

Ortner, S. B., *High Religion: A Cultural and Political History of Sherpa Buddhism* (Princeton: Princeton University Press, 1989).

Palmer, M., *The Jesus Sutras: Rediscovering the Lost Scrolls of Taoism Christianity* (New York: Ballantine Wellspring, 2001).

Penenchio, M., *Guide to the Tripitaka: Introduction to the Buddhist Canon* (Bangkok: White Lotus, 1993).

Pine, R., *The Zen Teaching of Bodhidharma* (New York: North Point, 1997).

Piyasilo, *Avalokitesvara: Origin, Manifestations and Meaning* (Malaysia: Dharmafarer, 1991).

Pradkar, B. A. M., "The religious quest of Ambedkar" in Wilkinsons, T. S. and Thomas M. M. (eds.), *Ambedkar and the Neo-Buddhist Movement* (Madras: CLS, 1972).

Prebish, C. S. and Tanaka, K. K., *The Faces of Buddhism in America* (Berkeley: University of California Press, 1998).

Rahula, W., *What the Buddha Taught* (Oxford: Oneworld, 1998).

Reichelt, K. L., *Truth and Tradition in Chinese Buddhism* (Shanghai, 1927).

Robinson, R.H. and Johnson W. L., *The Buddhist Religion: A Historical Introduction* (Belmont, CA: Wadsworth, 1997).

Salomon, R., *Ancient Buddhist Scrolls from Gandhara: The British Library Kharosthi Fragments* (London: British Library, 1999).

Samuel, G., *Civilized Shamans* (Washington: Smithsonian, 1993).

Shane, P., *The Warrior Within* (Colorado: Delta, 1983).

Skorupski, T., "The historical spectrum of the Bodhisattva ideal", *The Middle Way* 75 (2000), pp. 95–106.

Snellgrove, D., *The Nine Ways of Bon* (London, OUP, 1980).

Strong, J. S., *The Buddha: A Short Biography* (Oxford: Oneworld, 2001).

Strong, J. S., *The Legend of King Asoka* (Princeton: Princeton Paperbacks, 1989).

Subhuti, *Bringing Buddhism to the West: A Life of Sangharakshita* (Birmingham: Windhorse, 1995).

Suzuki, D. T., *Zen and Japanese Culture* (Princeton: Princeton University Press, 1959).

Suzuko, C., "Can yoga be reconciled with Christianity?" in Watt, J. (ed.), *The Church, Medicine and The New Age* (London: CCHH, 1995), pp. 105–122.

Swanson, P. L., *Foundations of T'ien-T'ai Philosophy* (Berkeley: Asian Humanities Press, 1989).

Sy, C. F., "A study of Tibetan culture and religion and of potential redemptive analogies which would heighten the Tibetans' receptivity to Christianity" (MA Thesis, 1987).

Syrdal, R., *To The End of the Earth* (Minneapolis: Augsburg, 1967).

Tambiah, S. J., *Buddhism and the Spirit Cults in North-east Thailand* (Cambridge: CUP, 1970).

The Buddhist Society Prospectus 1994–1995 (London: The Buddhist Society 1995).

Theo, Ven, D., "Samma Samadhi, Samatha and Vipassana", *The Middle Way* 77 (2002), pp. 67–80.

Thomas, E., *The History of Buddhist Thought* (London: Routledge, Kegan & Paul, 1933).

Thompson, L. G., *Chinese Religion* (Belmont: Wadsworth, 1989).

Vessantara, *Meeting the Buddhas* (Glasgow: Windhorse, 1993).

Waddell, A., *Buddhism and Lamaism of Tibet* (Kathmundu: Educational Enterprises, 1985).

Watson, B., *The Lotus Sutra* (New York: Columbia University Press, 1993).

Weinstein, S., *Buddhism under the T'ang* (Cambridge: CUP, 1987).

Welch, H., *The Practice of Chinese Buddhism* (Cambridge: Harvard University Press, 1967).

Wessels, C., *Early Jesuit Travellers in Central Asia 1603–1721* (New Delhi: Motilal Banarsidass, 1992).

Wijayaratna, M., *Buddhist Monastic Life* (Cambridge: CUP, 1990).

Williams, P., *Buddhist Thought* (London: Routledge, 2000).

Williams, P., *Mahayana Buddhism: The Doctrinal Foundation* (London: Routledge, 1994).

Williams, P., *The Unexpected Way: On Converting from Buddhism to Catholicism* (Edinburgh: Continuum, 2002).

Wilson, B. and Dobbelaere, A., *A Time to Chant* (Oxford: OUP, 1994).

Wood, T. E., *Mind Only: A Philosophical and Doctrinal Analysis of the Vijnanavada* (Honolulu: University of Hawaii Press, 1991).

Yampolsky, P. B., *Selected Writings of Nichiren* (New York: Columbia University Press, 1990).

Yu, Chun-Fang, *Kuan-yin: The Chinese Transformation of Avalokitesvara* (New York: Columbia University Press, 2002).

Zurcher, E., "Buddhism in China" in Kitagawa, J. M. and Cummings, M. D. (eds.), *Buddhism and Asian History* (London: Macmillan, 1989), pp. 139–149.

http://www.falundafa.org

http://www.fpmt.org/organization/history.asp (December 2002)

INDEX